I0817349

THE AFRICA SHIP

DOMINIC ETZOLD

Schiffer
Military History
4880 Lower Valley Road
Atglen, PA 19310

Other Schiffer books by the author:
Reaping the Whirlwind: The U-boat War off North America during World War I,
978-0-7643-6704-5

Library of Congress Control Number: 2025939992

Designed by Jack Chappell
Cover design by Jack Chappell
Type set in AgencyFB/Bradley DJR/Times New Roman
Cover artwork by Valeria Timofeeva (Lady Flamberg)

ISBN: 978-0-7643-7082-3
ePub: 978-1-5073-0653-6

Printed in India
10 9 8 7 6 5 4 3 2 1

Published by Schiffer Publishing, Ltd.
4880 Lower Valley Road
Atglen, PA 19310
Phone: (610) 593-1777; Fax: (610) 593-2002
Email: Info@schifferbooks.com
Web: www.schifferbooks.com

To my mother, Patricia,
my greatest advocate and critic.

Contents

Appendixes

Acknowledgments

OFTENTIMES, ONE MAY HAVE a lifelong fascination with a subject but still lack an expert understanding of its greater foundations. Just as a famous fashion designer isn't necessarily an authority on the mechanical workings of sewing machines, a historian writing about a particular Zeppelin may not always be an erudite spokesperson about the intricacies of lighter-than-air aeronautical science. Likewise, if one becomes obsessively hyperfocused on the specific subject of his/her research, it's very easy to gloss over some of the topic's more-general but equally important themes. Thankfully, I've had the help of numerous engineers and airship historians while writing this book to ensure its technical soundness and accuracy. Of these, there are some I'd like to recognize specifically.

Concerning the fundamentals of buoyancy and hot- and cold-air densities, and reintroducing me to Archimedes's principle, I'd like to thank an old acquaintance who wishes to be known only as "Dr. Anonymous Engineer." The fact that he took time out of his busy life of solving technical problems and attending ASHRAE conferences to answer silly questions from a simpleton in such a patient and uncomplicated manner was very much appreciated. Similarly, pertaining to the characteristics and commercial production of hydrogen (and other materials), I have to acknowledge my brother Dr. Anthony Etzold. Although much more condescending than "Dr. Anonymous," he still greatly improved my understanding of hydrogen's elemental and chemical properties.

In the realm of Zeppelin history, I was very fortunate to be able to consult airship mavens from around the world. Alastair Reid, in particular, helped fill important gaps in my knowledge of prewar DELAG commercial operations, early military flights, and Zeppelin factory history. He was an invaluable, encyclopedic source of information, not only through our email correspondence regarding this work, but through his own published works, translations of rare primary sources, and other vital contributions to airship scholarship.

In that same vein, I must also pay homage to the late Elisabeth Bliesener, whom I communicated with frequently until her passing in June 2024. *Frau* Bliesener was the granddaughter of Ernst Fegert, an airship veteran who served with Ludwig Bockholt on *L 23*, *L 57*, and *L 59* and focused part of her later life in preserving her grandfather's legacy as an honorable sailor instead of a "pirate." I had actually already completed the prologue and early chapters of this book prior to being introduced to her via Facebook, and although I sent her a very early, incomplete draft in May 2024, I'm uncertain if she was able to read it before her passing. I sincerely hope she had done so and that she entered eternal rest assured that her *Opa* Ernst's reputation had been presented fairly, if not wholly restored.

With regard to the cover art, I'm indebted to the talented artist Valeria Timofeeva (Lady Flamberg), whose other illustrations already adorn the walls of my home. She, with just a few basic postcard images and sample photos, conceived and produced artwork that I feel perfectly captures the mood of the book—far exceeding my already high expectations.

Tobias Weber, the administrator of www.buddecke.de, also must be thanked for his contributions to this book's images. The various photos from his collection, including those from Friedrich Engelke's personal album, add a never-before-seen (in print) insight into the personalities behind *L 59*'s story, to say nothing of being fantastic uniform studies.

Finally, I'd like to thank some of my personal friends for their own unique contributions to this work: Keith Hansen, for his continuous support and the help with some of the Norwegian translations and phrasing; Jake Iapicca (who is doing his own exciting research for a future book on World War I), for looking over early drafts of this work and generally being a bad influence on my collecting impulses; and Joseph Ciampitti, for his overall enthusiasm regarding my work.

Introduction

THROUGHOUT MY LIFE, I've gravitated toward niche subjects. This pull has existed for as long as I can remember and has affected nearly every facet of my existence, whether it be in music, art, or my greatest passion—history. As such, airships, particularly the ones built by the Zeppelin factory, have been fascinating to me since I was in elementary school. If I wanted to impress the reader, I could say my interest in them was kindled when one of my grandfather's old friends from the Seabees took me to the site of the *Hindenburg* disaster in Lakehurst, New Jersey. Visiting the spot of this tragic event indubitably made an impact on me and would certainly have been a commendable catalyst for pursuing a life of historical research, but, regrettably, the truth is far more mundane and, dare I say, childish.

I was eleven years old in 1995 when my friend Brian introduced me to the DOS computer game *Red Baron*. For a child with a nascent interest in the past, this was akin to giving a junkie his first fix. The game's impact cannot be exaggerated. Upon completion of my initial, keyboard-operated, VGA-colored flight mission, I was hooked. My obsession with air combat, and the First World War in general, came on immediately and absolutely. In fact, looking back on decades of education, research, and collecting, of which I still have an insatiable appetite, drug addiction probably would have been the cheaper course.

Very shortly after my first virtual dogfight, I began building rudimentary plastic models of Fokkers, SPADs, Sopwiths, and the only Zeppelin I could find, the *Hindenburg*—hanging them from my ceiling with fishing line. I replaced my generic, hooded winter jacket, worn by all "normal" middle-class children growing up in New Jersey, with a gray, wool, military surplus trench coat, complete with pinned-on medals. Completing the transition to a history nut, I swapped my interest in sports figures and video game characters for the aircraft and the pilots of the Great War. Not surprisingly, the first grammar school book report where I could actually pick my own topic was on *Ace of the Iron Cross*—an English translation of Ernst Udet's autobiography, *Mein Fliegerleben.*

I actually borrowed and enjoyed that book so much that I considered stealing it from the Woodbridge Public Library. Being that this was in the mid-1990s, the internet, as we know it today, didn't really exist, and out-of-print works like that were simply unattainable locally (I do own it legally now, coincidentally an ex-library copy from Canton, Ohio). They were, however, out there somewhere, and there was no shortage of new publications being released on the "knights of the air." Peter Kilduff's biography of Manfred von Richthofen, a birthday gift one year, was one such example, as were the numerous Squadron/Signal paperbacks that could be found at the local hobby shop. This wasn't, and still really isn't, the case for books on World War I–era airships.

Those who remember the old computer game will recall its "Zeppelin hunt" missions and, if you were like myself, were enthralled by the heavily pixelated, floating behemoths and eager to learn more about them. Proving that there continues to be a similar interest in the modern age, or perhaps merely a case of the "apple not falling far from the tree," my son has also become engrossed with these giants of the air through playing *Battlefield 1* on Xbox. Still, airship studies of the First World War remain quite rare, and there are few options within the academic and commercial markets for those yearning to quench their thirst for knowledge.

Even after the recent World War I centennial, when it seemed like every publisher was in a rush to get any book on the Great War onto bookstores' shelves, little arrived concerning the stories of lighter-than-aircraft of the period. Indeed, Douglas Hill Robinson's *The Zeppelin in Combat: A History of the German Naval Airship Division, 1912–1918* (Schiffer Military History, 1994), first published in 1958 and translated to other languages and remaining in print ever since—with Dr. Robinson continually making updates until his death in 1998—remains the end-all, be-all of wartime Zeppelin-related histories.

After repeatedly reading an early edition of that book, and inherently being drawn to the obscure aspects of everything, one story always stood out among the rest—*L 59*'s mission to German East Africa. That topic was a novelty within an already eccentric subject matter, and Robinson devoted a mere twelve pages of his magnum opus to her saga. On a cursory level, he succeeded in accurately and succinctly summing up her construction, record-breaking flight, and ultimate destruction but didn't venture much deeper. As a result, one couldn't help but feel that there was so much more to her story left buried within the archives.

Sadly, his short chapter seems to have satisfied the curiosity of other historians, since Robinson is cited almost universally when the topic of "*das Afrika Schiff*" is mentioned in modern English-language chronicles of the African Front. Even postwar German sources, some of which were written by men who actually took part in operation *China-Sache* (China Matter), leave us with only a superficial understanding of the Zeppelin, the mission, and the crew. Like a game of telephone, this often can result in problems.

The lack of extensive scholarship on this subject beyond Robinson's work has allowed numerous myths and "mistruths" about *L 59*'s mission to propagate, which have been repeated in several lesser-researched books and articles. While most of these could be attributed to more easily accessible postwar British sources that made extraordinary claims about fabricated radio signals or other fantastic intelligence masterstrokes, others came from German authors who themselves speculated about *L 59*'s fate or at other times gave credibility to some of the more fanciful British tales in order to preserve German prestige. Again, there simply aren't many historical studies available on airships, never mind one about a single airship designed for a very specific purpose.

Making this all the more scandalous is that the Imperial German Naval Office (*Reichsmarineamt*) very neatly compiled the "files concerning the undertaking of *L 57* / *L 59*" into a solitary, substantial volume. The fact that in the twenty-first century there is any debate about *L 59*'s African mission, particularly its conclusion, is inexcusable. Akin to my research into the German U-cruisers of the First World War (*Reaping the Whirlwind: The U-boat War off North America During World War I*, Schiffer Military History, 2023), I found that there existed a wealth of information, both within and outside the archives, just waiting for the right person to explore it.

What I discovered did not disappoint. The legend of *L 59* goes far beyond the *Kaiserliche Marine* and the *Reichskolonialamt*'s attempted rescue mission of the German Empire's sole-remaining, beleaguered colony.

It is a story that is inundated with political intrigue, both inter- and intraservice rivalries, drama, desperation, and, ultimately, tragedy. This book will deliver the first comprehensive history of the "Africa Ship" and her crew, beginning with their origins serving on board *L 23* and ending with the mysterious loss of *L 59* over the Mediterranean in 1918.

A chronicle of the colonial land and naval forces in German East Africa, while no less fascinating, will also be given, but to a lesser degree and largely in regard to their deteriorating position in late 1917. This should not, however, imply that they play only a minor role in the narrative. To adequately explain the situation in East Africa, and why a rescue mission was required in the first place, I've made use of numerous German and British memoirs and archival sources that go beyond the well-publicized, and often exclusively quoted, "reminiscences" of Lettow-Vorbeck—the commander of the *Schutztruppe*.

In the same vein, while there have been several published works that specifically concentrate on the African front during World War I, most seem to mention *L 59*'s enterprise only in passing—a mere sideshow. Correspondingly, the various books and articles written about period airships that describe the *China-Sache* mission, tend to present only a limited, peripheral analysis of the ground war—instead, and perhaps rightfully, placing their emphasis on the air campaign as a whole, Zeppelin raids on Britain, or the bare essentials of *L 59*'s singular, record-breaking flight. This book is the first to bridge the gap in both historical disciplines, analyzing both operations concurrently and in relation to each other.

It should be noted that this work, while far-reaching, does not intend to educate the reader on airship history as a whole or of Germany's various colonies. There are other books that do a much more thorough job of that. Since the focus of this work is on *L 59* specifically, it assumes the reader already has a basic understanding of World War I by the year 1917, the disintegration of the German Empire, and airships in general. This being said, a concise crash course on the aforementioned subjects will be given in chapter 1. Additionally, vignettes have been used extensively not only to draw the reader into the story, but also to introduce characters, expound on viewpoints hinted at in memoirs, and explain somewhat technical terms in a more easily accessible way—the "pressure height" being one such example. Obviously, poetic license had to be taken in many instances, but actual quotations have been used as much as possible and can be identified by their citations. The copious use of endnotes has also been utilized for more-in-depth explanations of topics so as to not interrupt the flow of the narrative.

Ultimately, I hope this book will prove to be a worthy addition both to airship and World War I imperial scholarship that will serve as an impetus for additional academic inroads into those subjects. For far too long, rigid airships have been considered little more than historical curiosities and failed experiments, beginning with the dismantling of *LZ 1* and culminating with the scrapping of the *Graf Zeppelin II* in 1940. Furthermore, the stigma of colonialism has sullied the legacies both of the European and Indigenous troops within the African continent, making their experiences during the Great War a taboo subject and their stories all but forgotten. Indeed, the umbrella of imperialism has cast a shadow on many important lessons whose impacts are still being realized in the modern day, but which the greater population no longer has the stomach to research. To the future historians who may be inspired by the saga of *L 59* and dare to keep digging, I say, "*Aufsteigen!*"

Author's Note

Throughout this work, there are numerous usages that may be foreign to the modern, English-speaking reader—namely, with locations, times, and imperial German ranks. In the case of European and Eurasian locations, the antiquated names of the era are typically used, with the modern designation given in parentheses or in the endnotes (e.g., Istanbul is referred to as Constantinople, and Smyrna is used in place of Izmir). For African locales, whose names were often butchered both in German and Allied primary sources, spelling has been corrected to modern usage without any notation, so as not to repeatedly interrupt the flow of the narrative. All times referred to in the work utilize military nomenclature, meaning that 0900 is used for 9:00 a.m. and 2100 is used for 9:00 p.m. Additionally, when airship operations based out of Germany are referred to, the Central European Time Zone (CET, or UTC+1) is used. When referring to operations based out of Yambol, Bulgaria, the local Eastern European Time Zone (EET, UTC+2) is used. Finally, concerning military titles, the original German ranks have been preserved, such as *Obersteuermannsmaat* (senior helmsman's mate), with American and British equivalents being cited in the endnotes and within the appendixes.

Prologue

April 22, 1917, Tondern, the German Empire.[1] *Kapitänleutnant* Ludwig Bockholt and his crew are enjoying what is now a three-day respite as their airship, *L 23*,[2] is being overhauled following a mine-searching mission on the nineteenth. Although they are fully committed to their duties, they are also cognizant that the tide has turned in the air war. Despite their Zeppelin being only a year old, it is woefully obsolete compared with the newer R- and S-class "height climbers" and even those have been failing to return to their hangars—*L 39* being the latest casualty, having been shot down by flak over France in March. With every new assignment, their chances of not coming back are increasing exponentially.

In the petty officers' mess, the men are trying their hardest to keep such morbid premonitions off their minds, and, despite the uniforms and the spartan furnishings, the scene is otherwise reminiscent of peacetime. Playing Skat, cracking jokes, and getting lost in their own thoughts are the orders for the night until a messenger abruptly interrupts the idyll, summoning *Obersteuermannsmaat*[3] Ernst Fegert to Bockholt's quarters. The geniality that has permeated the atmosphere up to that point is immediately spoiled.

As Fegert quickly makes himself presentable and heads toward the door, the senior machinist sardonically calls out, "Just no bad news!"[4] Although Fegert can hear the cynical remark, he doesn't react and instead stoically follows the messenger out of the mess.

In the few minutes the helmsman is gone, the remaining officers sit in silence, staring at the door, awaiting their fate, their cigarettes turning to ashes in their hands. Will this be another monotonous reconnaissance flight over an endless sea, or will they be participating in another perilous raid over Great Britain? When Fegert returns, he puts an end to their mental toil and gives a sober response to the comment directed toward him on his exit. "Well, gentlemen, it's not bad news for us this time, but we *are* heading out. One of our U-boats has gone missing and we're to find her; we have five hours to get ready."

With this announcement, the pessimism of moments before transforms into a firm resolve, and the relaxed pace within the airship base that evening suddenly becomes frantic. Gas bags are filled with hydrogen, a course is plotted, and munitions, equipment, and ballast are loaded, with the officers giving the final sign-off that the weight is properly distributed in the airship—a tedious but essential task to ensure proper buoyancy. By 0936 the next day, *L 23* is in the air, and at 0955 her radioman sends a message to Vice Admiral Reinhard Scheer: "Ascended. Course 158 . . . seeking *UC 30*."[5]

The U-boat in question, SM *UC-30*, is a UC II type minelayer that last reported her position four days prior about 60 miles west of *L 23*'s hangar in Tondern and 105 miles north-northwest of the 1st U-boat Flotilla's base in Wilhelmshaven. To make finding the missing submarine a certainty, the Naval Airship Division has also dispatched *L 30*. While *L 30* is to proceed on a line west of *UC-30*'s last known position, *L 23* is to search the eastern sector, hugging the western coast of the Jutland peninsula and as far north as Norway. Dashing any hopes of this being a short flight, the orders explicitly instruct both airships to "return in such a way that you land when it gets dark, or later if the weather is good."[6]

Thankfully, the weather is perfect for the task at hand—the horizon is clear, visibility is unobstructed, and the wind is varying between force 1.5 and 3, a gentle breeze. Conflictingly, the conditions that make finding a small vessel in the North Sea so favorable also make the large Zeppelin an enticing target for patrolling British seaplanes and surface vessels. With no cloud cover to hide behind, *L 23*'s only means of defense are her recently added machine gun platform and the complement of 50 kg bombs taken on board.

As *L 23* leaves the safety of the coastline behind, Bockholt, remembering his Goethe and thinking of the men in the missing U-boat, mutters to himself, "If one has not seen oneself surrounded by the sea, one has no concept of the world and of one's relationship to it."[7] He checks his watch, 1010, and gives the order to arm the bombs and climb to 3,500 meters—the pressure height. This will allow the hydrogen in the gas cells to expand with the decreasing atmospheric pressure and "blow off" so that when *L 23* descends to her normal operating altitude, no further venting will take place, and the machine guns can be used without any risk of igniting any flammable gases.

"All right, men, we're entering the witches' cauldron; descend to 1,000 meters, open the bomb traps, and double the lookouts. Let's see if we can find this tub." He doesn't want to take any chances today.

Hovering above the waves, the watch officers in the forward gondola strain their eyes peering through their binoculars, searching for any signs of their missing comrades. It is all in vain. At 1058, the wireless telegraph aboard *L 23* comes to life with a message from the Airship Division's headquarters in Nordholz:

> To *L 23* and *L 30*: *UC 30* has been reported south of Horns Reef; therefore, new orders: *L 23* reconnoiter area Great Fisher Bank, *L 30* reconnoiter area Dogger Bank.
>
> —FdL [*Führer der Luftschiffe*][8]

This news elicits a collective groan throughout the control car, and Fegert dejectedly turns toward the elevator operator, who smirks and mouths out the words "another wasted effort." Bockholt, unperturbed and pretending he didn't see the interaction, refrains from chastising his crew and orders, "Continue course north-northwest; if we're not on a rescue mission anymore, let's see if we can lighten our bombload a little. Increase altitude to 3,000 meters; keep your eyes peeled for British warships."

As *L 23* proceeds toward the Horns Reef Lightship, she passes over three groups of German blockade runners at 1119. Then, at 1402, she observes a fleet of at least forty steam trawlers and a sailing ship. Even though the Dutch emblem is clearly emblazoned on their hulls, their crews simultaneously raise their largest ensigns just to make sure the Germans recognize them as neutrals. Not wishing to compromise one of the few remaining supply arteries Germany has left at this point in the war, Bockholt orders the airship onward but radios back their position in case any patrolling surface vessels of the *Kaiserliche Marine*[9] want to investigate further.

So far, the hunt is proving fruitless, and Bockholt knows his men are getting restless. The more time spent in the air spotting innocuous fishermen above a vast, calm, blue sea means fatigue will set in and complacency will take hold. Something needs to be done both to break the monotony of the patrol and to salvage the high morale that predicated the onset of the original mission. In essence, the men aboard *L 23*, and the greater Naval Airship Division, for that matter, need a win.

Incredibly, just an hour later, as if Providence herself cast sympathy on the German airmen, the watches aboard *L 23* detect a lone, curious vessel, heading westward toward England. Bockholt also spots the sailing vessel and, seizing the moment, gives the order, "*Volle Kraft voraus!*" With this command the telegraph in the control room swings to "full speed ahead," and the crew immediately spring back to life.

On the water's surface, the Norwegian barque *Royal* is on a southwest course, about 90 nautical miles from her last logged landmark, the Lindesnes Lighthouse—a 261-year-old "Pharos" of the North Sea marking the entrance to the Skagerrak. Her helmsman, Karlsen, is at the wheel when he notices what he can only describe as a strange bird approaching from the southeast. "*Hva i helvete?* Captain Eriksen, look up over there! What is it, some kind of albatross?" The captain, along with the rest of the other ten crewmen, instantaneously cups his eyes and begins peering toward the heavens, desperately trying to make out the mysterious object through the sun's glare. "*Hva pokker!* It's Hræsvelgr,"[10] cries out Jens Christensen, the youngest member of the crew.

"Enough with that nonsense, both of you!" retorts the captain, himself taking a few more moments to calmly assess the craft. "Unless there's a bird shaped like a *pølse* that started flying with propellers, I think it's safe to say it's man-made." After a brief pause he grimaces and, without any satisfaction, concludes, "It's an airship, German. Keep calm for now; it's probably fishing for haddock, not herring like us. Stay the course and let me worry about it."

While the crew slowly return to their duties, subtly trying to hide their anxious, incessant gazes upward, Eriksen remains fixated on the Zeppelin, now utilizing his telescope to study it further. It continues to approach at speed and is now close enough that he can now make out its identity: "*L 23*." He ceases scanning the sky any further and instead begins pacing along the deck, thinking out loud about his next course of action. "They must be coming to get a better look. They've probably already radioed our position to a nearby submarine or torpedo boat, and in that case, we're done for." Stopping near the bow, he lowers his head. "*Faen!* It's no use . . ."

With this sudden outburst, his crew freezes. They put an end to their half-hearted attempt at feigning work and instead peer mutedly toward their captain, their stares burning a hole into his back. Eriksen, now painfully aware that his crew are awaiting his decision, turns to face them.

"Men, grab whatever provisions you can and take to the boats. We have a better chance of surviving this ordeal if we abandon ship right now instead of waiting for a torpedo to pick the moment for us."

Despite being under no immediate threat, panic sets in and the crew hastily clutch all the food and personal belongings they can hold. Within minutes they launch two of their lifeboats and begin rowing away from their ship.

Back in the air, the officers aboard *L 23* are incredulous to this sudden evacuation of the vessel. "What do you think, *Herr Kaleu*?"[11] asks *Leutnant zur See* Heinrich Maas, the watch officer. "This doesn't make any sense."

To Bockholt, the situation is eerily familiar. Months earlier he heard a story from a U-boat commander concerning a Q-ship encounter off the Irish coast. It described stopping what appeared to be an old, tramp steamer, observing its crew put on a show of fright and abandon ship. Once the U-boat approached the vessel to investigate, a hidden skeleton crew suddenly emerged, raised the ensign of the Royal Navy, and dropped the disguise, revealing large-caliber deck guns that opened fire on the submarine.

"I don't like this one bit," responds Bockholt. "Let's take her up another 500 meters and get a good, long look at her."

As *L 23* ascends to the higher altitude and begins circling the *Royal*, every officer on board leans out of the windows of the forward gondola, endeavoring to find any signs of hidden gun platforms or crewmen still lurking aboard the vessel. After completing two circuits, Bockholt orders one of *L 23*'s 50 kg bombs to be dropped near the barque, just to see if it provokes any reaction—there is no response. Bockholt too remains idle, pensively stroking his chin, contemplating his next directive.

In this period of anxious stillness, Fegert shares a glance with the elevator man, who is still exuding smugness, confident that this is, yet again, just another wild-goose chase. Then an unorthodox idea suddenly comes to him.

"*Herr Kaleu*, perhaps we can land next to the barque and take her as a prize; she certainly seems harmless from up here." Bockholt isn't keen on the idea.

"Helmsman, I'm not Treusch von Buttlar and this isn't the Alster.[12] Besides, just one flare from one of those lifeboats and we're done for."

It is, however, already too late. The idea spreads like wildfire through the airship, and Bockholt is assailed by eager volunteers wishing to be members of a prize crew. Realizing the morale-boosting effect such a feat would have, not only on his crew but the German populace at home, Bockholt acquiesces.

"All right, boys, I suppose sailors belong on the sea and not the air, after all. Break down one of the machine guns and prepare to take our prize!"

A loud "hurrah" follows this announcement that sounds through the gondola and up the hatch to the airship's envelope, reverberating across its duralumin frame.

"Fegert, since this was your idea, you'll lead the boarding party, take *Bootsmannsmaat* Wiesemann and *Obermaschinistenmaat* Engelke with you in the prize crew. Unfortunately, those are the only petty officers I can spare; find a fourth man among the enlisted."

Fegert can barely contain his excitement; however, as the airship corkscrews down toward the nearest lifeboat, reality sets in, and he begins to ponder the situation more sensibly.

"Only four of us, and close to three times as many of them," he thinks to himself. "No matter, we'll just let the machine gun do the talking for us if we have to."

Landing on the North Sea was proving to be easier said than done. After an initial attempt to stabilize the airship near the water's surface failed, Bockholt orders more hydrogen to be released from the gas bags to lighten the Zeppelin. Now, with *L 23*'s forward gondola wavering tenuously barely a meter above the swelling waves, the Germans observe one of the Norwegian boats approaching on their own initiative.

"Stop where you are and extinguish your tobacco!" orders Bockholt. "Nationality and destination, *bitte*."

Thankfully, there are two Dutch sailors among the Norwegian crew with a rudimentary understanding of German. One shouts back, "Norwegian. Cargo, pit props. West Hartlepool."

"Aha! England!" exclaims *Leutnant* Maas. His declaration prompts cheers from his comrades.

This detail seals the fate of the *Royal*—both the vessel and its goods are fair game for confiscation. However, before Bockholt can summon the launch to take on the German prize crew, *L 23* once again begins to rise, and more gas has to be vented to stabilize her.

The airship's sudden movement startles the helpless Norwegians, who react with a collective gasp. In their already frightened state, they assume they are about to be shot where they rest. To their relief, when *L 23* returns to the water's surface, they can make out four of the Germans, now equipped with life vests, approaching the door of the gondola, smiling.

Bockholt once again calls out to them, "Your vessel is carrying contraband to an enemy port and will be seized according to prize rules. It is now the property of the German Empire. Approach with your boat and make room for our boarding party!"

The Norwegians comply but are visibly perturbed when they observe a machine gun and ammo boxes being gathered within the control car.

Bockholt, seeing their apprehension, reassures them. "Relax; if you don't give us any trouble, no harm will come to you." Adding, "You should be thankful we came across you first, since our comrades in the U-boat service wouldn't have been nearly as amiable."

As Fegert and his party make their way toward the gondola's exit, Bockholt hands him an emergency flare pistol, which he then secures around his neck, using its lanyard.

"Let's hope you won't have to use that; it'll be just as likely to attract an English patrol out here as it would one of our torpedo boats," remarks Bockholt. "I suppose you could always use it to club one of the fish eaters if they get mouthy."

Fegert, knowing that there aren't any small arms allowed on the airship, retorts, "*In der Not frisst der Teufel Fliegen, Herr Kaleu*,"[13] and he carefully climbs down into the lifeboat. Wiesemann and Engelke follow, but the fourth member of the party doesn't make it.

In his haste to offload the prize crew, Bockholt neglected to account for the weight of the three absent men, who were essentially acting as ballast. Their exit once again lightens the airship, and it begins to climb, taking the fourth member of the prize crew and the machine gun with it. Rather than attempt to land again by venting any more precious gas, Bockholt instead allows the airship to continue its ascent and orders *L 23* steered toward the second Norwegian lifeboat. He then commands its crew, via megaphone, to return to the *Royal*. This time, the Norwegians aren't as compliant.

"Seems these ones don't fancy a cruise to Germany," he mutters to himself. "I think they need a little convincing, *Leutnant*."

The first watch officer implicitly understands his commander and barks an order into the voice tube, destined for the upper machine gun platform. As the directive completes its journey to the roof of the airship, the awaiting gunners atop *L 23* fire a burst of 7.92 mm rounds into the water near the obstinate lifeboat—it has the desired effect.

Meanwhile, Fegert and his party are left sitting in an uncomfortable silence on the other lifeboat. The Norwegians, huddled on the opposite end, are staring at them as if they were ghosts.

"Well, back to your ship!" yells Fegert, breaking the trance and shocking the crew back to life.

Within minutes, all are safely on board the deck of the *Royal*, and the lifeboats are tied off to the barque's stern. Leaving Wiesemann and Engelke, both unarmed, in charge of the *Royal*'s crew, Fegert escorts Captain Eriksen and helmsman Karlsen to their cabins and locks them in; he then returns to the deck and gives a wave back to the airship.

Bockholt, satisfied with the operation from above, yells out to his prize crew, "Hold out; we'll send help for you!"[14] He then orders *L 23* back to her operational height and radios a signal reporting the encounter and requesting a torpedo boat escort:

> Square 140 gamma IV. . . . Took as prize Norwegian barque "Royal" carrying pit props to West Hartlepool. Prize crew heading to Horn's Reef. Please expect tomorrow at 10:00 a.m.[15]

With this transmission completed, he gives a final, superfluous salute to his men below and orders *L 23* on a course back to base.

Back aboard the barque, Fegert, Wiesemann, and Engelke anxiously watch their comrades float away into the quickly darkening horizon and out of sight. They are now on their own.

Turning toward the remaining crew of the *Royal*, Fegert reiterates that their vessel is now a war prize and the property of the *Kaiserliche Marine.* He is met with blank stares. Flabbergasted, he then removes the flare pistol from his neck, cocks it, and exclaims, "At the slightest resistance, I will blow this ship sky high. Then this peaceful seafaring will be over! Understood?"[16]

The crew, somewhat confused at the odd display, remain where they stand in silence. It isn't until the Dutch sailors in their midst translate the instructions that they comprehend what the Germans are trying to convey, and they nod their heads. They then allow themselves to be ushered below deck while the prize crew secures the hatches above them. Fegert, Wiesemann, and Engelke, now alone on the deck of an unfamiliar vessel, are dumbstruck.

"What now, *Obersteuermann*?" asks Engelke as all three survey the vessel and their bleak situation. "Not much we three can do to get this ship to Cuxhaven . . . do we even know where we are?" opines Wiesemann. "*Scheisse* . . ." is all Fegert can articulate in response.

After a brief conference, the three decide to allow Captain Eriksen and the helmsman back on the deck to plot a course and to determine the minimum crew size that would be required to operate the barque. Having already observed the need for translators, both of whom were now locked below, the Germans use sign language, pointing at various parts of the ship and drawing symbols on paper. When they are confident that they have been reasonably understood and a course has been drawn on the Norwegians' chart, Fegert takes Eriksen aft and cuts the ropes securing the *Royal*'s two lifeboats. He utters, to no one in particular, "This should serve as a motivation to get us back to Germany safely."

The two men then silently watch their only means of emergency escape drift away.

Captain Eriksen, smirking, chooses this moment to reveal that he can actually speak some German. He turns to Fegert and, with a bit of self-satisfaction, posits a rhetorical question.

"Very wise, Mr. Prize Officer, but what shall we do when you sail us into one of your mines?" Adding, "Surely you possess a map of the minefields surrounding the German bight, don't you?"

He relishes the moment in which the anticipated reaction takes place, and begins to laugh out loud.

In that instant, the color drains from Fegert's face, and his jaw begins to drop. He *had not* given such a situation any thought. Now facing the second test of his leadership in less than an hour, he begins to feel a rage forming within. He clutches the barrel of the flare pistol as if getting ready to strike the insolent sea captain with its grip, but he pauses.

Regaining his composure, he retorts, "I suppose as master of the *Royal*, that's my concern and not yours, prisoner."

This jibe stuns Eriksen, piercing his heart more deeply than a cutlass. Before the scorned captain can offer a riposte, Fegert grabs him by the arm and forcibly turns him around, giving the Norwegian a rough push in the direction of his quarters, where he will remain for the duration of the voyage.

With Eriksen and Karlsen now reimprisoned in their respective cabins, the German prize crew carefully opens the hatch leading below deck, fully anticipating a final attempt by the Norwegians to take back their ship—it doesn't come. Instead, the Germans coax just enough men to return to the deck to man the vessel and sail her on a course south-southeast for Cuxhaven. It was to be the beginning of a very long night.

The mild wind conditions from earlier in the day diminished to naught upon nightfall, reducing the speed of the barque to a standstill. This, in turn, significantly delayed the *Royal*'s arrival at Horn's Reef, where the promised escorts expected to intercept her at 1000 the next day. When the next morning changed to afternoon and there was still no sign of the sailing ship, the awaiting torpedo boats gave up and returned to base. The *Royal* and the German prize crew were assumed lost.

It wouldn't be until the evening of the following day that the *Royal* entered German waters and happened upon a coastal patrol boat. Not surprisingly, it is suspicious of the unexpected vessel, and instead of welcoming Fegert and his party, it aims its deck guns at them. Not wishing to be sunk so close to his destination, Fegert decides to finally make use of his light pistol, firing his entire supply of flares into the heavens. The torpedo boat is unconvinced and circles the barque three times.

Finally, it pulls alongside the *Royal*, and, observing men in German naval uniforms, the watch officer calls over to them.

"What crew are you?"

Fegert responds, "Prize crew from airship *L 23*; aren't you expecting us?" The response is disconcerting.

"No. How did you get on board from an airship?"

Fegert, exhausted and now visibly frustrated, nearly loses his composure. "Why does it matter? Please tell your commander to radio the High Seas Fleet; we've been at sea since yesterday evening."

The watch officer remains unconvinced and calls out to a subordinate to corroborate the story; it takes only minutes to be confirmed.

"My apologies, *Obersteuermann*, you and your men are free to continue onward." Adding, "We'll radio your position and get you a proper prize crew."

"*Gott sei Dank*," mutters Fegert.

"*Wie bitte?*" retorts the watch officer.

"Nothing; thank you for all of your assistance."

The two men salute each other, and the *Royal* once again continues her southerly voyage toward Cuxhaven.

Upon passing the *Elbe IV* lightship, the promised help arrives, and a large, well-armed boarding party is transferred to the barque from another torpedo boat for the purpose of relieving the weary airmen. Although the additional manpower is welcomed, Fegert and his crew refuse to leave the *Royal*. After coming so far, they want to be at the helm when the *Royal* makes her glorious arrival in Germany—their wishes are granted.

When Fegert, Wiesemann, and Engelke finally arrive in Cuxhaven over forty hours after boarding the barque, they are personally greeted by the leader of the airships, *Korvettenkapitän* Peter Strasser, who takes them back to Nordholz in his personal car and treats them to a night of copious libations. Much like the hangover that would follow the proceeding day, however, their triumph is bittersweet.

Although the *Royal* was a welcome, albeit small, addition to German commercial shipping and a remarkable propaganda victory, the Naval Airship Division forbade any such feats from recurring—the risk-to-reward ratio was far too unfavorable. Adding insult to injury, the original objective of the mission, the missing U-boat, SM *UC-30*, which had been reported as being safe on the twenty-third, was later found to have been sunk by mines two days prior. Still, the men of *L 23* were heroes for the time being. Their bravery, or recklessness, depending on the viewpoint, would not be forgotten by high command or the larger German public, and illustrations and photos of the event would grace newspapers and magazines for the immediate future.

•••

Over 4,500 miles away in German East Africa, Lt. Col. Paul von Lettow-Vorbeck is oblivious to the happenings on the North Sea and the Western Front. It is the rainy season, and his elevated encampment now resembles "an island, from which access to the outer world [is] possible only by boat."[18] Peering out at the torrents from his leaky tent, all he can think of is the potential corn harvest and the British offensive campaigns expected to resume again in July. The lull in the fighting gives him no peace. He is outnumbered, surrounded, and woefully short on supplies.

Although optimistic, Lettow is also a realist. With a dwindling supply store that is already barely adequate for his troops, at the onset of the rains he had given the order for all noncombatants composing his army's retinue to be transferred to British occupied territory, where it was hoped they would be fed and conveyed back to their homes. A necessary but painful decision that did little in improving a diminishing morale among his troops.

Lost in solemn thoughts, his attention is broken when he notices his aide-de-camp, *Oberleutnant der Reserve* Walter von Ruckteschell, running toward the tent, hunched over his box of stationery, desperately trying to keep it dry. He smirks as the thirty-four-year-old captain stumbles in.

"Walter, you know better than to think my tent would somehow be any less holed up than yours. You can't possibly expect to get any sketching done here."

Von Ruckteschell doesn't reply. Instead, he places his box down and joins his commander near the shelter's aperture, letting out a sigh as he surveys the ragtag state of the camp. Although Lettow immediately senses his subordinate's moroseness, he says nothing and the two men continue to stare in silence, watching the raindrops saturate the ground.

Finally, the young captain speaks his mind.

"Paul, it's been over a year since the last blockade runner resupplied us. Even though I have complete faith in your abilities as our leader and our means to capture what we need, when we need it."

Von Lettow doesn't let him finish.

"Walter, I know it did nothing to improve morale by sending off non-essential personnel into the care of the enemy, to say nothing of this unrelenting rain. But I haven't let us down yet and have no plans for our unbeaten record to be blemished. I promise you. Conditions will improve again when things dry up—you'll see. We have to hold out for the Fatherland; I can't lose you to melancholy now."

Von Lettow, upset at both the young captain and himself, for briefly losing composure, turns away and lights a cigarette.

"I haven't given up," retorts Ruckteschell. "I trust you and truly believe we'll keep the colony in our hands by the end of this terrible war. It's just . . ."

"What, Walter? Out with it!"

"You don't think everyone at home has given up on us, do you?"

This was not a question that Lettow was expecting, nor one that he had given much thought to previously. After the shock wears off, he articulates a response.

"Well, if General Smuts is to be believed, I was awarded the Pour le Mérite back in November. I assured him that he must have confused this with the Order of the Prussian Crown."

Von Lettow involuntarily feels around his neck, where his newly awarded medal would be if contact was reestablished with Germany, and concludes, "If that Boer is right, it means someone is not only still thinking of us, but thinking we're doing a damn good job."

With this, he smacks Ruckteschell on the back, and the two men let out a hearty laugh, immediately snapping out of their funk.

Still, the young captain's query continues to linger in Lettow's mind, and returning to an optimistic outlook, he thinks to himself, "You'll see, Walter; they haven't forgotten about us. They just need some way to break through. They'll figure it out though; they always have. You'll see . . ."

1

The Wind and the Lion

THE YEARS 1916–1917 proved to be a turning point both for the naval airship service of imperial Germany and the *Schutztruppe* in German East Africa. Things were not going very well for either. While the former was experiencing dramatic setbacks in its bombing campaign of Britain, putting the continued use of Zeppelins as a combat arm in jeopardy, the latter was in a perpetual mobile war with a rapidly shrinking foothold in the colony and, consequently, critically diminishing supply stores.

During the tribulations of this period, two figures stood at the helms of their respective forces that, depending on the viewpoint, could be regarded as either military tactical geniuses or stubborn fatalists, determined to fight a battle whose outcome had long since been determined. Both were working toward a common objective in helping Germany emerge victoriously from the Great War, despite being continents away from each other and having entirely disparate means at their hands to do so. They were *Korvettenkapitän* Peter Strasser, chief of the naval airships (*Führer der Luftschiffe* or FdL) and the "lion of Africa," *Oberstleutnant*[1] Paul von Lettow-Vorbeck, commander of the Colonial Protection Forces in East Africa. To understand their situation in 1917, however, we must go back to the outbreak of war and analyze the events that shaped their mutual *Weltanschauung*.

In the skies, Count Ferdinand von Zeppelin's eponymous airships were playing a role that he could have only dreamed about back in 1863, when he first witnessed the advantages of aerial reconnaissance as a foreign observer during the American Civil War.[2] His craft were bringing the fight to the enemy far beyond the trenches and directly into the Allied home fronts, albeit with often-catastrophic results. Even before the war began, the hydrogen-filled airships proved to be quite delicate, with the losses of the first commissioned naval Zeppelins, *L 1* and *L 2*, occurring in 1913—both in noncombat situations and with significant fatalities.

In the case of *L 2*, during a test flight over Johannisthal on October 17 a carburetor fire in the forward gondola ignited venting hydrogen gas, which led to a huge tongue of flames that quickly engulfed and destroyed the airship, killing all twenty-eight passengers and crew on board. Notable among the deceased were three Zeppelin factory engineers and members of the Admiralty's Aviation Department, including its chief—*Korvettenkapitän* Max Behnisch. This was a cruel lesson in history repeating itself, since, six weeks earlier, an equally important figure, *Korvettenkapitän* Friedrich Metzing, the head of the Naval Airship Division (*Marine Luftschiff Abteilung*) was drowned on board *L 1* after that airship departed in bad weather and crashed into the North Sea. That event propelled the thirty-seven-year-old *Korvettenkapitän* Peter Strasser, at the time learning how to handle airships from the DELAG captain and naval reservist Ernst Lehmann,[3] into Metzing's former role and into history.

By 1914 the fragility and untried nature of the large, expensive dirigibles led the *Kaiserliche Marine* to utilize them in reconnaissance roles that played on their inherent advantages over surface vessels and seaplanes. In their favor, airships had an ability to quickly ascend to high altitudes, had a top speed comparable to period aircraft and nearly twice those of the era's scouting cruisers, and could remain in the air for extended periods of time, including overnight. They could hover in place, hide behind cloud cover, and fly above and beyond the British blockade with ease, due to their remarkable range.

Indeed, the earliest and most primitive naval Zeppelin to fly during World War I, the M-class *L 3*, had a maximum, unladen, operating radius of 1,381 miles, which was 3.75 times greater than that of the Friedrichshafen FF.33, the most common reconnaissance seaplane in production in 1914. This would exponentially increase throughout the war, reaching its zenith in 1917 with the subjects of this book, the W-class *L 57* and *L 59* airships, at 9,897 miles. Airplane ranges, on the other hand, would remain rather stagnant. The Gotha G.V, the most prolific long-range German bomber of the war, could manage only 518 miles despite being introduced in 1917, and even the Zeppelin-Staaken R.VI, the most numerous of the *Riesenflugzeug*[4] strategic bombers, still could not approach the rudimentary *L 3*'s range. Although able to operate in the air for seven to ten hours, its size and weight limited its radius to 559 miles.[5]

While the aforementioned strengths seem to paint the Zeppelins as ideal for offensive operations, significant shortfalls existed that made the German navy hesitant to send their flammable airships into roles beyond their regular, safer scouting duties. First, they were few in number, and none could be spared from supporting the operations of the High Seas Fleet. Second, since they relied primarily on buoyancy instead of dynamic lift, their large payloads had to be delicately balanced against other weight constraints such as the crew complement, equipment, and ballast. The number of machine guns, bombs, and even parachutes taken on board had to be limited for the sake of lift. Finally, since the lifting power of the airship was directly determined by the volume of its gas bags and, correspondingly, its overall size, larger airships could enter service only when larger hangars to house them were constructed. These would be problems that would plague the airship service throughout the war.

The army, while not outright ignoring these deficiencies, showed more willingness to "experiment" with utilizing Zeppelins for offensive purposes at the onset of the war, despite their apparent design constraints. While the naval Zeppelins were pertinently relegated to long-range reconnaissance missions over the North Sea, searching for mines in cooperation with surface minesweepers, and spotting enemy submarines and warships, the airships operated by "*das Heer*" were the first to attack military and civilian ground targets on continental Europe. Perhaps expectedly, they had an appalling attrition rate.

In the very first month of the war, bombing[6] and reconnaissance missions over Belgium, France, and Poland (then in the Russian Empire) resulted in the losses of the army Zeppelins *Z V*, *Z VI*, *Z VII*, and *Z VIII*—all being forced to crash-land after losing buoyancy due to hydrogen leaks incurred by shrapnel and small-arms fire. Their heavy loads forced them to operate at lower altitudes and thus were unable to escape the short ranges of the ground-fired projectiles.

Leutnant zur See Ernst Lehmann, commanding his former civilian airship *Sachsen*, now requisitioned by the army as *LZ 17*, very clearly illustrated this problem, and the compromises being made for buoyancy, when he recalled an attack on Antwerp on the night of August 25–26, 1914, noting,

> We had 2,000 pounds of bombs on board, a heavy load for the ship, which was supposed to rise to 6,700 feet above sea level [he was able to manage only 5,700 feet]. We had left the machine guns behind, but the crew was armed with automatic rifles and pistols.[7]

The fact that altitude and proper defensive measures had to be sacrificed for the sake of bombload may seem inexcusable to modern readers; however, it must be remembered that the army's Imperial German Air Service was still in its infancy and largely commanded by infantry and cavalry officers, not specialists.[8]

This disconnect between the tactics of the army general staff and the actual capabilities of the Zeppelins was further emphasized when, shortly after the Antwerp raid, the airship *Z IX* was given orders to bomb Antwerp, Zeebrugge, Dunkirk, Calais, and, on the return leg of the flight, Lille. Yet again, Lehmann pointed out that his superiors "were asking a little too much, for even under the most favorable conditions, the airship could not carry more than ten bombs for all five cities."[9]

Incredibly, the army's less-than-stellar record for early combat airship missions did little to dissuade certain ranking members of the *Admiralstab*, notably *Konteradmiral* Paul Behncke—deputy chief of the Admiralty staff, from abandoning their initial reservations about naval airship usage and planning their own offensive operations. Despite having only two Zeppelins in service with the navy in August 1914, *L 3* and *L 4*, Behncke set his sights on bombing England, beginning with London and the Thames estuary and proceeding even farther on to Manchester to destroy infrastructure and demoralize the population. His plans were justifiably shot down by his superior, *Vizeadmiral* Hugo von Pohl, who argued that the navy's limited airship supply could not be risked when they were more urgently required by the High Seas Fleet for scouting missions.

Nevertheless, the plans were revisited as early as October, when two additional Zeppelins were expected to be delivered. With a total complement of four airships, three would be available for reconnaissance duties in the North Sea, and the fourth could, theoretically, be spared for raids. Still, nothing materialized. In a sign of things to come, however, interservice rivalry with the army would finally spur the Naval Airship Division into offensive action, but only after both branches bickered over roles and wrangled over additional airship resources.

Independent of the imperial navy's plans, on October 10, 1914, the chief of the Army general staff, Erich von Falkenhayn, himself with only a single airship available for crossing the English Channel,[10] made it known that the army also had intentions for bombing "*das perfide Albion.*" Although he initially suggested a cooperative effort between army and naval airships, by the end of the month, with neither branch making headway in their plans, the army general staff requested that once the Naval Airship Division arrived at its expected strength of ten airships, seven be relinquished to the army, along with their crews, to raid England. Naturally, this led to loud protestations from the *Admiralstab*, and again, another month passed without any flights toward England.

On November 18, another conference between the army and navy took place to coordinate a combined attack on Britain. It was here that the naval representatives saw firsthand the incongruence between the army general staff and the airships they commanded, which was alluded to by Lehmann in August. According to historian Douglas Robinson,

> Admiral Philipp, attending with Strasser on behalf of the Navy, was not impressed: "Airship matters in the Army . . . are not handled and directed as is necessary in the interest of the war effort, considering the importance of the arm." Philipp met Major Köppen, of the General Staff, who "seemed to be" in charge, but "did not appear to be well oriented concerning the weapon he was representing at the conference." "No particular senior officer could be found directing the Army airships and their employment," Philipp alleged. "If any decision is required, the Army officers get together either spontaneously or by order of the Army Command and reach a decision after a conference."[11]

It was becoming more and more apparent that it would be the *Kaiserliche Marine* taking the leading role in long-distance airship operations in the future, though not without the army continuing to mount resistance.

When November and December also passed without any raids on England, and the army began focusing all their efforts on attacking targets in France, Pohl received clearance directly from Kaiser Wilhelm II for the navy to begin attacking England independently. Reinforcing this decision were Allied aerial-bombing raids on German cities, leading *Großadmiral* Alfred von Tirpitz, the chief architect of the imperial navy and one of the most influential members of the emperor's inner circle, to insist on retaliation with the entirety of the Naval Airship Division, forgoing keeping any airships in reserve for scouting.

Peter Strasser, having trained with Lehmann on board the *Sachsen* prior to being appointed to his position of *Führer der Luftschiffe*, held a significant advantage over his army contemporaries in terms of experience and strategy. He was not merely a ranking officer put in charge of a new branch; he was an airship maven. His expertise was thus reflected in his tactics when it came time to develop offensive plans of his own, which, not surprisingly, were already prepared in advance of the Kaiser's blessing. Unlike the army, his orders stipulated that attacks should be carried out from high altitudes during the "new moon" lunar phase—when his airships would be obscured by the darkness of the moonless night and more difficult to spot. Additionally, he emphasized a "west-to-east" attack plan when approaching targets in order to take advantage of the wind direction, minimizing the use of the engines and decreasing their noise output.

To ensure the soundness of his strategies, much to the chagrin of his superiors, he made it a point to participate in at least one raid a month. This allowed him to judge not only the capabilities of his airships, but how enemy defenses were evolving. Although considered a Jonah—it seemed that whatever Zeppelin he boarded was forced to turn around due to a mechanical difficulty of some kind—he became the military's greatest airship advocate (some would say a fanatic) and, unlike other staff officers, had an intimate relationship both with his airships and his men. He was keenly aware of their abilities and how to exploit them and would work directly with the Zeppelin factory to improve any deficiencies. According to *Vizeadmiral* Reinhard Scheer,

> Captain Strasser took part in most of the airship raids, although permission was often given to him very grudgingly. . . . I was always afraid that one of these days he would not come back, and he was too valuable to the airship service for such a risk. But just because the difficulties always grew, I had to admit that he was right in considering it necessary to see for himself what conditions were like on the other side, so as to judge what he could demand of his crews and how he could improve the efficiency of the ships.[12]

Vizeadmiral Adolf von Trotha, chief of staff of the High Seas Fleet, speaking on a more personal level, remarked that

> [he] was a man who could be hard to the point of ruthlessness toward himself, and who recognized but one necessity—duty. While

> he was the staunchest of friends to all those who served with him and under his command, he could also, when for a moment duty ceased to call, be the jolliest among his men.
>
> Endowed with an amazing natural understanding of the fundamental principles and dangers of airship flight, which, at the time he became acquainted with the Service, were still matters shrouded in mystery, he soon acquired such a sure grasp of his special arm, and . . . brought it to such a surprising degree of perfection that its outstanding successes . . . may well be regarded as his own personal achievement and as due entirely to his unbending will and unflinching faith.[13]

Indeed, such hands-on governance of the *Marine Luftschiff Abteilung* ensured that when the naval airships began their first combat operations, they had a far better survival rate than those of the army.

During the very first raid over England on January 19, 1915, *L 3* and *L 4* successfully bombed the port of Great Yarmouth and some smaller villages,[14] causing only negligible damage but returning to base safely. These minor victories were repeated by *L 9*, under the command of *Kapitänleutnant* Heinrich Mathy on April 14, and by *L 5* (Böcker), *L 6* (von Buttlar), and *L 7* (Peterson) the next day. Although an army airship, *LZ 38*, was the first to attack London on May 31, in June *L 9* bombed Hull and *L 10* bombed Newcastle, both successfully avoiding naval antiaircraft fire and the latter causing significant damage to a shipyard and chemical plant. Naval airships *L 10*, *L 13*, and *L 15* eventually reached their goal of London on August 17, September 8, and October 13, respectively, with *L 13*'s raid alone resulting in 176 casualties, including 44 killed, and £510,000 in material losses.[15]

As a testament to Strasser's leadership, between 1914 and 1915, only two, or 11 percent of the total complement of twenty-one (eighteen Zeppelins and three constructed by Schütte-Lanz[16]) airships in service with the *Kaiserliche Marine*, had been lost in combat.[17] In sharp contrast, eight, or nearly 30 percent, of the army's twenty-seven (including two Schütte-Lanz types) airships were shot down during the same period. These initial successes, however, would prove to be evanescent. By 1916, the relative invincibility of naval Zeppelins during the early raids on Britain had been obliterated as advances in ordnance designs and artillery allowed the Allies to close the technological gap and engage the vulnerable airships.

Up to that point, the defense of British cities relied primarily on a mix of antiquated artillery and naval cannons with insufficient ranges, shells, and firing arcs and intercepting aircraft armed with conventional munitions. According to the British official history of the air war, in 1915, of the "295 guns of all calibers" intended to defend the entirety of Britain, "53 were pom-poms of no fighting value, and, of the others, no more than 80 met the War Office definition of efficient anti-aircraft guns."[18] The situation was no better with the interceptors.

While the Royal Aircraft Factory B.E.2c, B.E.12, and F.E.2b planes composing the home defense squadrons could approach the Zeppelins' operational altitude if given enough time to climb—it took nearly an hour for them to reach 3,053 meters (10,000 feet)—their tactics were found to be completely insufficient to destroy the German dirigibles once they got there. In 1914–15, the only aerial stratagems to counter airships revolved around attempting to fly above them and bombing them or shooting either conventional or incendiary bullets into the airship's envelope. The former was completely impractical. The latter resulted in either lead bullets penetrating the gas bags and causing hydrogen to leak slowly or the incendiaries being snuffed out by the hydrogen-rich air in the cells, since the small .303-caliber ingresses failed to let in enough oxygen to cause ignition. Fortunately for the British, these shortcomings were both recognized and remedied quickly.

For ground defenses, vast quantities of mobile, French model 1913 75 mm antiaircraft cannons, which had nearly double the effective range of the earlier pom-poms at 6,500 meters (21,000 feet), were imported,[19] and the antiquated British 3-pounder and 6-pounder guns were replaced with modern QF (quick-firing) 3-inch 20 cwt (hundred weight) antiaircraft artillery, with an effective range of 4,900 meters (16,000 feet).[20] The complement of searchlights around urban areas was likewise greatly expanded. Although not realized during the war, Admiral Sir Percy Scott, then in charge of the London Air Defense Area, requested 475 guns and 500 searchlights be allocated for London alone![21]

For the slow-climbing, intercepting airplanes, special explosive and incendiary "anti-Zeppelin" .303 bullets were developed[22] for use in a vertically mounted machine gun. By staggering conventional, explosive, and incendiary bullet types in the magazine of the aircraft's Lewis gun and firing them upward into the Zeppelin's underbelly or side, the rounds would sequentially penetrate its canvas skin and blow large holes in the gas bags, allowing oxygen to amalgamate with the hydrogen, and then ignite the flammable gas mixture. These two important terrestrial and aerial advancements effectively negated the altitude advantage enjoyed by the M, O, and P/Q-class Zeppelins in 1914–15, rendering them woefully obsolescent. Indeed, in 1916 Strasser's tactics alone would no longer be enough to save his airships.

Aware of the progress being made in Allied anti-Zeppelin countermeasures, in early 1916 a commission of engineers and military personnel made strides at overcoming them by designing the R-class "super Zeppelins." These six-engined behemoths were commissioned in August of that year, with *LZ 62 / L 30* being the first to take flight, and then continuously developed through *LZ 90*.[23] They were initially 649.6 feet in length and 61.3 feet in diameter and had a useful lift of 61,600 lbs.[24] This translated to a 64-foot increase in length over *L 23* and *L 24* (the previous Q-class Zeppelins), more than a 50 percent increase in volume and lifting capabilities, and, most importantly, a 12 percent increase in the altitude ceiling to 4,000 meters (13,000 feet).

Obermaschinistenmaat Pitt Klein, serving under *Kapitänleutnant* Heinrich Mathy on *L 9* and *L 13*, was present at the Zeppelin works when their new R-class airship, *L 31*, was being constructed. He noted that Count Zeppelin himself would appear at the factory (he actually used the term "shipyard") daily and on one occasion told the crew "Now, I will build ever bigger and faster airships, so that you can properly ascend and deliver lots of bombs to the British!"[25] While appreciative of the old man's enthusiasm, Klein and his years of operational experience had more-realistic expectations of the R-class in relation to improved British defenses. Seemingly trying to convince himself, even years after the war concluded, that altitude alone would have been enough to escape, he stated,

> With *L 31* we could carry many more bombs and could climb thousands of meters higher than before. Also, the motors were stronger, and there were more of them. It would be easy for us to make our attack at a height of 4,000 meters . . . though, at that altitude the anti-aircraft fire could still go 1,000 meters higher. [Still,] We had the advantage of being a target that was difficult to hit at such a high altitude. Of course, when it came to defenses en masse, you had to take everything into account, but the speed with which we carried out our attacks further reduced the risk of being hit.[26]

As it turned out, it wasn't enough. Four of the initial R-class Zeppelins were lost almost immediately, and all at the hands of British B.E.2c aircraft armed with the new anti-Zeppelin ammunition.

Kapitänleutnant Wilhelm Ganzel, Bockholt's predecessor on *L 23*, bore witness to the destruction of one of these new Zeppelins, *L 32*, which was lost along with *L 33* on a raid over London on September 24—shot down by a B.E.2c piloted by 2nd Lt. Frederick Sowrey. Already on his journey home and having just escaped the searchlights and batteries of Lincoln, nearly 115 miles north of London, he recorded in his log: "Strong glow of fire observed towards Thames estuary. [It is a] Burning[,] crashing ship."[27] Despite his being so far away from the horror of the incident, the loss of *L 32* had a profound effect on Ganzel. When ordered to bomb England the very next day, he adjusted course a total of six times, three times heading toward his objective, and another three reversing, before finally giving up and retiring to base.[28] He justified this by claiming that he was having issues with his forward engine, but in reality he was suffering with what we would refer to in modern times as PTSD and could no longer bring himself to attack England. By November, he transferred out of the Naval Airship Division and spent the rest of the war serving in the Baltic on the cruiser SMS *Kolberg*.[29]

Ganzel wasn't the only one of Strasser's men who were beginning to lose faith in their airships. Even Pitt Klein, while on leave prior to the commissioning of *L 31* and experiencing similar symptoms, recalled:

> Is there still a quiet, civil life, life without the din of hell, shrapnel, and incendiary shells? I'm adjusting slowly. At night I dream of combat flights. . . . My nerves are frayed. I hear from my comrades that they are not doing any better.[30]

And again, after also witnessing *L 32* being shot down while on board *L 31*:

> We were disgustingly restless. Our way of expressing ourselves, which was already crude due to our nautical background, took on something violent.
>
> It was the nerves; for months they've been so worn out that you almost don't recognize yourself anymore. It's understandable that they give out after this striking blow.
>
> The horrific image [of *L 32*] cannot be shaken. The greatest skill of the commander and the most meticulous caution, extreme devotion to duty, and unconditional war-fighting ability of the airship are no longer of much use compared to the enormous array of people and material fielded by the English. It was luck, a total fluke, almost a miracle, when an airship came back after going through hell over there.[31]

These sentiments weren't just speculation or emotive hyperbole—they were backed up by hard figures. By the end of 1916, the British had reduced the material damage caused by raids in the prior year by more than 25 percent and sextupled Zeppelin losses.[32] In fact, 40 percent of the fifteen total airships destroyed in combat in 1916, across all fronts and including both military branches, were lost while bombing Britain.

Still, Strasser remained undeterred and continued to press on with repeated attacks against England, when it was already becoming apparent that Zeppelins would be better suited to their primary, naval roles—namely, long-range reconnaissance. Douglas Robinson, in assessing Strasser's obstinance, eloquently wrote, "With his heart and soul mystically identified with the gigantic gas-bags, [he] refused to accept the verdict of trial by battle, and clung to his illusions with unrealistic optimism."[33] Strasser's sanguinity, however, was not baseless. He interpreted the airship campaign against Britain in the very same vein as the *Admiralstab* did "unrestricted submarine warfare"—a means of defeating Britain through attrition. Writing to Vice Admiral Scheer, then commander in chief of the High Seas Fleet, he claimed,

> The performance of the big airships had reinforced my conviction that England can be overcome by means of airships, inasmuch as the country will be deprived of the means of existence through increasingly extensive destruction of cities, factory complexes, dockyards, harbor works with war and merchant ships lying therein, railroads, et cetera . . . the airships offer a certain means of victoriously ending the war.[34]

While many in the general staff and the *Admiralstab* no longer felt that airships were suitable for this task, interpreting Strasser's "unbending will and unflinching faith" as a liability, Scheer stuck with his FdL and continued to give him his support. However, if raids on Britain were to continue, just as before, airships had to be designed that could fly higher, beyond the range of enemy defenses.

In January 1917, a conference took place among the Naval Aviation Bureau, represented by its head, Admiral Wilhelm Starke, and *Oberleutnant* Dietrich Engberding; the Naval Airship Division, represented by Strasser; and the Zeppelin factory, represented by its chief designer, Dr. Ludwig Dürr, and director Dr. Wilhelm Dörr. The topic was extensive lightening of the R-class Zeppelins, including redesigning the control cars, in order to achieve a final useful operational altitude of 16,500 feet.[35] Although this was achieved and exceeded, Strasser and the Zeppelin factory continued to push for greater altitudes and the development of what would be known as the "height climber" classes. These began with the S-class in February 1917, with *L 42* easily reaching an altitude of 19,700 feet,[36] and culminated with the X-class in 1918, the final evolution of combat Zeppelins designed to reach an altitude of 6,200 meters (20,300 feet) statically.[37] Even these, however, failed to live up to expectations.

Although the S-class ships slightly restored the Zeppelins' imperviousness to anti-airship defenses when flying at their operational ceilings, these extreme altitudes introduced problems completely unforeseen at this early age of aviation. The weather and wind currents were unpredictable, the air was frigid, and the atmosphere was oxygen deficient—with the latter two being the most-serious issues. When flying in such a bitterly cold environment, the absence of any onboard climate control meant that crews were perpetually freezing, and frostbite became common on any exposed part of the body.[38] Additionally, the lack of oxygen, besides making the engines malfunction, caused altitude sickness and serious physical fatigue among the aircrew, who often became completely incapacitated. While the crews were eventually issued compressed oxygen in portable cylinders and bottles, nothing could be done to help the engines, which continued to run on reduced power or totally ceased operating. Still, even if the men remained alert and somehow managed to stay warm, and the engines ran perfectly, the incredible altitude was a problem in itself. As the airships became exceedingly difficult to hit at extreme heights, so did targets on the ground.

This became resoundingly apparent on the height climbers' very first raid on England, on March 16, 1917. During this mission, *L 35*, *L 39*, *L 40*, *L 41*, and *L 42* set out to bomb London, but bad weather prevented all from actually getting there. While all but *L 42*[39] made it across the English Channel and experienced nothing in the form of meaningful resistance, none of the airships were actually above the places they believed they were, and none correctly identified any targets on the ground. In fact, the seventy-nine bombs dropped at various points over Britain resulted in no casualties and material damages totaling only £163—two houses damaged by *L 39*.[40] Making matters worse, the raid became Pyrrhic when *L 39* experienced engine failures on her return leg and was forced southward by high winds. Immobilized and hovering at 3,500 meters (11,480 feet) over the town Estrées-Saint-Denis, *L 39* was lost with all hands after just one of over a hundred shells fired from French ground forces struck the airship, setting her alight and causing her to explode in two.

The second raid on London on the night of May 23–24, involving *L 40*, *L 42*, *L 43*, *L 44*, *L 45*, and *L 47*, was hardly any better and once again proved the difficulties of trying to attack from great heights. Despite it being spring, the squadron of airships encountered snow and hail at altitudes between 18,000 and 21,000 feet and, losing their bearings (radio triangulation from Germany was often unreliable), either gave up on London entirely or completely misidentified their objectives. *Kapitänleutnant* Hermann Kraushaar, commanding *L 43*, believed he was over the Greenwich section of London when he dropped all thirty-eight of his bombs (4,080 lbs. / 1,850 kg worth) from a height of 19,700–20,700 feet.[41] In actuality, he was nearly 90 miles northeast, and his futile attack resulted in the death of one civilian and some damaged cottages. Commanders Martin Dietrich and Waldemar Kölle, in *L 42* and *L 45*, respectively, dropped a few "probing" bombs into heavy cloud cover from 18,700 feet in hopes of provoking searchlights and establishing that they were over worthwhile targets. *L 42* was immediately met by a flurry of illumination, and although Dietrich dispensed of his entire bombload at that location,[42] he scored no hits. Kölle, on the other hand, saw nothing and continued onward until he eventually spotted beams of light on the horizon. Opting to drop his remaining complement in this area,[43] his attack also failed, since most of *L 45*'s bombs fell harmlessly into the sea. *L 40*, *L 44*, and *L 47* were likewise ineffective raiders, with *L 44*, cursed by Strasser's presence on board, suffering numerous mechanical failures and dumping all of her ballast, including the water for the radiators, to stay buoyant.

When the report of the May 23–24 raid made it to the desk of the Kaiser, he noted, "Despite the success, I still think that the time for airships to attack London is over. They are to be used as scouts for the High Seas Fleet and for strategic long-range reconnaissance, but not for bombing raids on England."[44] This verdict couldn't have come as a surprise to the *Marine Luftschiff Abteilung* at this point in the war. Indeed, the army—the pioneers of the combat missions—had decided to cease all airship operations altogether in February, dismantling all but four of their airships and eventually ceding the remainder, with their crews, to the navy.[45] Count Zeppelin, although passing away months before the May raid, had also given up on his invention being utilized as a bomber. While he appeared optimistic to Pitt Klein about the new airships' prospects in striking England back in 1916, in reality he had envisioned the role being fulfilled by the *Riesenflugzeuge*, or "R-planes" being designed and constructed at his Zeppelin-Staaken works in Berlin since 1914. As biographer Douglas Botting put it, he "steadily lost interest in his Zeppelins [as the war progressed], believing the era of the airplane had finally arrived, as he always forecast it would."[46]

Facing this seemingly insurmountable wall of criticism, Scheer nevertheless vehemently defended Strasser's policies and caused the emperor to make an about-face, allowing the navy to continue raiding England "when circumstances were favorable."[47] The actual argument made by Scheer, however, wasn't a merely a reiteration of the Naval Airship Division's objectives of 1916. Instead, it reflected the culmination of Strasser's firsthand experience from raids and the maturation of his tactics into something more viable than simply attempting to bomb England into submission. Now, Strasser

> advocated the necessity of airship attacks, above all with their substantial support for the U-boat war. In particular, he stated that England was compelled to keep large quantities of artillery, aircraft material, and personnel in the country which would otherwise be available for the Western Front and for anti-submarine warfare. The immediate military and economic damage, which provided valuable support for the U-boat war, was also highlighted.[48]

His airships, no longer capable of effectively hitting ground targets from such great altitudes, would be helping to win the war just by being present over Britain.

Kapitänleutnant Horst Treusch von Buttlar-Brandenfels, commander of six Zeppelins during the war, felt that, given the limited number of available airships, this was the only sound strategy. Writing in the postwar years, he recalled:

> An Englishman recently asked me whether I could honestly say that our air-raids had any major purpose. No. The chief purpose of the attacks was . . . to keep men and material at home for England's defense, and so to relieve pressure at the Front.[49]

Indeed, a substantial amount of manpower and resources, all of which could have been applied with great use on the Western Front, were relegated to home defense, specifically to guard against Zeppelin raids.

The official British history gave the Zeppelins quite a bit of recognition in this respect, noting that, although bombing raids on Britain were sporadic and largely ineffective in causing direct material damage,

> the threat of their raiding potentialities compelled us to set up a formidable organization which diverted men, guns, and aeroplanes from more important theatres of war. By the end of 1916 there were specifically retained in Great Britain for home anti-aircraft defense 17,341 officers and men. There were twelve Royal Flying Corps squadrons, comprising approximately 200 officers, 2,000 men, and 110 aeroplanes. The anti-aircraft guns and searchlights were served by 12,000 officers and men who would have found a ready place, with continuous work, in France or other war theatres. There was an observer corps of officers and men, and, in addition, some part of the energies of the police force and of the personnel of the telephone, fire brigade, and ambulance services was diverted to home defense activities.[50]

In addition to these incredible figures, it credits the Zeppelins with disrupting railway transports and factory output—again, not by explosives, but by air raid alerts. Given that blast furnaces were often doused to prevent being observed from above, or that workers simply fled for cover at the sound of a siren, the Germans were making an impact on the British war industries without actually delivering any blows.

So, in 1917, with the army completely removed from the airship campaign and the navy having to justify every raid on England, Strasser and the *Marine Luftschiff Abteilung* now found themselves pressing on with their "holy" cause and "sacred obligation,"[51] if for no other reason than to lessen the burden of the ground forces on the Western Front. Despite the occasional propaganda victory, such as *L 23*'s capture of the *Royal*—which was ordered never to be repeated—the Zeppelins had to continue trudging on with the undistinguished tasks of flying systematic, wearisome reconnaissance missions and, on the offensive side, simply keeping British resources away from the main theater of war through futile bombing raids. It was a duty that, although valuable to the war effort, appeared by all other tangible metrics to be a losing stratagem.

Far away in German East Africa (GEA), Lettow-Vorbeck saw his campaign in much the same light. He had been fighting a campaign against British, Belgian, and Portuguese forces since the outbreak of war in 1914, and, under his leadership, the ever-shrinking colony was enduring as the last bastion of Germany's colonial empire—albeit marginally. Unlike Strasser's view, however, being a diversion from the greater war in Europe had been his aim from the very beginning.

Having arrived in Dar es Salaam, the colony's capital, in January 1914 to take command of the Colonial Protection Forces—the *Schutztruppe*—he was responsible for a territory encompassing 384,180 square miles (this area now comprises parts of Burundi, Rwanda, and Tanzania). A keen political observer, or perhaps merely reflecting his emperor's belligerent nature, he immediately foresaw his remote new home potentially playing a role in a much-larger, global conflict. The establishment of the Entente Cordiale in 1904, the Anglo-Russian Convention of 1907, and the two Moroccan Crises of 1906 and 1911, respectively, certainly cemented his perspective that Germany's imperial rivals were unifying and effectively encircling the fatherland's nascent empire with aims to smother its "place in the sun." Taking a Bismarckian view, he noted in his memoir that

> during the past ten years the universal war had more than once seemed so imminent that I was obliged to seriously consider whether the force under my command would be called upon to take any part in that conflict, and, if so, what its task might be. Owing to the position of the Colony and the weakness of the existing forces . . . we could play only a subsidiary part. I knew that the fate of the colonies . . . would be decided only on the battlefields of Europe. To this decision every German, regardless of where he might be at the moment, must contribute his share. In the Colony it was also our duty, in case of universal war, to do all in our power for our country.[52]

Considering that German East Africa was only about 30 percent smaller in area than the *Kaiserreich* within continental Europe, it is not surprising that Lettow found the strength of the *Schutztruppe* to be inadequate for the conflict he was anticipating.

Across twenty-eight districts, there existed a peacetime army of only 95 European officers (including medical officers), 119 noncommissioned officers, and 2,542 native Askaris.[53] While seemingly an insignificant force for such a vast area, in actuality this was comparable to the King's African Rifles (KAR) in German East Africa's northerly neighbors, British East Africa (now Kenya) and the Uganda Protectorate, which posed the most likely and immediate threat in a "universal war." In August 1914 the KAR consisted of 70 British officers, 2 British noncommissioned officers, and 2,177 Indigenous troops.[54] In Britain's other nearby African colonies, the situation was no better. Northern Rhodesia, on GEA's southwest border, and South Africa, on the continent's southern extremity, had only police forces at their disposal, which numbered no more than 576 European and 1,170 Natives with the appropriate military training.[55]

German East Africa's other two adjacent neighbors, the Belgian Congo to the west and Portuguese East Africa (Mozambique) to the south, were far better manned. In 1914, the Congo's *Force Publique*, comprised of 15,200 men, was the largest army in the region, and the latter's four-thousand-strong army was nearly double that of the *Schutztruppe*; however, neither were considered to be potential adversaries, since both pursued neutral policies.[56] While the Second Moroccan Crisis had occurred only three years prior to 1914 and exhibited that the scramble for Africa remained alive and well, it also indicated that any future colonial conflagration in Africa would likely be between Germany and the combined forces of France and Britain—both with powerful navies and vast colonial expanses from which they could draw resources.

Aware of the military weakness of the colony and wishing to remain out of European politics, Dr. Heinrich Schnee, the governor of German East Africa, sought to avoid conflict altogether. Coming into office in 1912, he aimed to continue the reformist policies of his predecessor, Albrecht von Rechenberg, who in turn was attempting to make up for the scorched-earth, genocidal courses of action taken by Gov. Gustav Adolf von Götzen during the Maji-Maji Rebellion of 1905–07. Schnee, although being the most progressive colonial governor in the territory up to that point, realized that his rule over the colony, even in peacetime, was still tenuous, and he didn't want to negate the headway being made on the relationship between the German and native populations by involving them in a European imperial conflict. Writing about the prewar situation, he recalled:

> Only eight years ago, a large-scale native uprising had raged in a considerable part of the colony, and the forces of the entire military unit had to be called upon to suppress it. Since then, it had been possible to maintain peace without resorting to violent measures through a firm and at the same time benevolent administration that took the natives' views into account. But no one could know to what extent the trust and loyalty of the natives had been achieved. A major uprising and even passive resistance on the part of the native population would have paralyzed the entire war effort. For we were barely 6,000 whites (including women and children) among almost eight million blacks and depended on the cooperation of

> our natives as Askari, as porters[,] and as war suppliers. If the natives actually remained loyal to the German cause throughout the war, this was based[,] on one hand[,] on the experiences they had had in peacetime with the German administration and with us Germans in general; on the other hand, with the maintenance of an appropriate native administration even during the war by experienced officials who were familiar with the natives. This would not have been possible if the colony had been stripped of troops.[57]

Furthering Schnee's pacifist position was his belief that German East Africa would be protected under the General Act that emerged from the Berlin Conference of 1885, specifically Chapter III, Article 10. This article stipulated that the area comprising the Congo Basin would "be placed . . . under the rule of neutrality, and considered as belonging to a non-belligerent State, [with] the belligerents [the European colonial powers] thenceforth abstaining from extending hostilities to the territories thus neutralized, and from using them as a base for warlike operations."[58] Since Schnee interpreted this territory to be inclusive of "German East Africa and considerable parts of Cameroon,"[59] he was shocked when, upon the declaration of war, it became apparent that few others shared his viewpoint. He later lamented that, almost immediately, "all German colonies, whether covered by the Congo Act or not, were attacked by far superior enemy troops,"[60] and blamed Great Britain specifically for going on the offensive.

Historian William Roger Louis, in his analysis of the fall of the German colonial empire, found that Schnee's suspicions about Britain initiating these assaults were justifiable. He noted that as early as the day after Britain declared war against Germany, a committee was formed to plan campaigns against all of Germany's territories, and, like many wars of conquest, they claimed their goals were defensive in nature. Their primary argument was that Germany "had planted strategic colonies in the Pacific and Africa to use them eventually as bases for attack against British territories,"[61] and felt that "one of the main goals of the war was to destroy Germany's 'place in the sun,' thereby securing their own safety."[62] Taking advantage of the alliance system and their global empire, the British orchestrated their campaign quickly and on a worldwide scale.

In the Pacific, the Germans lost their colonies at Kiaochow (also known as Tsingtao, in China), Samoa, German New Guinea, Nauru, the Bismarck Archipelago, Kaiser-Wilhelmsland, and the Marshall, Caroline, Palau, Marianas, and Solomon Islands within the first four months of 1914—falling to combined British, Australasian, and Japanese forces. With the added annihilation of the entire German East Asia Squadron that same year, the Allies effectively neutralized Germany's influence in an entire hemisphere. In Africa, German South-West Africa fell in 1915, followed by all of German West Africa (Togoland and Cameroon) in early 1916, to Anglo/French troops. German East Africa was the only colony, and military asset, outside Europe to hold out, largely due to Lettow's prewar preparations and his discounting of Schnee's rather naive and dovish ambitions.

Indeed, Lettow-Vorbeck, upon arriving in East Africa and inspecting his meager forces, had already strategized about the eventuality of an invasion. He proposed concentrating his forces in the northern parts of the colony around Mt. Kilimanjaro and the border with British East Africa and Uganda. Here, his forces would be in a position to launch a preemptive strike against the British, thus tying down the KAR units and forcing the greater British Empire to divert its resources away from a war in Europe in order to reinforce their colony.

Schnee, however, completely disagreed with these tactics and pressed the secretary of state at the Imperial Colonial Office (*Reichskolonialamt*, or RKA) for guidance in May 1914. It was only the British declaration of war on August 4, and the lack of a prompt response from his superiors, that caused him to relent on his program. He later claimed, "As the holder of the highest military authority, I determined that [von Lettow's] previous guidelines should prevail: defensive with offensive strikes, nondefense of the coastal areas."[63] The latter caveat was added by Schnee after an intense argument with Lettow, who conceded only due to "an ordinance, which certainly did not contemplate the case of a foreign war,"[64] placing "supreme military power" in the hands of the governor and not the *Schutztruppe*. Indeed, the two would be completely at odds during the initial stages of the war.

When Schnee secretly petitioned the United States to ensure that the Great Powers respected the vague neutrality outlined in the Berlin Conference, the differing aspirations between the governor of the colony and his protection forces truly came to light.[65] Schnee, a committed imperialist and reformer, was trying to do everything in his power to safeguard his colony and its people; Lettow-Vorbeck, part of the nobility and a loyal son of Germany, sought only to save the fatherland. It took only one day of the conflict, however, to prove that the might of the global British Empire would be forthcoming, and that Lettow's strategy of drawing British resources away from Europe may have been more than he bargained for.

Following the British declaration of war, on August 5, a British joint naval and army "Offensive Sub-Committee" recommended raising two Indian expeditionary forces (IEF) for an invasion of German East Africa. IEF "B," consisting of two brigades and a total strength of 7,973 men,[66] was to make an amphibious landing at Tanga, while IEF "C," with 3,048 total strength,[67] was to reinforce the KAR battalions and invade from the Kilimanjaro region—they wouldn't begin their offensive until November. Additionally, the Royal Navy ordered the Cape of Good Hope Station's cruisers, HMS *Astraea*, *Hyacinth*, and *Pegasus*, to isolate and destroy the only German warship in the region, the cruiser SMS *Königsberg*. By contrast, the *Schutztruppe* didn't actually find out about the state of war until an overseas wireless telegram arrived at 0630 on the fifth, were delayed in establishing a war footing, and had to scramble to mobilize. Although Lettow appeared to exude confidence amid the chaos in his memoirs, his adjutant, *Hauptmann* Karl Ernst Göring (older brother of Hermann Göring), admitted that the outbreak of war "caught the colony completely unprepared and by surprise."[68]

Nonetheless, the *Schutztruppe* was able to efficiently mobilize and likewise rapidly took up positions on the northern, western, and southern borders of the colony. On August 15, it was actually the Germans and not the British who opened the ground offensive, when Captains Tom von Prince and Albrecht Hering and two companies of Askari and European volunteers crossed the border into British East Africa and captured Taveta. Additionally, and flying in the face of Schnee's argument about neutrality in the Congo basin, units on and around Lake Tanganyika raided Belgian outposts and attacked vessels in an attempt to establish German control of the lake. These attacks brought the Belgian colonials, who up to that point honored the Congo Act and wished to remain neutral, into the war against German East Africa. Going even further, on August 24, the *Schutztruppe* crossed the Rovuma River and entered Mozambique, attacking the Portuguese fort of Maziua despite Portugal not aligning themselves with the Entente until 1916. They were essentially "poking the bear," and these early successes would prove to be fleeting.

Following the loss of the SMS *Königsberg* as a military asset in September 1914[69]—she had to retire from commerce-raiding operations to conduct engine overhauls in the Rufiji River and was eventually surrounded, attacked, and scuttled—the Royal Navy very quickly came to dominate the waters off East Africa. Indeed, without the *Königsberg*'s presence off the colony, the HMS *Hyacinth* was able to enter Dar es Salaam's harbor and destroy the capital's powerful wireless station. Even worse, the subsequent British naval blockade essentially cut German East Africa's only lifeline with Germany. This meant that the colony's only means of replenishing ammunition, medical supplies, and clothing would be from an occasional blockade runner (see chapter 2) or by raiding enemy supply dumps. Meanwhile, just as Lettow had anticipated, the Allied forces were actively intensifying their presence around German East Africa with assets from abroad.

While the Germans were able to repel the initial amphibious landing of IEF "B" in November, resulting in what the British Committee of Imperial Defense regarded as "one of the most notable failures in British military history,"[70] and were ultimately able to increase their total forces to a peak of 17,121 men in January 1916 (3,026 Europeans, 11,465 Askaris, and 2,630 porters and auxiliary troops),[71] the British, to say nothing of the Belgians and Portuguese, soon committed a total of 73,300 men to the campaign,[72] including the King's African Rifles, the 2nd Battalion of the Loyal North Lancashire Regiment, the 25th Battalion of the Royal Fusiliers, the 2nd Rhodesia Regiment, and the Indian and South African Expeditionary Forces. Indeed, in 1915, Bonar Law, the British colonial secretary, "demanded the conquest of German East Africa 'once and for all,'"[73] partly to restore British prestige but mostly to prevent the Belgian Congo's formidable *Force Publique*, now invading from the west, from impeding potential territorial gains for the British Empire.

Facing such numerical superiority, when the *Schutztruppe* entered into a conventional battle, they often had to pay a significant, and disproportionate, cost than their enemy. In one such example, on January 19, 1915, Lettow led an offensive with nine field companies to retake the coastal town of Jasin, then occupied by four companies of the Indian Expeditionary Force. Although the Germans emerged victorious, Lettow lost 15 percent of his army's total strength to casualties and used up 200,000 rounds of his protection forces' precious ammunition supply—capturing only 70,000 rounds from the enemy to replenish it.[74] If he genuinely wanted to continue the fight and divert resources from the war in Europe, his forces would have to resort to guerrilla tactics and ambushes deep within the hinterland.

In the three years that had elapsed from the outbreak of war to 1917, the *Schutztruppe* had been forced to make continual strategic withdrawals inland and southward toward Mozambique while the Allies maintained their advances, occupying most of the coastal, western, and northern areas of German East Africa. As Alfred Schöffler, a German settler in the colony and cavalryman with the *Schutztruppe*, admitted,

> The enemy continued its slow advance. Their progress would have been faster had it not been for our . . . hit-and-run tactics. This kept the enemy off balance. . . . Although we were able to slow the enemy forces down, we could not hold them back indefinitely. Our force was just too small, too ill-equipped, and poorly supplied. As a result[,] we were always on the move.[75]

Indeed, by 1917, the areas of the colony still occupied by German forces had shrunk by over 80 percent and now amounted to just 74,565 square miles.[76] Additionally, being entirely cut off from the fatherland, the survival of the *Schutztruppe* depended on unreliable, seasonal local corn harvests and capturing Allied supply dumps. While these requisitioned resources often satisfied immediate needs, as mentioned by Schöffler, they were barely adequate for sustained operations. Although Lettow noted that during this year his attacks continued to inflict a greater loss upon the enemy than the *Schutztruppe* sustained and that "the enemy's forces were once more getting exhausted," without more reinforcements they "would before long be worn out and his operations end in failure."[77] He too had to admit his situation was bleak.

In the same month that the *Marine Luftschiff Abteilung* was being lauded for the inconsequential capture of the *Royal*, Lettow's Askaris were on half rations, and the Europeans within the *Schutztruppe* were being decimated by malaria and blackwater fever. Exacerbating an already bad situation, in March 1917, one-third of the Germans' supply of quinine fell into British hands, and an ersatz concoction called "Lettow Schnapps" had to be derived from the bark of the cinchona tree.[78] Additionally, the wheat supply was completely depleted, boots were wearing out and their soles could be replaced only by using pieces of leather from captured saddles, and clothing had to be sacrificed and sterilized in order to make bandages. Still, morale remained good within the *Schutztruppe* both among Germans and the indigenous soldiery. Thanks to the Allies' imperial greed and competition among themselves, the protection forces' limited and erratic resistance continued to draw a considerable number of resources away from the European and the Mediterranean theaters of war. A secret report from the *Reichskolonialamt* concluded that as of September 1917, "100,000–120,000 enemy troops are said to be present in German East Africa. The longer the *Schutztruppe* succeeds in resisting and tying down these forces, the less likely is the possibility of their use in other theaters of war."[79]

This was a valid assessment. At this point, the British, Belgians, and Portuguese had already wasted billions in today's currency and lost tens of thousands of soldiers to combat, disease, and capture[80] in pursuit of an army less than 10 percent of their strength. Still, the German High Command, obviously appreciative of these figures, also needed German East Africa to hold out for less quantifiable reasons. As the same report from September noted, it was "of great political importance" that a "piece of German colonial property still [be] firmly in Germany's hands when peace is concluded."[81] As the last colonial vestige still flying the *Reichsflagge*, German East Africa had essentially become a bargaining chip.

Thus, in 1917, the *Marine Luftschiff Abteilung* and the *Schutztruppe* in East Africa unwittingly found themselves bound to the same cause. Although Strasser and Lettow had never met, their stubbornness and adherence to policies that many others interpreted as hopeless meant that the Germans could continue fighting in Europe with significantly less manpower and resources directed at their already surrounded position. Unbeknown to them, by the end of the summer the two dissimilar combat arms would become even further conjoined when an obscure, recently repatriated POW would make a radical proposal to the RKA. He believed he had found a solution to the *Schutztruppe*'s supply problems, and, with it, a ride back home.

2

Feasible and Promising

JUNE 20, 1917, GERMAN-OCCUPIED VILNIUS. Far from the seasonal rains of sub-Saharan Africa, *Oberstabarzt* Dr. Maximilian Zupitza is now serving in the medical corps on the Eastern Front. Although being stationed just over 400 miles from his place of birth, Bauerwitz in Upper Silesia (now Baborów in Poland), he finds the Baltic climate to be both foreign and uninviting. Having spent nearly half of his life in the African colonies, he likewise feels like a refugee among his peers in the German 10th Army. He can only marvel in disbelief at the meandering route that brought him to the East. This wasn't where his path in life was supposed to lead.

As early as 1895, he committed himself to service within the African colonies, joining the *Schutztruppe* in East Africa just a year after earning the rank of *Oberarzt* in the Royal Saxon Army, essentially a first lieutenant in the medical staff. By all indications, this truly seemed to be his calling in life. Given that the Great Powers were still relatively at peace in the late nineteenth century, Zupitza spent his initial years in the medical service of the protection force not tending to wounded soldiers, but studying local plagues in the vicinity of Lake Victoria and treating the indigenous population. When he was recalled to Berlin to serve in the administration of the *Reichskolonialamt*, he lasted only a year before finding a way to get back to what contemporary Europeans referred to as the "Dark Continent." After initially volunteering with the *Schutztruppe* in Cameroon in 1901, he returned to East Africa by 1903, once again responsible for researching and treating local diseases and providing medical assistance to European troops, Askaris, and ruga-ruga (auxiliaries) during the Maji-Maji uprising. A promotion following the rebellion brought him back to Cameroon in 1905, and in 1908 he was transferred to Togo to assist in combating trypanosomiasis, or African "sleeping sickness"—a devastating parasitic infection caused by the bite of an infected tsetse fly. It was here that he was captured by the British in the opening month of the Great War, forcing him to spend the next two years both in British and French colonial POW camps. In 1916 he was eventually freed by the latter in a prisoner exchange and repatriated to Germany.[1]

Now continuing his service with the *Heer* in the East, his comrades in Africa are always on his mind. Knowing firsthand the conditions being endured by the remaining *Schutztruppen* in East Africa, he is painfully aware of the suffering caused by diseases and a lack of provisions but can only feel helpless being so far away from the action. His free time is spent poring over local newspapers for news of "back home" and mulling ways to render relief to his compatriots still fighting it out. Being stymied, both physically and mentally, by the British blockade, he can only sulk in quiet contemplation in his quarters. His assistant, seeing the stack of newspapers on his desk, breaks the stifling silence.

"Well, *Herr Doktor*, any word from the colony yet?"

"Nothing. Every day it's just more of the same old." Zupitza grabs a paper from the middle of the pile. "Look at this, it says in April our submarines sunk over a million tons of Allied shipping, but we're still no freer from the stranglehold of the Royal Navy. Or how about this? Kerensky is warning that Russia is about to collapse . . . probably should've thought of that before revolting against the czar. Or on the southern front, the 10th Battle of the Isonzo is underway; it may as well be the thousandth.[2] All these supposed victories, yet we're still here in Vilnius and East Africa is still cut off."

He grabs another newspaper and turns to a dog-eared page. "It seems like the only news I can find from Africa is from the British; see this?" He holds up the page, pointing his finger at the column.

"According to Reuters the British are already planning on dividing up East Africa after the war. It seems General Smuts hopes that, and I quote, 'Britain would not only receive the aforementioned inland connection from one end of the continent to the other, but that the sea route around the Cape and through the Red Sea would also be secured for her.'[3] Our poor boys have to hold out, if for nothing else than to make Smuts eat his words."

He puts the paper back down and stares blankly out the window, once again deep in thought.

"Well, *Herr Doktor*, three years in and still persevering; I'd say the *Schutztruppe* must be doing something right. Besides, you can't rely on the British press for honesty; remember how little they had to say about the Somme last year?"

Zupitza perks up. "You're right, or about our airship raids. It looks like there was another successful bombing mission on London at the end of May, this time with massive 'super Zeppelins.' Unfortunately, it seems we may have already lost two of them this month, but with every year of this war we seem to be making them only bigger and better, or so the experts say."

Zupitza reaches for the morning's issue of the *Wilnaer Zeitung* and hands it to the assistant. "Look at the bottom of page 3. According to a specialist magazine, with the current state of the art in airship construction, even America would be reachable from Germany. They seem to think that it would take only about 100 hours to get there, and since our present airships are already more than half the size of what would be required to make the trip, future ones' capabilities to reach the New World would be 'almost guaranteed'!"[4]

He pauses. "A trip of nearly 6,000 kilometers, almost guaranteed . . . that's it!"

Following this "eureka moment," Dr. Zupitza immediately got in touch with the *Reichskolonialamt*,[5] which was, at this point in the war, accepting both oral and written relief proposals from military and private citizens alike.[6] His report, titled "Relief for the Protection Force in East Africa," suggested that instead of sending blockade breakers in the form of steamships, the RKA utilize an airship. He also placed an emphasis on the delivery of medicines above ammunition, with the Colonial Office later noting,

> Statements from prisoners who have recently been exchanged to Germany [Zupitza] avow that "the sufficiency of the available medicines alone would determine the continued performance of the troops and thus their further successful perseverance, while weapons and ammunition would be very desirable; they would be of only secondary importance, since the order issued by Colonel

> von Lettow-Vorbeck to not seek replenishment [from Germany] when there is a lack of ammunition, but to capture some from the enemy, was always successfully carried out by his subordinates."[7]

Sending an airship for the purposes of resupplying the army was not without precedent. In February 1917, the naval Zeppelin *L 16*, under the command of *Kapitänleutnant* Hans-Karl Gayer, reinforced a *Landsturm*[8] company on the East Frisian isle of Juist in the Wadden Sea when the extremely cold winter caused pack ice to block access to the island. Taking off from Hage, the airship carried "a large amount of food and also a considerable volume of post and packages," since aeroplanes would have been "totally insufficient to meet the needs of the islanders and the military . . . stationed there."[9] The distance from Hage to Kalfamer (a sandy area on the northeast of the island), however, was less than 11 miles and in no way comparable to a flight to GEA.

Indeed, when the RKA's proposal reached the desk of Ernst von Hoeppner, commanding general of the army *Luftstreitkräfte*, it was nixed as being entirely impractical. Up to this point in the war, airships had not yet demonstrated an ability to remain aloft for multiple days on end, and it was doubtful that they could successfully cover the nearly 4,000 miles from Germany to East Africa. Specifically, it was believed that the change in climate from temperate central Europe to the "scorching hot weather" and "tropical sun" of Africa would cause too much hydrogen to vent, and there simply wasn't enough volume in the Zeppelins' gas cells to last for a journey of that length.[10] This should not imply, however, that no attempts were being made to resupply the *Schutztruppe* up to that point or that other options weren't being explored. Although the British had established a naval blockade in the North Sea since 1914 and along the coast of German East Africa by March 1, 1915, between 4°41' and 10°40'S (largely to prevent the rescue of the entrapped SMS *Königsberg*), the Germans were able to send blockade breakers with limited success.

The first of these was the SS *Kronborg*, a 3,587-ton British cargo ship originally named *Rubens* that was impounded in Hamburg upon the outbreak of war and later disguised by the Germans to represent a neutral Danish vessel. Under the command of *Kapitän Oberleutnant zur See der Reserve* Carl Christiansen, a German of Danish ancestry (and Danish speaker) from Schleswig-Holstein, she departed Germany on February 19, 1915, avoided the British patrols in the North Sea, and arrived in Manza Bay off German East Africa on April 14. Her mission was twofold.

Primarily, she was there to resupply the *Königsberg*; thus the bulk of her cargo consisted of items for the cruiser and its officers and men. It amounted to: 2,000 metric tons of coal, 1,000 tons of boiler water, 50 tons of lubricants, two 6 cm cannons for use in landing boats, four 8.8 mm heavy machine guns, three hundred Gewehr 98 rifles, one thousand 10.5 cm rounds for the ship's main deck guns, three thousand 6 cm rounds, three thousand 3.7 cm rounds, 500,000 rounds for the Gewehr 98 rifles and machine guns, five hundred 8.8 cm rounds for the cruiser's secondary guns, five hundred packs of work clothes (for the naval crew), five hundred white (summer/tropical) naval uniforms, five hundred items of underwear, five hundred pairs of shoes, one thousand socks, three hundred sets of landing-party equipment (including backpacks, mosquito nets, canteens, etc.), 2,000 kg of provisions and gifts for the crew and officers, and 1 ton of trinitroanisole (explosives).[11]

Her secondary mission, largely due to aid requests sent by Governor Schnee to the *Reichskolonialamt*, was to resupply the *Schutztruppe*. Reflecting the lack of prioritization of this task by the *Reichsmarineamt* (Imperial Naval Office, or RMA) in comparison to the former, this cargo was appreciably smaller. It consisted of 1,500 Gewehr 98 rifles to replace the antiquated, black-powder model 71/84 rifles still largely in use with the protection force, four million rounds of ammunition, two hundred tents, medical supplies, telegraph and telephone equipment, 2 tons of machine oil, 3 tons of spirits (alcohol), 5 tons of gasoline, and a "small amount" of provisions.[12]

Given that the *Kronborg*'s only means of contacting the *Königsberg* was through radio communications, as she approached German East Africa her numerous messages were being intercepted both by French and British stations on the African continent—with the latter already being in possession of the German cipher keys for the signals. When the *Königsberg*'s commander, Max Looff, instructed Christiansen to proceed to Manza Bay on the morning of the fourteenth, Admiral Herbert King-Hall, commander in chief of the Good Hope Station, had already broken away from monitoring the *Königsberg* with the HMS *Weymouth* and was instead lying in wait for the *Kronborg* with his flagship HMS *Hyacinth*. As he put it,

> We arranged to stand in from sea at such a time that at daybreak we should make the entrance to the channel which . . . led to the entrance of Manza. Everything worked out according to plan, and, as . . . dawn approached we made out a dark shape inshore of us, and at once realized it was our quarry.[13]

Contrary to his statement, things did not go according to plan.

Although the *Hyacinth* was in an optimal position to intercept and sink the steamship, shortly after engaging the blockade breaker with her 6-inch guns, a wrist pin in one of the starboard engine's connecting rods broke, and she was only able to limp along with her portside engine. This allowed Christiansen to temporarily outrun his pursuer, steer the *Kronborg* to shallow water, scuttle her, set the deck of the steamer alight with gasoline, and escape to German East Africa with his crew. When the *Hyacinth* finally caught up with the stranded *Kronborg*, King-Hall "opened fire with shell . . . with the result that three or four immense explosions took place," and concluded that although "guns and rifles might be saved [from the wreck], there would be little or no ammunition for them."[14] When a British boarding party reported back to the *Hyacinth* that the *Kronborg* couldn't be boarded or salvaged due to the raging fire on the deck, King-Hall departed the area, satisfied that he prevented valuable reinforcements from arriving in GEA. Nothing could have been further from the truth.

In reality, the only significant loss, besides the steamship itself, was nearly three-quarters of the coal supply intended for the *Königsberg*. When the Germans returned to the wreck with divers to begin salvage operations, all 1,800 rifles on board were recovered, as well as the larger-caliber cannons, machine guns, and the entire complement of ammunition, explosives, and provisions on board. Although the Mauser caliber (7.92 mm) ammunition for the rifles and machine guns was fouled from being submerged, when the supply was transported to New Moshi, each cartridge was subsequently, and painstakingly, disassembled. Then, the powder and firing caps were either cleaned and dried or replaced. Lettow noted that after testing the "remade ammunition," the batches of cartridges that had a rate of 20 percent or less being misfires were retained for use in machine guns in frontline service, and the remainder were used as practice rounds.[15] The memoir of Alfred Schöffler, a cavalryman within the *Schutztruppe*, gives the impression that such batches were likely few and far between, noting,

> Though exposed to salt water for only a short time, the salvaged arms and ammunition were not totally usable. The guns were rusted, and the ammunition could not be depended on. This salvaged ammunition was unacceptable [Schöffler's emphasis] for use in machine guns. The large number of misfires caused the guns to jam at the most-critical times. We had to turn in our good rifle ammunition for use in the machine guns. The corroded ammunition from the sunken ship was restricted for use in rifles. We soon found out that this ammunition was a problem. . . . One night as we made camp,

> a lion threatened an askari sentry. He fired one of these rounds. The lion, frightened by the noise of the shot, ran off. . . . In checking his rifle, he found that the bullet was lodged in the barrel. . . . We test-fired some of these rounds and noted immediately that you could not predict the range or accuracy of these cartridges. . . . It was a hell of a way to fight a war.[16]

These limited supplies, along with the addition of Christiansen and his thirty crew members to the fighting strength of the *Schutztruppe*, were certainly welcome, but the modest resupply could not be sustained if fighting was to continue for years instead of months. If the forces in East Africa were to hold out, they would require consistent reprovisioning.

A second blockade breaker, the Woermann Line steamer *Muansa*, was intended for this purpose. She had already escaped German East Africa and arrived in Buenos Aires, Argentina, on January 8, 1915. Technically, the *Muansa* was supposed to be the initial vessel to resupply the *Schutztruppe* and was loaded and reported ready for sea as early as February 2, 1915, but was advised by the foreign office not to depart until April, when "special orders" would be issued. Unfortunately, when the SMS *Dresden* was scuttled off Chile on the morning of March 14, 1915, and the political situation in South America began to deteriorate, the RKA abandoned any plans for the *Muansa* to sail for Africa. Instead, they opted for another British steamship detained in Hamburg at the beginning of the war, the *Dacre Hill* (2,674 GRT), which would become the blockade breaker *Marie* and depart on January 16, 1916.

Like the *Kronborg*, the *Marie* was commanded by another Danish-speaking German from Schleswig-Holstein (Flensburg), *Leutnant zur See* Conrad Sörensen.[17] Unlike the initial blockade breaker, however, her freight was determined solely by specifications outlined by Governor Schnee for use in the colony. Schnee requested that the 1,500 tons of cargo be packed in 50,000 porter loads to allow for ease of offloading and subsequent transporting by rail throughout the colony, and besides war materiel, he also desired it include creature comforts such as "European everyday items of all kinds; large quantities of medicines; clothing for Europeans and Blacks; materials for mail, telegraphy, and railway construction; European food and beverages; and semifinished products made of iron and metal."[18] Additional morale boosters in the form of Iron Crosses (1st and 2nd classes) and decorations for the Askaris were also included in this complement.

Since the *Königsberg* had been scuttled and her officers and men (and salvaged deck guns) became part of the *Schutztruppe* in the period between the arrival of the *Kronborg* and the dispatching of the *Marie*, the weapons and ammunition supplied on the *Marie* were almost entirely intended for use on land. They consisted of four 10.5 cm light field howitzers; two 7.5 cm portable mountain guns with equipment for carrying by mule; four 8.8 mm machine guns with telescopic sights, replacement barrels, and mounts; four caterpillar-wheeled mounts for the SK L/40 deck guns salvaged from the *Königsberg*; two thousand Gewehr 98 rifles with three million cartridges; 1,500 egg grenades; and two thousand rifle grenades (all of which arrived unusable due to their powder becoming damp from condensation in transit), plus five naval mines to block the harbor entrance in Sudi Bay off Kiswa.[19] An army artillery officer, *Hauptmann* (Captain) Roland von Kaltenborn-Stachau, was also added to the naval crew list on the *Marie* for the purpose of leading the sailors in defense of the vessel in the event of an attack at sea or upon landing (utilizing the items in their cargo) and staying on in East Africa to train the *Schutztruppen* how to operate the new models of field guns, mountain guns, and grenades being supplied.

Despite the best efforts of the Royal Navy, *Leutnant* Sörensen was able to completely avoid the blockade[20] and successfully land within Sudi Bay on March 15, 1916. In lieu of a dock, the *Marie* was met with floating platforms that allowed for the offloading of the cargo to the shore. While the British were eventually alerted to the *Marie*'s presence, sending two armed whaling ships into the bay to attack the *Marie* on April 11, and two cruisers on April 15, none were able to sink the vessel, and any damage incurred was successfully repaired. When it became time for the *Marie* to depart of April 23, Governor Schnee requested that *Leutnant* Sörensen not return to Germany, but instead sail to Batavia in the Dutch East Indies (now Jakarta, Indonesia) to take on additional supplies and return to East Africa—he agreed. Unfortunately, after reaching the harbor of Tanjung Priok in Batavia after twenty days of sailing, Sörensen was met by the "unfriendly attitudes of the Dutch colonial authorities, who seemed to be entirely under the political influence of the English consul."[21] His observation was astute. Unbeknown to Schnee or Sörensen, the English consulate took out an ad in the city's most popular newspaper that threatened any Dutch company that was willing to assist the *Marie* by putting them on a British "black list."

Despite the exclusively humanitarian nature of the provisions being requested by Governor Schnee, which consisted of clothing, medicine, quinine, food stocks, and the request for a loan of three million marks, the neutral, but threatened, Dutch refused to allow the Germans to take on any cargo or carry out any additional repairs on the *Marie*. She was thus interned in August, with many of her crew, including Sörensen, becoming POWs when they tried to escape the island and make it home. Although two more blockade breakers were approved to sail for GEA, and vast quantities of supplies, weapons, and ammunition had been ordered for the purpose and loaded onto the vessels, the British land forces' occupation of the coastal areas of German East Africa that occurred in the subsequent months led the RKA and RMA to abandon the operation by December 1916. The *Marie* would be the last steamship that sailed for GEA. Still, the RKA didn't yet consider *Schutztruppe*'s situation as being hopeless and refused to give up on the concept of resupplying them.

In April 1917, Wilhelm Solf—the secretary of state of the *Reichskolonialamt*—penned a lengthy memo to the German Admiralty staff, the army general staff, and the state secretary of the Foreign Office, very much in the offensive spirit of Lettow. In it, he claimed that "at least part of the protectorate can be held against the enemy onslaught," with reports from GEA convincing him that the *Schutztruppe* would be able to "hold out until at least mid-July."[22] Incredibly, he felt that the possibility of the protection force persevering had "not worsened, but rather improved" as a result of the several-month gap in fighting due to the rainy season. He did concede, however, that this would be achievable only if morale was revived by the arrival of another relief operation.

While admitting that it would be impossible to repeat the exploits of the two previous relief ships with future vessels sent under the same circumstances (i.e., solitary and defenseless), a U-boat with a large radius of action could instead be sent as a vanguard to attack British vessels and clear a path. He was, no doubt, familiar with the large U-cruisers operating off the North African coast and the Azores at this point in the war, themselves derived from the *U-Deutschland* cargo submarine, which had successfully made two separate trips to the United States in 1916. Interestingly, he pitched the idea in the very same phrasing that Admiral Holtzendorff used in his orders for SM *U-53*'s separate long-distance cruise to the US in September 1916.[23] His justification for sending a U-boat was as follows:

> 1. To bring fear and unrest into the blockade fleet by sinking blockade ships
> 2. To disrupt the replenishment of the English expeditionary corps' supplies by destroying transport and merchant ships
> 3. To increase the confidence and endurance of the German troops by transmitting messages

> 4. To announce and prepare the immediate material aid shipment planned for the autumn[24]

Given that Lettow was emphatic that the arrival of the *Kronborg* elicited "tremendous enthusiasm since it proved that communication between ourselves and home still existed,"[25] such an act would be a definite signal to the *Schutztruppe* that they had not been abandoned by Berlin.

If the proposed U-boat mission proved to be successful, Solf felt that in the autumn, additional auxiliary ships could make the trip to GEA, with "active support" from an additional submarine. He stressed that although U-boats were much more useful to the war effort in the North Sea and the Atlantic in 1917, the German Empire must, for political purposes, retain at least one of its colonial possessions when peace is concluded. Unfortunately, while finding sympathetic ears in the army and navy high commands, he did not find any support for his plans.

General Ludendorff, chief of staff of the army, was the first to respond to the memo on April 28, 1917, stating that although he appreciated "the value of an operation on the East African coast, I must nevertheless take the view that a submarine for this purpose should not be deprived of its role at sea, which is crucial for the war."[26] Admiral Holtzendorff, responding the following day, concurred, albeit with a more empathetic tone. He wrote,

> I am fully convinced . . . that it is necessary to prevent the loss of our most important and most valuable colony, German East Africa, by all means possible and to relieve the pressure on our heroic troops there. However, for technical reasons and in view of the fact that the coast of our colony is in enemy hands, it is not possible to achieve this goal either with lighter boats alone or in the autumn with steamers working together with submarines.
>
> As no other means of naval warfare are available, I find myself, to my deep regret, unable to provide the colony with the requested assistance.[27]

Noticeably absent from his memo was any mention of his other combat arm, the Naval Airship Division. In fact, he never even consulted Strasser on the matter.

Thus, when Zupitza submitted his proposal to the RKA in June 1917, he did so at a time when both the army and navy had effectively already given up on aiding German East Africa by land and sea. Although there wasn't any British blockade of the skies, Hoeppner and Holtzendorff very logically assumed that airship technology was not yet up to the task of performing such a long-distance trip. No one had yet attempted to remain aloft for days on end, and the airships' motors had already shown themselves to be consistently unreliable for trips across the English Channel, never mind over the Mediterranean. As such, when the RKA forwarded Zupitza's report to the army on July 24, 1917, the army's Inspectorate of the Airship Troops ruled out participating in the operation and instead forwarded it to the navy, which, although not outright dismissing the proposal, shelved it pending a review of its viability.[28] Incredibly, just two days after the army received Zupitza's pitch, a completely unrelated endurance flight took place over the Baltic that effectively proved the concept of his idea.

Following the army's retirement from airship combat missions in February 1917, the four airships that were not dismantled and scrapped were transferred to the *Kaiserliche Marine*, where they and their army crews assisted with naval reconnaissance over the Baltic Sea. In an odd juxtaposition of roles, the army airships would be performing the duties allocated to the navy at the beginning of the war, while Strasser's airships continued their bombing raids, initiated by the army, against enemy ground targets. *Leutnant* Ernst Lehmann, now commanding the R-class Zeppelin *LZ 120*, was one of the army officers to remain with his ship.

Stationed in Seerappen in East Prussia (now Lyublino, near Kaliningrad, Russia), his missions revolved around twenty-four-hour flights "to determine whether enemy forces were on the Baltic, to watch the Anglo-Russian submarine base in Finnish waters, and to search for mines and commercial ships off the coast of Sweden."[29] For Lehmann, these missions, besides resembling uneventful peacetime flights for DELAG, were the embodiment of operational inefficiency. He noted that in order to reach the submarine base in the Åland Islands off Finland, one-third of the total flight consisted of traveling to and from base—a complete waste of his time aloft that he could have otherwise spent patrolling.[30] Lehmann felt that it would be more militarily advantageous if his airship could instead remain in flight for one hundred hours or more and return to base only when fuel and provisions had been exhausted. He thus petitioned his superiors to put his airship to the task, and, largely owing to the fact that the army abandoned their airship battalions and Lehmann himself was soon to leave the service to take up a position with the Zeppelin factory in Friedrichshafen,[31] his request was granted. According to the man himself,

> One night the conversation in the officers' mess turned on the question of whether . . . an airship [could] remain out on patrol . . . for a hundred hours or more. The hovering capacity of an airship is theoretically unlimited, but there were some doubts that the motors and crew could endure such a prolonged strain. Though the question popped up again and again, it remained unanswered, for no such endurance flight had ever before been attempted. Then, I decided to settle the matter and within two days had equipped *LZ 120* for the test. After we had taken aboard 2,640 pounds of bombs; 6,160 pounds of arms, provisions, and spare parts; and about 7,700 pounds of water ballast, I found that, counting the crew of thirty men at about 5,500 pounds, we could still take on 37,000 pounds of gasoline and oil, which would be sufficient to run the motors, at reduced speed, for at least a hundred hours.[32]

Taking off shortly before midnight on July 26, 1917, he and his crew began what would become a record-breaking endurance flight over the Baltic.

Of all his concerns, Lehmann found dealing with his crew's fatigue to be the easiest. He put his mechanics on four rotating shifts and the remainder of the crew on two, varying between eight-hour, four-hour, and eventually six-hour rotations. The mechanical equipment, too, for the most part held out. Lehmann decided to maximize his efficiency by utilizing only three to four of the Zeppelin's six motors at a time but, even so, struggled with one particular engine that vibrated so badly that he had to stop the airship twice so his mechanics could replace the bolts securing the propeller to the drive-shaft.[33] The warm summer temperatures also proved to be challenging. When *LZ 120* ascended from Seerappen, Lehmann found that the air became warmer with every foot of altitude, thus diminishing his buoyancy and static lift. Although he successfully utilized his motors for dynamic lift, he was only barely able to pass over the hills and houses surrounding the airfield without dropping any ballast. These issues, however, proved to be only minor inconveniences, and the remainder of his flight was reported to be enjoyable by most of those who took part in it. The fact that Lehmann and his crew installed comfortable wicker furniture, hammocks, a bathroom, a rubber tub, and served hot meals by utilizing the hot engines as griddles certainly contributed to the illusion of this patrol being a pleasure flight.

Communication to the base in Seerappen was maintained throughout the trip by using the airship's wireless antennas, which allowed for both weather reports to arrive and experimental radio-compass positioning to be tested.[34] While both were essential for plotting approaching weather systems and the airship's heading on the charts, the former actually prompted the ending of the patrol. When a storm warning was received on the night of July 30–31, Lehmann, not wishing to push the limits of his already strained Zeppelin, set a course for home. Upon landing back in East Prussia at 0440 on July 31, Lehmann proved that R-class Zeppelins could remain aloft for at least 101 hours. In fact, he found that while the patrol used 34,750 lbs. of the initial 37,000 lbs. of gasoline taken on board, the remaining 2,250 lbs. would have allowed for an additional fourteen hours of flight.[35] Even more impressive, Lehmann calculated that *LZ 120* landed with "a useful load of 11,880 pounds, which, if converted into gasoline, would have made possible another thirty-three hours of flight."[36]

To the desperate RKA, an additional thirty-three hours of flight time was inconsequential. What mattered to them was that Lehmann and the crew of *LZ 120* had realized and exceeded the one hundred hours that experts predicted would be required to reach North America. Such a flight to German East Africa was now no longer, as the newspaper put it, "almost guaranteed," but already attainable with the military's existing airships.

Kurt Strümpell, heading the High Command of the *Schutztruppe* within the *Reichskolonialamt*, was quick to seize on this news and, in September 1917, sent another appeal to the RMA. He didn't mince his words. Emphasizing the critical need for relief by airship, he stated,

> With tenacious resistance and extreme exertion, the *Schutztruppe* for German East Africa, whose strength can be assumed to be about 1,300 Europeans in addition to the colored people, held the sole remaining piece of the German colonial possessions against an opponent far superior in numbers and resources.
>
> Since the beginning of this year[,] they have maintained, and in some cases expanded, an area confined to the east by the coast, to the north and northwest by the Rufiji-Kilombero-Ruhudji, to the west by a line drawn about 130 km east of Lake Nyasa, and to the south by the Rovuma. . . . Through powerful advances far into enemy territory, they have repeatedly proven that their offensive spirit was unbroken and their combat power unimpaired.
>
> Only lately have the enemy forces deployed from all sides succeeded in gaining some ground; after all, around 120,000 square kilometers of the protected area are still firmly in the hands of the tough defenders.

> Insofar as the German armed forces will be able to offer long and successful resistance to the advancing enemy, in addition to having the remaining stock of weapons and ammunition on hand, depends primarily on maintaining the physical fitness and the state of health of the European and colored members of the troop. . . . Although the last relief ship dispatched has brought out copious quantities of medical supplies, there can be little doubt that the stocks on hand have been heavily used and will soon be exhausted. . . . Sending further auxiliary ships or establishing contact with the troops by submarines is now prohibited by the war situation since the coast has been abandoned [by the *Schutztruppe*].
>
> The airship remains the only means of bringing help from home to the brave defenders; it will be in a position to supply the *Schutztruppe* with the urgently needed medicines, thus contributing to increasing its resistance and enabling the last piece of German colonial property to be held.[37]

The RKA estimated that after accounting for fuel, ballast, and crew, the airship making the trip to German East Africa would be able take on a payload of 14,700 kg (32,430 lbs.) comprising 3,000 kg of medical supplies and bandages, 1,200 kg of MG08/15 machine guns (thirty guns), 10,000 kg of ammunition (400,000 cartridges), and 500 kg of miscellaneous cargo, including binoculars, sewing kits, mail, and radiotelegraphy equipment.[38] Strümpell, likely foreseeing resistance from the RMA in sending what seemed like an insignificant quantity of materials via airship in comparison to what was already sent via steamship, already had his justifications prepared.

He noted that the machine guns being sent would not only replace the worn-out guns already in service in Africa but would also greatly improve the combat strength of the protection force—essentially acting as additional riflemen. The ammunition, while appearing to be "extraordinarily small, especially measured by European standards," was actually quite considerable, since the *Schutztruppen* were trained to use ammunition "sparingly" and to be selective with their shots. The mail would be of "moral importance," bringing news of the war in Europe, which was then still going well for the German army, and urging them to fight on. Additionally, it would deliver the numerous awards intended for Lettow and his European troops and Askaris so they would realize how proud the fatherland was of their continued resistance and that they were far from being forgotten. Finally, he rationalized the inclusion of sewing kits in a cargo that did not include any fabric or uniforms.

Since there was no means of replenishing the airship's hydrogen supply upon its arrival in East Africa, the mission would be a "one-way" trip. As such, the RKA intended to cannibalize and recycle its components. The gas bags could be converted into waterproof clothing, sleeping bags, and rain jackets worn by the *Schutztruppen*, the airship's walkways were made of leather that could be cut into soles for boots, and the canvas "outer shell" could be cut up and fabricated into tents, clothing, and bandages. Later, it would be determined that even the duralumin frame of the airship could be disassembled and utilized as a wireless antenna or cut into pieces to fabricate stretchers, and the motors could serve as generators.[39]

In concluding his missive, Strümpell reiterated the enduring argument about the importance of the East African campaign tying down enemy forces that could otherwise be employed in other theaters of war, but he also made a final, almost despairing entreaty about the mission's value to the *Schutztruppe*. He wrote,

> The medical and war material to be sent out is not very large in quantity, but it is of inestimable value for the maintenance and strengthening of the troops' power of resistance. If it succeeds in making it possible to keep the most-important stocks replenished, even for just a few more months or possibly until the end of the war, the goal set for sending out an airship will have been achieved.[40]

Certainly, he made both a convincing and heartfelt argument, but unbeknown to him, he didn't have to be quite so persuasive.

Following the success of *LZ 120*'s endurance flight, the *Reichsmarineamt* had also begun reexamining the operation. They calculated that if a Zeppelin departed from the Central Powers' most southerly airship base in Yambol, Bulgaria, a trip to East Africa would cover less distance than Lehmann had already proved possible over the Baltic. On August 3, the RMA submitted a report to FdL Strasser for comment, in which *Korvettenkapitän* Müller-Berneck, departmental head of the RMA, noted,

> At first, the idea of flying by airship from Yambol to East Africa seems fanciful and risky. The distance from Yambol and Lake Tanganika is 5,300 kilometers [3,293 miles]. Since, however, the *LZ 120* has just recently flown 5,700 kilometers [3,542 miles], the concept is worthy of a close and detailed examination into its feasibility, especially since an intermediate landing in Syria is not

> impossible. It would take only 12 railway cars to resupply the airship. From Syria to Lake Tanganika is only roughly 4,000 kilometers [2,485 miles], as is Yambol to Aden.[41]

He also raised concerns about potential landing sites, whether or not the navy would be willing to sacrifice an airship for a "one-way" mission, and whether the operation's morale-boosting effect in itself made the mission worthwhile. In an obvious dig at the army, he added the additional viewpoint that "since the army have already started to dismantle their airship support facility, and since the army airships are generally not capable of such long flights from a navigational and airmanship point of view, the mission should be attempted only if the navy is capable of carrying it out."[42] Müller-Berneck's selective memory apparently forgot that *LZ 120* and her crew were originally army assets.

Upon viewing the report, Strasser requested additional calculations and feasibility studies to be conducted, particularly about the elevations of mountain ranges to be crossed and subtropical wind and weather conditions, which were, as of yet, unavailable. He also insisted that if the mission were to take place, it must depart from Yambol and be a direct flight, since a stopover would not extend the range of the airship unless hydrogen was also supplied. When he was eventually provided with a nine-page meteorological study that concluded "conditions, as far as they can be judged from the sparsity of observations at higher altitudes, are considered favorable for the undertaking . . . especially in the months of the October and November,"[43] Strasser was prepared to give his judgment about the mission to the RKA. Responding on September 16, 1917, he wrote,

> I consider the undertaking to be feasible and promising.
>
> The possibility of losing the airship as a result of enemy counteraction is present in the first part of the journey. However, the probability of this is low if the journey is started during a new-moon period.
>
> The meteorological conditions are favorable for the undertaking in October and November. Unfavorable meteorological conditions, which cannot be determined beforehand, and which can cause the undertaking to fail, are of course not excluded. With a bit of luck, however, the trip must succeed.
>
> The implementation of the undertaking will be, in addition to the direct relief for the brave *Schutztruppe*, an event in which the German people will be enthusiastic again and which must arouse admiring attention all over the world.

> Compared to this overall goal, the use of an airship with a crew of 20 seems trivial.[44]

By the nineteenth, the RMA officially gave the "green light" for the relief mission and, after conferring with the RKA and the Zeppelin factory in Friedrichshafen, drew up plans at an "accelerated pace"[45] so that an airship would be ready to fly by the end of the month. The Zeppelin, *L 57* (factory designation *LZ 102*), which was then nearing completion, was chosen for the flight but would first need to be modified from its original design.

Given that, unlike *LZ 120*, the Africa ship would be carrying additional loads and would likely not be able to take a direct route to GEA, its gas capacity would have to be increased from 55,000 m^3 (1,942,307 ft.^{3}) to 67,500 m^3 (2,383,740 ft.^{3}), resulting in a usable lift of 27,700 kg (61,068 lbs.).[46] To accomplish this, *L 57* would have to be lengthened by 30 meters (98 feet) from its original length of 196.5 meters (645 feet) to allow for the inclusion of two additional gas cells. A fifth 250 hp, six-cylinder Maybach HS-Lu ("Lu" indicating *Luftschiff*) engine would also be added to increase the airship's speed from 22 m/sec. (49 mph) to 25 m/sec. (56 mph).[47] Finally, the bomb bays would be eliminated and converted to cargo holds, and all the steel cables would be replaced with bronze substitutes in order to eliminate any possible magnetic interference with the Zeppelin's compass.[48]

While the RMA had agreed with the Zeppelin works on a fixed price of 3.2 million marks per airship in 1917 (just over 13.6 million USD in 2024), *Luftschiffbau* Zeppelin requested an additional payment of 50,000 marks to convert *L 57* to the new specifications—a bit of price gouging, since the gross profits made on the delivery of *L 57* came to 1,202,128.55 marks[49] (over 5.1 million USD in 2024).

In order to keep the actual destination of the mission a secret, the operation's code name referenced another colony lost back in 1914, Tsingtao. This dramatic undertaking would henceforth be referred to as "*China-Sache*"—the China matter.

3

The China Matter

EARLY SEPTEMBER 1917. *Kapitänleutnant* Horst Treusch von Buttlar-Brandenfels and his crew are in the air, en route to the Zeppelin factory from their base in Potsdam. They have been flying this circuit for months, carrying out various airborne tests on an airship that, despite it still being wartime, is no longer relegated to combat duty. Their Zeppelin, originally commissioned by the army in 1915 as *LZ 88*, was now—upon being ceded over to the navy in January 1917—"re-Christened" *L 25* and serving as the Naval Airship Division's lighter-than-air test bed for various aerial inventions, armaments, and equipment. Buttlar was entrusted with this "experimental" airship due to the fact that, at that point in the war, he was one of the *Kaiserliche Marine*'s most experienced and successful commanders. It was another notch on his rapidly widening belt.

As early as November 1914, he was given command of *L 6*, by June 1915—*L 11*, and in May 1916 took over the first-ever R-class "super Zeppelin"—*L 30*. He even had a short stint with the Parseval blimp *PL 6*. His years of reconnaissance flights over the North Sea and raids on England made him one of Strasser's most prized officers, valued by the FdL not only for his operational proficiency, but for his candidness. He was, in essence, the navy's equivalent to Lehmann and certainly the *Marine Luftschiff*

Abteilung's most qualified candidate for a potential long-distance mission that would push the limits of rigid-airship technology.

Upon landing in Friedrichshafen and making his way out of the airship hangar with his executive officer, *Oberleutnant zur See* Hans von Schiller, Buttlar's attention is drawn to a group of "very stern-looking gentlemen" wearing "strange uniforms."[1] As the two men draw closer, the mysterious congregation is recognized as being members of the *Reichskolonialamt* and officers of the *Schutztruppe*, conferring with engineers from the Zeppelin factory. Schiller, turning to his commander but speaking to no one in particular, brusquely blurts out, "So, what's with the brown shirts?" The guests from the Colonial Office don't even turn to cast a disparaging stare; they are engrossed in their discussion and transfixed on another Zeppelin under construction, but nearing completion, *L 57*. Buttlar, too, offers no response.

Choosing to be more tactful, the *Kapitänleutnant* silently thinks about the party's purpose at an airship factory as he and Schiller continue to walk out of earshot and toward the mess. Only then does he pull aside a Zeppelin factory employee and jestingly posit the rhetorical question "Surely, they are not going to try to fly to Africa?"[2] Both Buttlar and Schiller are dumbfounded when a response in given in the affirmative—that is exactly what the RKA intended to do. While Schiller gives the matter no further thought and continues onward to grab a bite to eat, Buttlar remains in place, stunned. Although he is shaken out of the trance by his returning, ravenous *Oberleutnant*, the concept of a flight to Africa continues to linger in his mind. "If only I could be entrusted with the job!" he thinks to himself. "Everybody would watch the flight with their hearts in their mouths, and, if it succeeded, I should be the bravest navigator in the whole world, including even the enemy."[3]

The idea does not diminish over the passing days, and on his return flight back to Potsdam, Buttlar continues to have his head both literally and figuratively "in the clouds." He imagines looking down at the "pyramid of Cheops, the Nile, and Victoria"[4] from great heights but, most of all, fantasizes about his glorious arrival in East Africa and the cheers from the grateful colonials. These whimsies go into overdrive when Strasser visits him at base days later and nonchalantly asks if he'd be willing to take command of *L 57* and head the mission to East Africa. Not giving the matter any thought, Buttlar spontaneously and enthusiastically agrees.

Strasser, taken aback by the swiftness of the twenty-nine-year-old lieutenant's response, decides to rein in his eager officer and inject a dose of reality into the conversation. "Treusch, I think you're the best man for this job, but remember this is a one-way trip. What would Ilse think of you fighting out the rest of the war in Africa? You've been married for just over a year. I wouldn't hold it against you for declining; besides, you know how much we need you in the air over here."[5] Buttlar, however, cannot be dissuaded and reaffirms his willingness to follow through with the mission.

"Very well, Treusch . . . *Wo keine Versuchung, da ist kein Ehre.*[6] Find out who of your crew wish to join you on the trip; we're accepting volunteers only. We can't expect all your men to be as keen as you to abandon the skies for the bush." Shaking his head and revealing a barely discernible smirk, Strasser then takes his leave and departs for home. Buttlar, still in a state of shock, immediately assembles his men and imparts the good news. Not surprisingly, none among his crew wish to sit out the expedition and are unanimously enraptured by the thought of the undertaking. Then, things go silent. For several days, nothing is heard from Strasser or the *Reichsmarineamt* about the mission, and Buttlar and his crew begin to discount the offer to participate as nothing but a cruel joke.

Finally, on September 16, Buttlar receives an encouraging telegram from Strasser instructing him to report to Nordholz immediately—surely this must mean he will be given command of *L 57*. When he arrives, however, he senses an ominous mood in the office, and Strasser looks uncomfortable. Gesturing to the seat in front of him, the FdL says, "Please, sit down, Treusch." Already deflated, Buttlar readies himself for the bad news.

"My dear Treusch, it pains me to tell you this, but you won't be going on the African trip." Strasser, seeing Buttlar agape and ready to protest, raises his hand and gives the young officer the signal to pause. Taking a moment to recollect his thoughts, he renews his speech: "The aerial warfare in the North Sea is, unfortunately, going to continue, and in the circumstances, I cannot possibly spare a commander and crew as experienced as you and your men.[7] You are to report to Tondern to take command of *L 54*." As a means of lightening the blow, Strasser promises that should the African mission prove to be successful, an even-bigger airship will be constructed, specifically for Buttlar, to make round trips to GEA. Neither man actually believes that to be true. The air in the room becomes heavy, and the two men remain seated, staring at the floor, in silent, deep contemplation.

Sounding as if he is on the verge of tears, Buttlar then addresses his superior. "Sir, if not me, may I ask who will be making the flight?"

"I suppose I owe you that at the very least, Treusch," Strasser concedes. "I'm sending Bockholt and his crew; in fact, it was they who delivered *L 54* from Staaken to Tondern. They're on their way to Friedrichshafen now to begin preparations for the mission."

As Buttlar discovered, the prospective commander of the flight was *Kapitänleutnant* Ludwig Bockholt, and the airship being allocated for the African adventure was *L 57*. The former was a curious choice, and the latter was, in its original design, not yet suitable for the trip. Perhaps expectedly, given the immediacy of the concerns about the *Schutztruppe* and the fluidity of the situation in East Africa, at this early stage the "China matter" operation was itself, likewise, in a state of flux. Although approved by the RMA, Germany's supreme warlord—the Kaiser—had not yet given his stamp of approval, and the army was actively voicing their concerns against the venture. Indeed, in the time that elapsed between September 19, when the navy green-lighted the operation, and October 1, when Strasser sent his appeal to Kaiser Wilhelm II, many details still needed to be worked out and bureaucratic battles had to be fought.

While all these niceties will be elaborated on in the proceeding pages, due to the frenetic nature of the planning phase and the various changes that had to be made in a matter of weeks, it's best to begin to explore one of the simpler particulars about the mission—Strasser's choice for the airship's commander. In this case, it appeared the FdL was opting for daring instead of experience.

Ludwig Bockholt was born in Heerdt (Düsseldorf) on March 1, 1885—neither was he of noble descent nor was his naval career terribly noteworthy. While just three years older than Buttlar-Brandenfels and two years younger than another famous naval airship commander, *Kapitänleutnant* Heinrich Mathy (killed on *L 31* during a raid on England on October 2, 1916), he was not in the Naval Airship Division from the beginning of the war. Instead, he joined the *Kaiserliche Marine* in 1903 and spent the first two years of the war as a watch officer on board the Kaiser-class battleship SMS *Prinzregent Luitpold*. It was on this dreadnought that he experienced action during the epic battle of Jutland, but otherwise he saw little else apart from training exercises, aborted attempts to draw out the British Grand Fleet, and numerous uneventful sweeps of the waters inside the confines of the British blockade. Seemingly bored by the monotonous, frequent sorties into the North and Baltic Seas, he transferred into the airship service in October 1916. This was by no means an unusual move at the time.

Seaman Richard Stumpf, an enlisted man on the SMS *Helgoland*—another battleship whose service history mirrored that of the *Prinzregent Luitpold*—often lamented that all the best officers, similarly frustrated by their lack of utilization in the war effort, were transferring out of the High Seas Fleet because they sought actual combat against the British.[8] Echoing these sentiments, his detailed diary is replete with tedium and the disappointment with almost never engaging the enemy. Interestingly, his incessant complaints of boredom on the battleship were often interrupted by the presence of a Zeppelin overhead. In one of his more poetic descriptions of the allure of the Naval Airship Division, he wrote,

> While I was occupied with my writing, one of our Zeppelins flew over with a thunderous noise. It blew away all my sad thoughts and worries. Its proud shape refreshed my heart and renewed my courage. . . . Although our ship was moving very fast, the shimmering giant soon vanished into the infinite distance. England, England, you are about to receive a surprise from the air.
>
> I fluctuated between two extremes. My imagination and the power of suggestion soon changed what had earlier seemed too difficult and depressing into dreams of victory. O Zeppelin, please come more often to banish my sadness![9]

From this perspective, it is understandable why such an attraction to the airship service existed. Unfortunately, not all missions were dramatic raids on England, and, as Bockholt soon found out, his transfer yielded little in the way of change from his earlier battleship excursions, despite being in the air.

He became the fourth commander of *L 23*[10] at the end of January 1917, and his war diaries read much like that of his former battleship's. Given that the Q-class *L 23* was already antiquated by 1917, and the R-, S-, T-, and U-class Zeppelins were now the only airships raiding Britain, Bockholt's missions almost exclusively consisted of assisting minesweepers and North Sea patrols. There were a few blips of excitement, such as escorting the submarine *U-53* through minefields on May 1 and then searching for *L 44* (with Strasser on board) after she encountered engine troubles on the infamous May 23–24 raid, but it was hardly the change of pace that he sought. This is perhaps why he became the only airship commander not only to attempt, but to successfully capture a surface vessel when *L 23* sent a prize crew to the *Royal* in April—the temptation for a tangible impact on the war proved too irresistible. When Bockholt was finally given command of a Zeppelin capable of bombing England, the newly commissioned U-class *L 54* in August 1917, his only mission was to deliver it to Tondern in September so that Buttlar could take command—he had already been earmarked to head the operation to East Africa.

Robert Gaudi, in his book *African Kaiser*, which I hesitate to cite because of its heavy reliance on English-language secondary sources and repetition of various myths, claimed that Bockholt was selected "for his boldness and also because he was expendable."[11] He also added that Bockholt "was not popular with his immediate superiors or his fellow officers—many of whom thought him a selfish careerist."[12] Rather paradoxically, he finally accused him of pulling strings in naval high command to preserve his role in the "China matter" when his "poor understanding of basic Zeppelin mechanics"[13] later resulted in the destruction of *L 57*—an allegation disproven by archival records.[14] With all these purported demerits, one must ask why Strasser would even consider such a man not only for a technically challenging and untried adventure, but for one of the most enviable charges in the entire *Marine Luftschiff Abteilung*.[15]

His bravery certainly helped get him the job, but the other sentiments, being expendable, unpopular, and incompetent, ultimately fail to hold water under scrutiny. While it was true that Strasser wished to retain the most-experienced commanders for raids on England, giving them the newest and best airships, Bockholt was awarded with just such a Zeppelin in the form of *L 54,* then under construction, when he turned over command of *L 23* to *Oberleutnant zur See* Bernhard Dinter in June 1917—long before being slated for operation *China-Sache*. His six months of experience with *L 23*, which consisted of no fewer than thirty-five successful flights, including test exercises, reconnaissance as far as the Norwegian coast, searching for and marking minefields, escorting U-boats, and training his replacement commander, seemed to have proven his abilities to Strasser, who now felt he was ready to cross the Channel on offensive operations.

As far as popularity was concerned, testimonial evidence exists that goes against Gaudi's assertion. When Buttlar, the scorned commander for the "China matter," later recalled his thoughts about Bockholt, he naturally expressed envy but claimed that there was "perhaps . . . no man better fitted for such an undertaking."[16] The Yambol-based army officers, engineer Johannes Göbel and meteorologist Dr. Walter Förster, whom Bockholt met after being given command of *L 57*, professed that Bockholt was far from being an opportunist, or a man given command due to cronyism, but instead "an extremely determined soldier who could not be dissuaded from a decision when he made up his mind."[17]

Photos too show a more congenial relationship among Bockholt, his peers, and Strasser, although these are admittedly open to the interpretation of the viewer. Of these, one taken on September 4, 1917, to celebrate Peter Strasser being awarded the Pour le Mérite on August 20, does this quite well.

It shows Bockholt standing not on the fringe of the group, but instead smiling near the center, to the immediate right, rear side of Strasser and two men away from *Kapitänleutnant* Franz Stabbert, the man who ceded command of *L 23* to Bockholt and who himself was one of the most experienced men in the assemblage.[18] This should not imply, however, that the relationship between Bockholt and Strasser was always affable and that no tension ever existed between the two men. Bockholt did have an aggressive nature, and, as archival correspondence reveals, he was willing to bypass the FdL and go straight to the *Admiralstab* when critical decisions had to be resolved, and time was of the essence—particularly in the later phases of the "China matter."

Finally, as a testament to his competence, Bockholt did not immediately commit to the African flight and instead brought up very real concerns about accepting command of the mission. In fact, he and his crew would research and consider the mission for over a month before ultimately accepting the responsibility.[19] In a top-secret telegram forwarded to the chief of the Admiralty, Admiral Henning von Holtzendorff, Bockholt very astutely raised the following queries requiring an immediate response:

> (1) What is known about the guarding of the North African coast by destroyers, submarine hunters, etc.?
>
> (2) Has Pola [the base of the Mediterranean U-boat Flotilla] already been in contact with the submarine flotilla for weather reports, wind directions, approaching storm centers, etc. to Yambol?
>
> (3) What types of aircraft are based in the Aegean Sea? Seaplanes or land-based planes? What altitudes?
>
> (4) What temperatures, during the daytime and at nighttime, did our pilots, who used to operate on the Suez Canal and on the Sinai front, find at the different altitudes?[20]

While the first three were answered quickly, with updates given frequently from this point onward, the most-important concerns, the weather conditions and the situation on the ground in East Africa, not addressed by Bockholt, were still largely speculative.

Concerning the weather in Africa, the RMA and RKA had only reports from the previous years to base their predictions on, but these were useful only for pressure systems and ground temperature within the continent. As such, the initial meteorological reports submitted to Strasser were based on expectations at low altitudes, while the anticipated winds and temperatures at high altitudes could be ascertained only by the "subtropical" conditions already experienced by army airships previously operating out of Yambol and naval seaplanes currently flying in the Mediterranean and Near East theaters. Dr. Förster, the expert being consulted for meteorology, and himself also taking part in the *China-Sache* operation, noted that at Yambol, summer temperatures typically averaged about 104°F (40°C),[21] making Bulgaria warmer than German East Africa in October (where temperatures were between 77°F and 86°F) and a good basis for predicting airship behavior upon reaching GEA. Still, he and his Yambol colleague Göbel noted that for every 262 feet (80 meters) the airship ascends, the air pressure drops by 1 percent.[22] Additionally,

> In an area where certain basic features of a subtropical climate are already noticeable: intense radiation with mostly very low air humidity during the day, correspondingly strong heat radiation at night, leads to a stratification of the atmosphere, in which the temperature, in contrast to normal conditions, starts to decrease from a certain layer and then suddenly increases again. For the vertical movement of an airship, such atmospheric phenomena as barrier layers, which suddenly impede the ascent, endanger the descent, so that if the lower air masses are too heavy, the ship can hardly be landed, and if they are too light, [the airship] falls into the danger of sagging [this is a literal translation of the word "*durchsacken*" used by Göbel to describe a loss of buoyancy].[23]

He ultimately concluded that the "Balkan subtropical zone" (i.e., Bulgaria) must be considered separate from the "Central European climatic zone," and that both were themselves completely different from the zone over the Mediterranean Sea,[24] to say nothing of the extreme temperatures an airship would encounter over the Sahara. In other words, even the most experienced Zeppelin commander operating over Europe would have his work cut out for him during a flight to Africa.

Compounding these issues was where to land the airship if it actually made it to German East Africa. Since the *Schutztruppe* had steadily retreated inland and in the direction of Mozambique, Mahenge, a mountainous region 175 miles west of the coastline and about 200 miles north of the border with Portuguese East Africa, became their stronghold. This meant that after consistently losing hydrogen through venting throughout the journey, the Zeppelin would still have to traverse high ground elevations, with some mountain peaks reaching 19,000 feet, to reach the colonial outposts. Making matters worse was that, even at this point, very few radio communications from the *Schutztruppe* were making their way to the *Reichskolonialamt*, and the Germans were already relying on intercepted reports from the British colonial forces and Allied public news broadcasts for their military intelligence. Strasser put particular emphasis on one such telegram from September 19 that reported the following:

> In the vicinity of Mkonda (53 miles south of Mahenge) [this is incorrect and is probably Makanda or Mkingira to the east] our columns are engaged with the enemy and several German counterattacks have been repulsed with severe losses. On September 6th, our aircraft cooperated successfully with the infantry, setting fire to the enemy's abattis [a defensive barrier constructed of wood and sharpened sticks pointed toward the enemy] and engaging the defenders with machine gun fire from a height of 700 feet.[25]

This was not misinformation being broadcast to deceive the Germans. As of May 1917, besides probing ever farther into the interior, the British had, in fact, established an aerodrome on the German East African coast at Kilwa for the South African No. 26 Squadron. Here, there were four B.E.2c reconnaissance/bomber aircraft available, along with two 150 hp Voisin III planes absorbed from the No. 8 Naval Squadron in Zanzibar, and a Short Type 827 seaplane from the Royal Navy's requisitioned cargo ship turned balloon ship, the HMS *Manica*.[26] They had already been harassing Lettow's headquarters as they supported the infantry in their push westward, with Lettow recalling that

> they had evidently found out the exact site of our headquarter camp. . . . I remember one day when four aeroplanes, against which we could do nothing, circled over our camp for hours and dropped bombs . . . the European employed in the telephone hut was so badly hurt that he lost his hand. An adjourning hut full of valuable documents was set alight by an incendiary bomb.[27]

Although these aircraft would undoubtedly *not* be armed with anti-Zeppelin ammunition, they still posed a threat to the vulnerable airship, especially when it made an approach to land.

While the presence of enemy aircraft and a rapidly shrinking viable landing zone were certainly major issues within the African continent, the

Reichsmarineamt encountered an even-bigger obstacle to the relief mission much closer to home—*das Heer*, the army. As a secret memo from September 26 revealed, the *Reichskolonialamt*'s initial appeal to the army back in July was now having an undesired effect on the navy's taking ownership of the operation. As *Korvettenkapitän* Müller-Berneck, departmental head of the RMA, and Major Döhring of the RKA discovered,

> For the purposes of the "China" expedition, the Reich Colonial Office first turned to the Inspectorate of Airships, which is subordinate to the commanding general of the [army] air force. They [the army] had [subsequently] submitted the request of the *Reichskolonialamt* directly to the *Reichsmarineamt*, which has followed the proposal up to the present day and has now submitted it to the *Admiralstab*.
>
> In the meantime, the Reich Colonial Office had asked *Hauptmann* von Bentingen, who is currently employed at the front for air force purposes, to take part in the expedition. As a result, the [army air force's] chief of staff [Lt. Colonel Hermann von der Lieth-Thomsen] informed the Inspectorate of Airships of the project and said the following in a telegram to the Reich Colonial Office:
>
> 1. That *Hauptmann* von Bentingen could not be requested.
> 2. [He] reported the project to the Supreme Army Command and spoke out against the feasibility of the undertaking.
> 3. The High Command of the army then expressed the desire to attend a lecture [on the matter], in which H.M. [his majesty Kaiser Wilhelm II] will be involved.
>
> RMA and RKA fear, given Colonel Thomsen's aversion to airships, that this could jeopardize the undertaking, and asked the Admiralty for a statement on how this possibility could be countered.[28]

The RMA, however, was unwilling to back down from going forward with the mission and felt that they needn't be concerned with the Kaiser, since "if the matter could be represented militarily," he would agree with the plan.

As a means of placating the army somewhat, the navy allowed their rival to nominate another potential candidate, in lieu of Captain Bentingen, for "possible consideration" by the RMA. Not wishing to be excluded from the glory, the army eventually proposed *Feldwebelleutnant* (2nd junior lieutenant) Emil Grussendorf, a prewar DELAG pilot described by Göbel as an "overbearing and capable helmsman who could find his way out of bad situations,"[29] for the job. While the RMA acquiesced, they emphasized that he could take part in the *China-Sache* mission only as the watch officer, and not the commander—terms the army air force was willing to accept.

These interservice challenges to *China-Sache* would continue to percolate in the coming weeks and would even reconvene with greater rigor weeks after the RMA made their appeal to the Kaiser, but ultimately, politics could be overcome with diplomacy, finesse, and time. As it was, there were still, quite literally, concrete issues putting the success of the mission in jeopardy that required a quick infusion of money, material, and effort to fix.

The final impediment to the success of the enterprise was the choice of the army airship station in Yambol, Bulgaria, as the launching point for the operation. As the RMA was soon to find out, in September 1917 the base was in a very poor state and was hardly capable of supporting the gigantic, W-class *L 57*, or its crew complement. According to a telegram forwarded to the *Admiralstab* on September 25,

> Harbor commander [at] Yambol reports that there is a complete lack of operating materials, fog-landing equipment, night-landing equipment, gag collars for landing. Only a limited amount of ballast material available in the hangar for loading onto an airship. No spare parts for S [Schütte-Lanz] and Z [Zeppelin] ships here. No ammo here. For airship defense [there are] only two machine guns with practice ammunition here. For crews to be sent[,] [there exists] no barracks equipment such as beds [or] cutlery. Final addition: regarding ground crews as well as accommodation and meals will [still need to] be reported. Recommend hammocks under all circumstances and [that the naval crews] bring eating and cooking utensils.[30]

This should not have come as a surprise to the *Reichsmarineamt*. Yambol was already a very minor base[31] prior to the army ceasing airship operations in February, with that decision only accelerating its obsolescence. In fact, when *Korvettenkapitän* Joachim von Arnim, the naval attaché in Sofia, was informed of the navy's plan to take over airship operations there, he telegrammed the RMA in Berlin to advise that the wireless transmitter at Yambol was already in the process of being dismantled, and its operators were set to return home—a process he immediately halted.[32] He reiterated that "only very primitive accommodation can be expected." Things only got worse when naval personnel actually arrived to inspect the base weeks later, but by the end of September, Strasser and the RMA had a decision to make.

On October 1, 1917, the *Reichsmarineamt* officially sought the Kaiser's blessing to go forward with the *China-Sache* undertaking. The request, delivered in person (*von Hand zu Hand*) and requiring an immediate response, began rather innocuously, reminding the emperor of the "heroic struggle" of the *Schutztruppe* and the navy's commitment to "leave no stone unturned" in any attempt to resupply them. While admitting that there were initial doubts about the mission's feasibility, the successful endurance flight of *LZ 120* coupled with the fact that *L 57* had been lengthened to support two more gas cells and lightened from six to five engines meant that *L 57* would easily be able to supply the colonial forces with 3,000 kg of medical supplies, thirty machine guns (accounting for 1,200 kg), 400,000 cartridges (10,000 kg), and mail, awards, and other miscellaneous material weighing 500 kg.[33] The plan to utilize Balkan weather stations and U-boats in the Mediterranean to supply weather updates was shared, as was the navy's intention to use wireless telegraphy for navigation. Then, given the evidence already available to the *Reichskolonialamt* and *Reichsmarineamt*, the wording of the request became wildly optimistic.

First, the RMA assured the Kaiser that the "only military danger to the airship will be from enemy air stations on the Aegean Sea," but this would be somewhat negated by departing in the new-moon phase between October 10 and 20. Next, they insisted that because the *Schutztruppe* would be available to serve as a landing party, there was no concern about a potential landing area within German East Africa. This disregarded the facts that no one in Africa was aware of the mission, and none of the European colonials or native Askaris had any training in handling airships. The most confident language, however, was left for the conclusion of the missive, with *Vizeadmiral* Eduard von Capelle, secretary of state for the *Reichsmarineamt*, stating,

> In summary, it can therefore be said that technically, based on human judgment, success is guaranteed and that there are no military dangers that could force an otherwise necessary war operation to be abandoned. An opinion which, as I would like to mention, is fully shared by the prospective commander, *Kapitänleutnant* Bockholt.
>
> After due consideration, the airship can be dispensed with from the main theater of war. Its commitment here is justified because it will give our defenders of East Africa, who are fighting so gloriously for Germany's honor, a tangible sign that home had not forgotten them, a new incentive for the future, and the politically

important opportunity to utilize the remainder of our colonial possessions till the end of the war, despite all the deprivations. In addition, the bold undertaking will, if successful, revive the Germanic pride in arms among our people and contribute to the further strengthening of our reputation in the rest of the world as an expression of the unshakable German will to fight. And even in the event of failure, the sacrifice of people and property, which is small in relation to the chances of success, will compel even our most bitter opponents to respect the attempt in which Germany's technical ability and the willingness of its sons to make sacrifices in the service of their fatherland were so completely united.

Therefore, I humbly ask Your Majesty to approve the sending of a naval airship to German East Africa.[34]

Missing in the telegram were the numerous, and quite serious, issues with the choice of using Yambol as a launching point for the operation. Unfortunately, these were discovered only after the army ceded command of the base to the navy weeks after the RMA made its appeal to the Kaiser. The most serious of these were as follows:

- Equipment and tools for the landing and maintenance of *L 57* had to be imported to Bulgaria from Ahlhorn—what was left over from the army was found to be entirely inadequate. Large items such as lifts, frames, and harnesses had to be shipped by rail in pieces and assembled upon arrival.
- The outer walls of the existing airship hangar were found to be rotten due to exposure and had to be refurbished.
- Construction in the base was being carried out by Serbian prisoners of war, and means of housing and guarding them had to be established.
- The "gasometer," used for pumping hydrogen into the airship's gas bags, had problems with its seal and thus leaked. This meant that the gas bottles storing the hydrogen required a replenishment of "several hundred" cubic meters of hydrogen every two weeks. New rubber hoses and a new aluminum nozzle would also have to brought along by the Zeppelin when it arrived.
- No gasoline storage tanks existed on-site, and therefore railway tanker cars had to be imported. Since the only means of transferring the fuel to the airship at Yambol were "a 500-liter Martini-Huenecke car along with 12 small carbon dioxide bottles and a 300-liter open

tanker with a hand pump," the process of refueling the Zeppelin would take an unacceptable amount of time. To fix this, barrels were filled with fuel and moved toward the staging area, where they could be operated with a hand pump.

• Weather reports for the Middle Eastern climate zone, supplied by the Ottoman forces in Constantinople (Istanbul), arrived irregularly or were delayed to the point that there were no longer useful.

• Foodstuffs confiscated by the Bulgarian government, such as "meat, fats, legumes, flour, cheese, sugar, salt, and potatoes," had to be requested from the Bulgarian Requisitions Commission in Yambol, using three separate forms. After the Bulgarians received the requests, they calculated what could be supplied to the Yambol base, and required immediate payment for the provisions via a monetary transfer to the Bulgarian National Bank. The process was lengthy, and often proteins and fats could be obtained only weeks after the requests were made. Since the Bulgarians forbade any private purchases of foodstuffs from Yambol, the former army personnel were discovered to have subsisted solely by gardening and keeping their own livestock within the base for slaughter.

• The construction of infirmary and hospital barracks was not completed, and, since the limited available facilities were already being taken up by army personnel afflicted with malaria, dysentery, and typhus (typically 35 percent of the German base during the summer months), there would be no means to house any naval personnel who got sick. Although one civilian hospital within Yambol was made available to the Germans, under the condition that Bulgarian forces would also be treated for free by a German doctor, it seemed "very questionable whether German patients would receive the careful and correct treatment they needed if the German doctor left." Given that a second city hospital was already full of Bulgarian civilians and military personnel, it was recommended that the navy take precautions to avoid getting sick by regularly using mosquito nets, taking quinine, and abstaining from eating any local fruits or pastries from Yambol.[35]

It will never be known whether the Kaiser would have given his approval for the mission had these details been known previously, but since they weren't brought up, the Kaiser immediately granted permission for *China-Sache* to go forward. It was not a moment too soon.

In the weeks that followed the enterprise's official "go ahead," the situation on the ground in German East Africa became ever more tenuous. Yet again, the Germans were relying not on reports from their own forces but on intercepted Allied transmissions to ascertain the deteriorating situation in the colony. The first of these arrived just a day after the RMA submitted its plan to the Kaiser, but it was already outdated.

On October 2 the RKA notified the RMA that on September 27 the British had launched an offensive on Lindi, and, according to a Reuters report from September 29, they had occupied a German staging area on the north bank of the Mbwemkuru River, capturing a cannon.[36] The *Reichsmarineamt* disregarded the report since they believed that the relief mission was still viable due to the "large areas of land" still occupied by the *Schutztruppe*. Then, on October 6, the RKA informed the navy that another Reuters report from October 3 indicated that the *Schutztruppen* were retreating from an area 35 miles southeast of Liwale and were being pursued by British forces. Again, these were not false reports intended to deceive the Germans; they were factual representations of the conditions on the ground. Still, the RMA felt that the situation had not changed dramatically and that a landing in the area was still possible.[37]

Indeed, the RMA seemed confident enough in the mission that on the very same day they received news of the British advances, they notified Yambol to anticipate *L 57*'s imminent transfer to the base. The airship had been fully converted to the specifications for the mission a week earlier and, on September 28, flew to Jüterbog to be loaded with its complement of supplies. The weight of every item and person on board had to be accounted for in detail, and the comprehensive inventory is shown on the opposite page.[38]

Simultaneously, the RMA sent another telegram advising Governor Schnee to expect the arrival of an airship carrying ammunition and medicine "from mid-October onward," with an intended landing area near Liwale.[39] Critically, they also included the cipher key (number 376) that *L 57* would be using to establish contact with the colony. While Schnee never received the telegram, later informing British intelligence officers after the war that any such mission was pure "fantasy,"[40] British cryptoanalysts in Room 40[41] had.

The implications of this will be discussed at length in the next chapter, but for now, despite all the hurdles, Bockholt, his crew, and *L 57* were in Jüterbog, preparing to begin the first leg of their mission—the flight to Yambol. Time was of the essence, since the success of the operation rested on the swiftness the airship's departure. Operation *China-Sache* had officially begun.

Size of the ship - 67,500 cubic meters (2,383,740 cubic feet), carrying capacity - 78,500 kg (173,063 lbs)			
Nr.	Type of weight	Kgs. (lbs.)	Remarks
1	Hull, engines, and gondolas	27,700 (61,068)	After discussion with Luftschiffbau Zeppelin construction supervision and Reichsmarineamt
2	Gasoline	19,662 (43,347)	For 108 hours and 4 engines and 90 hours and 1 engine. 43.5 kgs. per motor/hour
		1,500 (3,307)	Special addition for rain exposure
3	Oil	1,356 (2,989)	For 108 hours with 4 engines and 20 hours with 1 engine. 3 kgs. an hour per engine.
4	Crew	1,760 (3,880)	22 men at 80 kgs. (176 lbs.) per man wearing flight uniforms. The original estimation called for 20 men, but 2 were added later.
5a	Food	300 (661)	3 kgs. (6.6 lbs.) per head for 5 days
		240 (529)	Iron supplements. 1.5 kgs. (3.3 lbs.) per head for 8 days (for emergency landing)
5b	Drinks	200 (441)	2 liters per head for 5 days
		100 (220.5)	5/8 liters per head for 8 days (for emergency landing)
6	Clothing	-	
a	Flight uniforms	-	Included in weight in number 4
b	Tropical equipment	520 (1,146)	Including 2 woolen blankets per head
7	Reserve parts	300 (661)	For engines and navigational equipment
8	Coolant/Water	500 (1,102)	100 kgs. (220.5 lbs.) per engine to also serve as drinking water reserves
9	Water ballast	-	
a	At 500 m altitude	3,925 (8,653)	
b	At 1,000 m altitude	3,227 (7,114)	Taking into account fuel consumption over 5 days
10	Temperature factor	2,600 (5,732)	Assumed at 10°C (50°F)
11	Miscellaneous	60 (132)	Toilet boxes, cooking pots, crockery, etc.
	Total	63,950 (141,008)	Service load
	Carrying capacity	78,500 (173,063)	
	Remaining for cargo	14,550 (32,077)	Buoyancy calculated at 6°C (43°F), 760 (mmHg), and 0.1 specific weight (hydrogen)
	Actual payload	13,930 (30,710)	Including 311,900 rounds of loose ammunition, 57,500 rounds of machine gun ammunition in 230 belts, 13,500 rounds of machine gun ammution in 54 boxes, 30 MG08/15 machine guns, 9 spare MG08/15 barrels, 4 Gewehr 98 rifles with 5,000 rounds, 61 sacks of medical supplies and bandages, 3 sacks of sewing equipment, mail, awards, telescopes, replacement locks, bush knives, and belts

4

Disaster over Jüterbog

OCTOBER 7, 1917, JÜTERBOG, NORTHERN GERMANY. In a process that lasted nearly the entire morning until noon, the outfitting of *L 57* and loading of the "Africa ship's" special cargo has finally been completed. *Kapitänleutnant* Bockholt is anxious to get a two-hour test flight in to determine how the fully laden giant will handle prior to setting off toward Yambol. Despite arriving at the airship base over a week prior, up to this point the only times that *L 57* had been in the air were a two-hour-and-thirty-six-minute, low-altitude, round-trip factory trial flight between Friedrichshafen and Ravensburg on September 26; another short military acceptance test over the Allgäu on the twenty-seventh; and the subsequent nearly eight-hour, 400-mile transfer from Friedrichshafen to Jüterbog on the twenty-eighth. Each of these, however, was completed with an airship devoid of its cargo and much of its equipment.

Given that the lengthened *L 57* was already expected to handle quite differently from the existing U-class Zeppelins it was based on, even without its payload,[1] the initial test flight on the twenty-sixth was completed by a factory crew under the command of Captain Bernhard Lau—a navigator and pilot employed by the Zeppelin works since 1908. Representatives from the RMA, as well as Bockholt and his crew, were also present but acted merely as onboard observers.[2] The complement of crew and passengers likewise remained the same on the twenty-seventh, when *L 57*'s prescribed twelve-hour military acceptance trial took place, but this too was not an accurate representation of how the Zeppelin would behave on its way to Africa.

For one, the airship was flown only to an altitude of 4,000 meters (13,123 feet), far short of its ceiling of 7,620 meters (25,000 feet).[3] Additionally, the planned twelve-hour assessment of the airship's capabilities had to be dramatically reduced to a mere three hours and eighteen minutes due to time constraints. While *L 57* achieved a cruising speed of 23.6 m/sec. (52.7 mph) with four engines and 26.2 m/sec. (58.6 mph) with the supplemental fifth Maybach HS-Lu engine[4]—slightly exceeding the 22 m/sec. (49 mph) to 25 m/sec. (56 mph) anticipated by the *Admiralstab*—its actual performance in tropical heat, at extreme altitudes, and under load remained largely unknown. Still, even with the limited testing, the Zeppelin factory and the RMA concluded that *L 57*'s trials were successful, and the command of the airship was transferred to Bockholt and his crew. Alas, their only chance to test their new airship for themselves occurred on September 28, when they flew the airship from Friedrichshafen to Jüterbog—again, without any cargo.

Showing the prudence that he exhibited in the planning phases of *China-Sache*, Bockholt wants to eliminate any variables that he can actually control prior to departing for Yambol. First and foremost, he needs to know how *L 57* will fly under load. Only then can he prepare himself for all the other obstacles he will encounter on his arduous relief mission within a combat zone. With the Bulgarian base being notified of *L 57*'s imminent departure on October 6, and the new-moon period rapidly approaching, he knows that if a true test flight is going to take place, it has to happen after the airship finishes taking on cargo on the seventh.

Unfortunately, the weather forecast doesn't look favorable. The morning's report shows a low-pressure system moving in from the English Channel and, if accurate, promises high winds and instability. Bockholt, however, is impatient. After conferring with his officers and Hugo Eckener, a manager at the Zeppelin factory, an expert airship captain, and the man responsible for training the officers of the Naval Airship Division,[5] the men concur that the forecast is no different than the two previous days, when the winds "completely subsided in the evening."[6]

"Do you think we can at least get two hours of flying time in today, Herr Eckener?" posits Bockholt.

Eckener, the subject matter expert, assures the commander that given "the steady lull in the wind this morning, I expect that this evening it will become completely still, albeit temporarily."[7]

Bockholt wastes no time making his decision. Turning to his watch officers, *Leutnant* Maas and *Feldwebelleutnant* Grussendorf, he commands, "Prepare the crew; it looks like we'll have a narrow window if we're going to fly today, I want to make the most of it. This may be our last chance before the operation begins in earnest."

As the airship crew don their flight gear and board the Zeppelin, and the officers sign off on *L 57*'s ballast distribution chart, the wind continues to subside. By four o'clock in the afternoon, it is nearly still, just as it was the two previous days. Bockholt, sensing that his opportunity has finally arrived, orders his men to their stations and for the ground crew, led by the airship's officers in the forward and rear gondolas, to prepare to walk the airship out of its "shed."[8] The massive doors of the hangar are slid open, and, for the first time, the fully equipped Zeppelin's stern is directed toward the enticing horizon. The time is 1710.

L 57, hovering just a few feet off the ground, is slowly guided toward the opening in the 787-foot, double-wide airship hangar. In many ways, the scene resembles the entrance procession of a Sunday mass, with teams of men gripping the gondolas and others securing loose tethers, walking in synchronized, rehearsed movements in the cavernous, cathedral-like space. Bockholt, however, notices that the march isn't proceeding with the mechanical perfection he desires. Sensing the inexperience of the men, he uses the voice tube to call out to *Leutnant* Maas, then supervising the aft crew: "Make sure your men are holding those lines tightly!" Maas responds, "Aye-aye, *Herr Kaleu*!" and barks commands to his squad. While he receives confirmation that his orders are understood, the men seem awed by the giant airship and make no noticeable corrections. After all, the lines are still slack at this point, resembling a "U" shape, and won't become taut until the airship needs securing outside the hangar.

The wind conditions continue to remain still as *L 57*'s rearmost extremity now begins to peek out of the shed, but this is the most dangerous stage in the entire maneuver. Since differences in atmospheric pressure exist between the enclosed, inner shelter and the outside environment, the ground crew must remain on their toes. Indeed, once two-thirds of *L 57*'s hull has advanced beyond the safety of the enclosure, a sudden gust of wind from the southwest, 6 points to the hangar and blowing around 12 mph,[9] buffets the airship, causing the aft end to swing out, back toward the building. The abrupt change in direction takes the ground crew by surprise, and they lose their grip on the tethers. As *L 57* continues to sway to and fro with the prevailing wind, it is now in danger of contacting a hangar door, causing significant damage to the airship's frame. Bockholt must act quickly.

Feeling that "an accelerated exit"[10] would be safer than attempting to bring *L 57* back into the shed, Bockholt orders his men to carry on leading the airship onto the field. It is the right decision for the moment. The ground crew is able to regain control of the airship and keep it stable despite the sustained wind gusts. With the situation again under control, Bockholt and his officers man their flight positions in the control car and order *L 57* upward to begin its two-hour test flight. Unfortunately, with one crisis averted, another was looming in the west.

After the airship had spent nearly an hour aloft, the wireless receiver on board *L 57* comes to life, sounding off rapid Morse code dots and dashes from the base below. The radio operator, *Funkmaat*[11] Kettner, immediately transcribes the message and hands it to his subordinate, *Funker* Wilhelm Müller, for delivery to the commander. It is now 1830.

Müller enters the helm of the control car and reports, "*Herr Kaleu*! We've received a report on the current ground conditions at Jüterbog."

Bockholt, seizing the paper from his hands, looks it over and reads it out loud: "Wind SSW, 5 m/s [11 mph] . . ." He pauses and turns to *Leutnant* Maas. "Well, Number 1, it doesn't look like it's getting any better on the ground; probably best to stay up here and wait things out for a while." The watch officer nods in agreement, and *L 57* continues to remain aloft, cutting wide rings in the sky over Brandenburg. As the airship continues its flight, the planned two-hour test has now nearly doubled in length. This would, in any other circumstance, have been desirable, given that this was the very first trial involving the actual service load of the airship. This time, however, the one-off Zeppelin was stuck flying in a holding pattern while the weather at the landing zone was continuing to deteriorate.

At 2140, another wireless signal from Jüterbog arrives, warning that the wind has increased and the barometer has suddenly plummeted—the anticipated storm is now arriving, and Bockholt's short window of opportunity has suddenly slammed shut. With no other options, he decides to land.

Upon returning to base, Bockholt finds the ground conditions to be precarious but not yet perilous. The wind speed is moderate, blowing steadily between 13 and 18 mph, and for the time being, the nearly four hundred men composing the various ground crews are able to keep *L 57* secure on the landing field. They are, however, unable to guide the airship back into the hangar due to the prevailing wind. For now, it can only be held in place. Bockholt assembles his officers in the control car.

"*Meine Herren*, it doesn't appear that we'll be able to get back into the shed for the time being. I'll see about getting help. For now, I want the men ready in case we have to depart again quickly. Officers, return to your landing stations and resume ground duties. *Alles klar*?"

"*Verstanden!*"

"Good, dismissed!"

As Bockholt makes the rather clumsy exit from the door of the control car to the ground nearly 4 feet below, Maas and Grussendorf head to the aft and forward gondolas of the Zeppelin to resume their previous responsibilities of supervising the "holding crews." Bockholt, proceeding away from the field, intends to confer with the base's commanding officer and Hugo Eckener about returning the airship to safety. He requests that an additional two hundred men be mobilized to support the existing ground crews and guide *L 57* back into the shed. This, he is told, can be done, but it will take approximately an hour for the men to arrive.

He then proceeds to the telephone to report his situation to headquarters at Ahlhorn and to hear the latest news about the incoming weather. All present remain silent as Bockholt puts down the receiver and quietly curses to himself: "*Verdammt* . . ." Turning to his captive audience, Bockholt imparts what all were already expecting, and makes a decision that will either save or doom his airship.

"Ahlhorn confirms that very strong storms continue to approach from the west. With the additional ground support teams not arriving for at least an hour, I don't think *L 57* can remain here."

"Well, *Kapitänleutnant*, if you're not staying in Jüterbog, where do you intend to go?"

Bockholt pauses for a moment and then addresses the officer. "Kovno, in Lithuania. The weather remains calm to the east. If that isn't feasible, then perhaps we'll head directly to Yambol. Do you think the necessary charts could be obtained for the trip?"

"Certainly, but it will take us some time to fetch them for you."

"Good. See to it that it's done as quickly as possible. In the meantime, would it be possible for blankets, warm clothing, and additional provisions to be brought to the airship for the men?"[12]

"*Natürlich*, but are you sure this is the best course of action?"

"I don't see any other choice, given our options. Besides, Yambol has already been notified of our impending flight since the sixth; it shouldn't come as a surprise if we land there early. I'll head back to the airship now, to advise the crew."

With the decision made, Bockholt salutes and returns to *L 57*, still held securely by the ground crews despite the steady wind gusts. It is now 2300.

Although the additional cold-weather items and provisions were immediately made available to *L 57*'s crew, the matter of supplying the necessary maps took longer than expected. When they were finally obtained and the course could be plotted, the weather had once again changed for the worse. With everyone on board *L 57* and now preparing to depart, droplets of rain began to fall, and the wind suddenly grew in strength to 20 mph. Even worse, it also changed direction.

At 2350, just as *L 57* began her ascent to escape the storm, "a gust of wind hit the ship from above, pressing the gondola so hard onto the ground that most of the struts and the portside attachment of the middle stays broke."[13] As a result of the impact, the steering wheel, both rudders, the ballast controls, and the engine telegraphs became inoperable.[14] Subsequently, another blast of air caused the rear gondola to also touch down and was similarly damaged. In a single moment, all of *L 57*'s primary flight apparatuses had been rendered useless, and Bockholt himself could only lament that "it was impossible to get up in this state."[15]

Incredibly, the violent bursts of wind that single-handedly grounded *L 57* began to abate just as quickly as they arrived, and what was drizzling rain had evolved into a heavy shower. This brought its own complications, since *L 57*'s canvas shell was now becoming saturated with water, causing the airship to become heavier and driving it ever farther into the dirt. However, at 0040, with the wind continuing to die down and the rain coming to an end, Bockholt wants to salvage his airship and attempts "to bring the ship [back] into the hangar, albeit as a wreck."[16]

To facilitate this operation, *L 57* must be made lighter; therefore, Bockholt gives an audacious order: "All men except for *Leutnant* Maas get off the airship! It appears that the gas cables are still working, and I alone will remain in the control car to operate them. Maas, head to the rear gondola and, if you can, try to resecure the stern tethering lines."

At this command, the men aboard *L 57* hastily begin disembarking from the airship, leaping to the ground from every man-sized aperture in the forward gondola. The sudden loss of ballast seems to do the trick, and *L 57*, once again buoyant, frees itself from the soil. Maas, after making his way to the stern of the airship and climbing through the tangled remains of the rear gondola, is able to resecure the four toggle clips that had become loosened during the crash. Finding that despite the damage, the "stern was relatively easy to guide with the aft gondola,"[17] he returns to the control car to assist his commander. For the time being, the giant Zeppelin is making slow but steady progress back to its sanctuary. Then, yet again, the wind suddenly gains in strength.

Just as *L 57* is nearing the entrance to the shed, another lateral gust impacts the airship, turning it sideways and redirecting the giant Zeppelin on a course toward the hangar's doors. With no means to steer the dirigible and with the forward gondola in danger of being smashed, Bockholt and Maas leap out and stare as *L 57* comes to rest about 50 meters from the opening in the shed. The two men let out a sigh of relief, but their mutual confidence that disaster had been avoided is premature.

Almost immediately after they finish exhaling, the Zeppelin, now made lighter by the canvas shell continuing to dry, as well as the departure of the two officers from the control car, suddenly rises 20 meters into the air and is being drawn toward the interior of the shed by the low-pressure vacuum within it. As *L 57* is being sucked in, she turns horizontally, parallel to the open gates, and smashes her nose into one of the doors—pushing in the bow section of the Zeppelin. Another gust of wind then pushes the airship away from the hangar and back into the landing field. *L 57* moves with such velocity that she travels 200 meters, dragging her anchor cable and the men securing it along with it. Before the ground crew can finally reestablish a hold of the Zeppelin, five members of the holding team are injured, including one with a serious spinal injury.

Seeing that the airship is becoming ever lighter as the water continues to evaporate from its canvas layer, Bockholt jumps back into the control car and begins anxiously tugging at the gas toggles in an attempt to vent hydrogen and make the airship heavier. He loses his composure, repeatedly yelling, "*Komm schon!*" as he tries to will the gas bags to release their contents. It is to no avail. As *L 57* is once again pushed toward the ground, Bockholt leaps back off and, lying motionless, watches the Zeppelin rise, come to a stop, and then make its way back toward the earth.

He quickly comes to his feet and escapes the danger of being crushed. Taking in his surroundings, it seems the situation is unfolding in slow motion. He observes the ground crew frantically trying to regain control of the airship, the five injured men of the anchoring team writhing in pain, and his own crew staring incredulously at the scene. Out of sheer desperation, Bockholt orders a futile, last-ditch directive in order to bring *L 57* to rest.

"Any man not holding on to a tether, grab a rifle and shoot into the top of the hull. We have to get the gas out of the bags!" Without questioning the order, his men hastily depart and, after removing Gewehr 98 rifles from their crates, return to the landing field and begin shooting. Although the projectiles cause some hydrogen to leak, each hole made by every singular 8.22 mm diameter bullet equates to only "one forty millionth of the surface of a gas cell"[18]—far too little to have a meaningful impact.

Completely forlorn, Bockholt considers having an opening cut into the hull of *L 57* and sending a team inside the airship to physically slash the gas bags,[19] but this would mean essentially ordering men to their deaths. With the airship continuing to rise and fall in 30-meter spurts, it would be far too dangerous to attempt. He watches helplessly as the Zeppelin persistently pounds into the earth. Eventually, the rear car completely caves in. Next the airship turns on its axis, and the starboard engines are driven into the soil. This time, one of the engine nacelles anchors itself into the ground. This, however, succeeds only in acting as a pivot point, causing *L 57* to rotate its hull, "transversely to the wind."[20]

Since the entire length of *L 57* now faces the squalls, her frame breaks apart at "ring 85" and then her stern straightens up "as a result of its excess buoyancy."[21] The airship, now impossible to hold, is once again adrift. Free of all of its tethers, *L 57* floats toward the wire fence along the perimeter of the landing field and breaks through, becoming "completely horseshoe-shaped." As the airship continues to fold into itself, a red glow is observed in the upper half of the gas cells, and, due to the "entire interior" of the airship having now been filled with leaking hydrogen, it explodes. At 0200 on October 8, the "Africa ship" was destroyed. Its crucial cargo for the beleaguered *Schutztruppen* continued to burn until dawn.

The investigation into the loss of *L 57* began immediately. On the very same day of the explosion, Bockholt submitted his testimony, in which he detailed the sequence of events leading up to the destruction of the airship. He took full responsibility, concluding,

> The behavior of the holding crews was good. Unfortunately, five men, who were thrown up when the ship went loose, were wounded and one of them has since died of a spinal injury. The behavior of the [airship] crew was also exemplary.
>
> I blame myself for not sufficiently taking the morning [weather] map into account when I started the journey. The afternoon map arrived here only at 6:30 p.m., and thus I could only guess the afternoon wind measurement [when he made his decision to fly earlier that day].[22]

At no point did he claim that rifle fire led to ignition of *Knallgas*—literally translating to "explosive gas," or, by its technical term, "oxyhydrogen"—the extremely combustive mixture of hydrogen and the atmosphere that led to the explosion. Instead, he attributed the loss of the airship to "sparks from the breaking of the [frame] ring"[23] igniting the flammable mixture.

This sentiment was echoed by *Leutnant* Maas, Hugo Eckener, *Feldwebelleutnant* Grussendorf, *Steuermann* Wald, and *Maschinist* Busch when they were interviewed by *Kapitänleutnant* Sommerfeld[24] the following day. While all agreed on the unpredictable weather playing the dominant role in the loss of the airship, and that rifle fire had not led to the explosion, unlike Bockholt, Maas and Grussendorf placed the source of the sparks in the airship's high-tension wires. The former testified that

> the whole ship flared up, in my opinion[,] not by the gunshots[,] but by sparks from the rupturing tension wires, as I had already observed sparks visible in the destroyed sections [of the airship]. The events from the breaking of the ship to the ignition followed one another very quickly.[25]

And the latter:

> The ship drifted on the wire fence, remained there at the point in which it broke, the stern and nose folded[,] and in a moment the explosion took place. Since I noticed sparks at the point of fracture . . . I believe that the cause of the ignition must be found in the tearing of wires.[26]

Although some modern scholars disregard earlier examples of airships being difficult to destroy with conventional ammunition and blame Bockholt for being reckless in ordering his airship to be shot at, the Admiralty in Berlin agreed with its officers on the scene.

A hearing chaired by Rear Admiral Starke (also on October 9), in which other members of the *Admiralstab* and Bockholt himself were present, concluded that

> in order to prevent it [*L 57*] from flying away, the commander now had to have rifles pierce holes in the hull. When the skeleton of the airship burped and buckled, it caused the airship to catch fire, and it was completely destroyed.[27]

Furthermore, while not entirely absolving Bockholt from the blame of the incident, the Admiralty empathized with him and deemed him worthy of remaining in command of another potential "Africa ship," finding that

> although the commander cannot be spared the reproach of endangering the airship when the weather was too unfavorable, given the great importance of the task assigned to him, it must be taken into account that, on the other hand, he was asked to speed up his test run, and therefore under less favorable weather conditions and circumstances than a test run would otherwise have been undertaken. It must also be taken into account that at the time of the ascent the weather conditions were not such that an ascent, which he said he had undertaken numerous times under the same circumstances, could not have been accomplished.
>
> In view of the fact that Kplt. Bockholt has now familiarized himself thoroughly with his task and is not personally deterred from repeating the experiment by the accident, it is advisable to leave him in command of the new airship.[28]

The group subsequently debated whether or not it would even be possible for another airship to be constructed in time to repeat the same mission in the following month. When the "question was decided in the affirmative," Yambol was notified to remain available for an airship landing until December 1, and the naval attachés in Vienna (Austria-Hungary) and Sofia (Bulgaria) were informed that *China-Sache* was to be delayed for about three weeks.[29]

L 59, already nearing completion in Staaken, was chosen as the new airship for the mission, and Bockholt and his crew were to await its transfer to Jüterbog to resume their former duties. Given that in its current state it would require only the same lengthening and converting that had to be done on *L 57*, it would be much quicker to bring into service than constructing a brand-new, purpose-built Zeppelin. While historian Wolfgang Meighörner-Schardt lamented that the policy of extreme secrecy surrounding *L 59*'s conversion, in which "only urgent cases should be written . . . everything else should be discussed verbally,"[30] causes problems for researchers, what is known from archival records is that this entire discussion concerning the utilization of *L 59* and *L 57*'s former personnel initially took place only among members of the *Admiralstab*, the *Reichsmarineamt*, and Bockholt. Incredibly, Peter Strasser was not present for any of these preliminary discussions!

It is unknown why the *Führer der Luftschiffe* wasn't consulted about the resumption of *China-Sache* at this early stage, but there are hints within the files of the *Reichsmarineamt*. A sometimes-repeated theory among some historians is that Bockholt went above the head of his superior and used his own personal influence and contacts in the *Admiralstab* to remain in command of the mission. Although evidence exists in the German naval archives that indicates Bockholt was not averse to disregarding the chain of command in particular (usually rushed) situations, the accusation, I feel, is a bit of a stretch. Given that Strasser was based in Ahlhorn, nearly 450 miles west of the Admiralty's headquarters in Berlin, and Jüterbog was only about 70 miles south, in the interest of expediency, haste, and logistics, it was easier to summon Bockholt for an issue that had to be investigated, discussed, and decided on in person and without delay. Indeed, Strasser was neither flouted nor kept in the dark about the matter.

Following the hearing on the ninth, the RMA noted that Bockholt "will submit the accident report to the FdL, who has been asked to respond to it here with his opinion."[31] When it arrived, however, Strasser was far less forgiving of Bockholt than his superiors and gave his honest, reproachful assessment of the matter.

In Strasser's official response, dated October 11, the FdL made numerous handwritten notations on the report but agreed that *L 59* should ultimately be the new "China ship." He didn't, however, concur that Bockholt and his crew should be left in charge. Perhaps feeling offended that Bockholt was given an audience in Berlin before he was, despite being responsible for the loss of the only W-class Zeppelin in existence, he felt that *L 59* should remain under the command of its previously designated commander, *Kapitänleutnant* Herbert Ehrlich,[32] and his crew. His rationale was certainly justifiable. His response read as follows:

> Attached is the report of the loss of the airship *L 57*. *L 59* is to be the new China ship. The commander of *L 59*, *Kapitänleutnant* Ehrlich, is ready with his crew by the ship in Staaken. He asked me to remain with *L 59* and be allowed to carry out the mission. Kplt. Ehrlich is one of the most experienced airship commanders and has a well-established crew. Since the *L 57* was lost, albeit without justifiable fault, before it began the undertaking, and the crew is still freshly impressed by this loss, I do not consider it advisable for the *L 57* crew to be transferred to the *L 59* and intend to propose it for Kplt. Ehrlich.

I ask for a telegraphic consent to this.[33]

Consent was not forthcoming. Instead, it appeared that Strasser, whether being pressured by his superiors, as other historians have suggested, or simply rethinking his initial evaluation under further analysis, changed his mind about Bockholt and his crew.

When a final appraisal of the resumption of *China-Sache* was presented to Holtzendorff, chief of the Admiralty, by the RMA on October 15, Strasser is noted as having an entirely contrary, more understanding opinion of Bockholt's role in the loss of *L 57*. It reads:

> As can be seen from the FdL's decision, [the RMA] does not accuse the commander, Kptlt. Bockholt, of justifiable guilt. In agreement with the FdL [Strasser], Kptlt. Bockholt should continue to be in command of the airship intended for the China operation. At the same time, this also has the advantage that Kptlt. Bockholt, after he had only a very limited period of time for technical preparation up to the original time of the first planned trip, can now improve his preparations considerably. This preoccupation with the [accelerated] execution of the undertaking, which is now taking place more calmly, has already brought about the result that he initially intends to take a slightly different route than previously planned.
>
> For the repetition of the enterprise the situation is now as follows:
>
> a.) The conversion of the *L 59* will be completed by the 25th of the month at the latest and will then be transferred from Staaken to Jüterbog for the test flight with the old *L 57* crew.
>
> b.) The cargo to be taken along will be made available by the Imperial Colonial Office at the same time and will be transported there. The flight to Yambol is planned for the first days of November. Departure from Yambol no later than November 10th.
>
> c.) The moon and meteorological conditions will not have changed significantly up to this point in time.
>
> d.) The Yambol airship hangar, belonging to the Ministry of War, is expected to remain occupied by an army force of about 70 heads; there are also a naval airship squad of 1 officer and 30 men. Also, by the time the airship arrives in Yambol, another naval airship

> maintenance crew of about 20 will be sent there. For the rest, the Bulgarians [will] provide the holding teams.
>
> e.) The actual execution of the undertaking remains[,] of course[,] dependent on the news that will come in from the China area, where according to the latest reports a certain deterioration in the situation has occurred.[34]

The report being referred to in the evaluation was, again, not from a German source, but instead another intercepted Allied transmission from Le Havre, in Normandy. Received on the same day that Strasser submitted his response to the RMA, it noted that

> the Belgian troops under Major Bataille continued their offensive east of the Kilombero-Rivers. On October 7th they broke through the enemy positions set up on an extensive front. The front is designated the Huegel line and is situated from the northeast and west through Mahenge. The German forces were thrown back from the first line of defenses and so retreated to the second line of ridges in front of Mahenge, on which retreat positions were prepared. On October 9th, Major Muller, the leader of the right column, entered Mahenge, which the troops occupied. The pursuit began in the mountainous region south of Mahenge, where the enemy had withdrawn. Beyond this area, the British columns from Songea and Lupembe advanced; Mahenge was the last capital of the district still in German hands.[35]

This certainly painted the situation of the *Schutztruppe* rather bleakly. Nonetheless, the *Admiralstab* felt that regardless of how unfavorable ground conditions seemed, as long as there still appeared to be resistance from the colonial forces, a relief mission would still be necessary and possible in Mahenge. All preparations for the mission were to continue as planned while awaiting further news from the front.[36] November 10 remained the new anticipated departure date from Yambol, and, "for the purpose of secrecy," the RMA was going to put on the facade that the *China-Sache* operation had been abandoned and that *L 59* was going to be transferred east for bombing missions in Türkiye (formerly known as Turkey).[37] The problem with this was that the British were already aware of the mission, partly from intercepts, but largely due to the fact that no one within Germany or Bulgaria could resist from publicly speaking about it.

While the RMA tried to maintain a strict policy of silence within its own ranks, going as far as noting "vacation in Yambol" on the military passes of the *L 57/59* crew members,[38] it had very little control over the Zeppelin factory workers or the general public within the area. Just four days before the final plan to utilize *L 59* for the mission was presented to Holtzendorff, Lt. Elias, an inspector of the airship troops, reported that a foreman named Bohne and a mechanic for the Bosch company, Frick, came to him because they were "visibly moved with a feeling of indignation at the carelessness with which they and other bystanders were given knowledge of things to be kept secret."[39] Specifically,

> the crew of the naval airship based in Staaken and the maintenance squad, as well as naval crews in Ahlhorn, spoke publicly of the fact that the ship should go to East Africa in order to bring medicines and ammunition to our protection troops fighting there, and because of this purpose, there are no bomb-drop mechanisms, the airship is extended by two compartments, and the possibility of replacing the two-engine gearbox while driving exists. Arabic-speaking people are also assigned to crew, and several ships are being equipped for the same purpose.[40]

Although Bohne and Frick were warned to remain quiet, it was already too late. Even Captain Lau, the pilot for the Zeppelin factory, noted that his son had been told about the Africa mission by boys on the street in Friedrichshafen.[41] In Yambol, things were no different.

According to Edwin Thomas Woodhall, a police officer who joined British counterintelligence in 1915, loose talk in Bulgaria confirmed the purpose and destination of *L 57*'s mission to the Allies. In his fanciful memoir, *Spies of the Great War*, he described how he accompanied another agent, Sgt. Tony Mortimer, to Italy, where the latter was to be flown and parachuted into Austria-Hungary. Here, Mortimer was to make his way to a hotel in Vienna in order to meet with an "American Secret Service man" who had been spying for the Allies in Bulgaria under the guise of being a businessman because "America [was] not at war with that nation."[42] Allegedly, this unnamed American agent informed Mortimer that many of the parts and equipment for *L 57* had already been transported to Yambol for a relief mission to Africa, and that when *L 57* crashed and burned in Jüterbog, its replacement was being constructed in Staaken to resume the operation.[43] Whether the details of this story were true or not are undetermined, but what is certain is that the British already knew incredible details about *China-Sache* by mid-October 1917.

Following the crash of the Zeppelin *L 45* in Sisteron, France, on October 20, after a raid on England, her commander, *Kapitänleutnant* Waldemar Kölle, was captured and transferred to England to be interrogated by Major Trench from the Naval Intelligence Division. While Kölle refused to answer any of the major's probes, he later recalled that Trench "tried to trick me into conversation."[44] Instead of continuing to directly grill Kölle, Trench attempted to use reverse psychology to draw out responses from the German officer by awing him about just how much the British were already aware of. Kölle claimed that Trench "showed astonishingly detailed knowledge of even the most recently joined personnel of the Naval Airship Division . . . bragging of his extensive information . . . accurate in the most minute detail, causing petty officers to declare it made their heads swim."[45] Regarding the *China-Sache* operation,

> The Major knew all the commanders by name; all the school commanders with opinions as to which were the best pilots; the change of command between Buttlar and Bockholt, and the destruction of the *L 57*. Here he suggested that the ship had been lengthened, and for what purpose. Surprise questions as to why Buttlar lost out as commander of the *L 57* [and] the general opinion of Bockholt [were asked].[46]

Unfortunately for the Germans, this intelligence lapse wouldn't become known to them until April 25, 1918, when Kölle's report was smuggled back to the fatherland, hidden in the heel of a repatriated prisoner's shoe. According to Douglas Robinson, the revelation resulted in three men being "tried and shot in Tondern, Kölle's home base, and two in Nordholz."[47] Much too late to have any impact on the pending resumption of the "China matter" mission.

As such, while the Germans continued with the conversion of *L 59* and the allocation of the various, already scarce, supplies lost in *L 57*'s inferno, the British began notifying their forces in East Africa about the potential arrival of a Zeppelin "coming to East Africa from Palestine"[48] in early November. While Captain Downes, serving with the Nigerian Brigade in German East Africa, thought this news was merely "a startling rumor . . . thought to be merely somebody's joke,"[49] other forces took the matter more seriously and took precautions. As historian Edward Paice uncovered in the records of the 5th Mountain Battery of the South African Mounted Riflemen, "aeroplanes were put on standby and two mountain guns were 'dug in for [*L 59*'s] reception.'"[50] Even more shockingly, the British were also aware that *L 59*'s original proposed landing site in Mahenge was, in all possibility, going to be altered.

As the movements of the *Schutztruppe* continued to change with each passing day and their situation became ever more tenuous, the *Reichsmarineamt* and the *Reichskolonialamt* struggled to make sense of the various, conflicting reports reaching them both from Allied and German sources. In the delay between *L 57*'s loss and *L 59*'s conversion and expected departure in early November, Lettow's forces appeared to be forced farther and farther inland and toward the border with Portuguese Mozambique. If *China-Sache* was going to proceed, the RMA would have to pin down the location of Lettow's main forces and reevaluate *L 59*'s course and landing site.

5

The Battle of Mahiwa and a Change of Plans

THE VILLAGE OF MAHIWA lies in the southeastern corner of modern-day Tanzania. It is located approximately 45 miles west of the coast, 49 miles north of the Rovuma River, and more than 200 miles southeast of Mahenge. A small place today with a population in 2012 of fewer than two thousand people,[1] in 1917 it was even more minuscule, with fewer than an estimated two hundred inhabitants residing there. Although essentially an insignificant position in the mountainous, rural district of Lindi, it was here that a large contingent of the depleted *Schutztruppe* faced off with the British Nigerian Brigade,[2] the Kings African Rifles, the 25th Royal Fusiliers, and Punjabi infantry—all under the command of Brigadier General Percival Scott Beves, a South African. The three-day battle would prove to be one of the bloodiest engagements of the East African conflict and the most pivotal for Lettow's forces. For Lettow-Vorbeck, it began in earnest on October 16, 1917, after a cup of coffee and a peaceful lunch.

Following continuous pressure from British advances in the Lindi district, the nine German colonial companies under General Kurt Wahle—the Wahle detachment—retired to Mahiwa. Here, Lettow correctly sensed that the British would attempt to encircle Wahle's units but, owing to information gleaned from captured mail and intelligence reports, understood that they had not yet identified the location of the bulk of the

Schutztruppe's forces. As Lettow put it, "In spite of his extensive intelligence and spy systems, the enemy was groping in the dark."[3] As such, Lettow felt that his limited assets could make a decisive counterattack and change the tide of the campaign.

To support Wahle, he ordered the strategic withdrawal of the German colonial 4th, 13th, 17th, and 21st Field Companies, the 8th Rifle Company, and the 2nd Mountain Battery through the mountains in Likangara toward Mnacho—a process that began on October 10 and concluded on the evening of the fourteenth. During the night of October 14–15, rifle and machine gun fire heard in the vicinity of Mahiwa alerted Lettow that contact with the enemy had been established, and orders were issued to march at daybreak. *Hauptmann* Karl Ernst Göring was to lead the main force, consisting of the 4th, 13th, and 17th Field Companies, Lettow's aide-de-camp, *Oberleutnant der Reserve* Walter von Ruckteschell, was to lead the 21st Field Company in the vanguard.

Although the distance between Mnacho and Mahiwa was less than 20 miles, the terrain was extremely difficult to traverse. According to Göring, who was already familiar with the route, having crossed it earlier in September, "The march on the narrow tribal path on the slopes of the mountains was strenuous and time-consuming; the guns were often left behind because the pack animals failed; our Askari and porters had to help out."[4] Thus, the exhausted German forces didn't reach Mahiwa until late in the evening on the fifteenth and were immediately thrust into battle.

Upon arriving within 500 meters of Wahle's units' left wing, Lettow's forces found themselves being fired at from two sides—they were in the midst of being enveloped. To counter the encirclement, Lettow ordered Göring and Ruckteschell to press forward with the 13th and 21st Companies and force the enemy back. Despite having been on their feet since daybreak, the Germans and Askaris fought hard and successfully repelled the British advances. They subsequently entrenched themselves, sent out parties to retrieve water, and, with rifles in hand, laid down and tried to get some rest to resume fighting the following morning. Only sporadic rifle fire was heard throughout the night—it was the calm before the storm.

On the morning of the sixteenth, Lettow ventured to the front lines to assess the situation. He later recalled:

> I found that the enemy had also entrenched himself immediately in front, at a distance of 60 to 100 meters. When Lieutenant von Ruckteschell offered me a cup of coffee, care had to be taken, as

> the enemy was keeping a fairly sharp lookout and shot with terrible accuracy. I thought the opportunity favorable for a determined surprise attack. It was decided to launch the attack at noon, on the left (north) wing, and try to turn the enemy's flank. Göring's detachment was to lead the attack.[5]

He then sat down to have lunch with his officers, summoning Göring to the meal to explain his plan of attack.

"Karl, I know it's been an exhausting last couple of days, but I feel the time is right to surprise the British. This may be our last chance to strike the decisive blow. How are your men holding up?"

Göring, taking a moment to sip his coffee and survey the meager rations on the makeshift table, responds. "General, it hasn't been easy leading up to this point, but the men are ready. When we departed Likangara, the British fliers were nice enough to drop fléchette arrows the size of pencils on our columns; many of the Askari's women were seriously injured.[6] I feel they, more than any of us, are eager for payback."

This is exactly what Lettow wanted to hear.

"Good, being that the morning's greetings from the British have mostly abated, an advance with your forces could potentially catch them completely off guard. At noon I want you to attack the enemy's left wing with the 4th, 17th, and 8th Companies, since they are still fresh. The 13th can join up once you've already begun your advance. As always, you'll be facing superior numbers, but this hasn't impeded our success in the past."

Göring, placing his now-empty cup of coffee on the table to be filled by a native porter, agrees.

"We're not quite positive where the enemy's left flank is, but I assume it to be opposite Ruckteschell's detachment. I think it would be wise to let things cool off a little more, and then, at 1400, I'll proceed forward with the flanking force. Once we ascertain where the enemy's perimeter is, I'll instruct *Leutnant* Brucker to lead a frontal assault with the 13th to disguise our encirclement."[7]

Finding the tactics to be sound, Lettow nods. "Very well. *Meine Herren, Mahlzeit!* I'm certain this is going to be the last quiet meal we'll have in some time."

Unbeknown to Lettow and his officers, the reason behind the lull in the fighting was that the Nigerian Brigade was in the process of bringing "considerable reinforcements" to the 1st Nigerian Battalion and the Gambian company already in position at Mahiwa. The reserve 3rd Nigerian Battalion, consisting of "twenty-five Europeans and five hundred and twenty native rank and file,"[8] set off at 0930 and reached the combat zone at 1300. Column IV of this battalion arrived first, just in time to face Göring's offensive, while column III remained in a reserve position. Göring was about to march head on into a hornets' nest.

Upon the commencement of the assault at 1400, Lettow moved into a position near the enemy's suspected left flank in order to observe the operation. It was immediately apparent to him that something was wrong. Watching Göring's forces advance, he wrote that when Göring "crossed a wide depression in the ground, to my surprise he changed direction still farther to the left."[9] Elaborating further:

> Only gradually I realized the significance of this surprising move. Captain Göring had come unexpectedly upon a new enemy who had come from Nahungru and was now attacking from the north. The force consisted of the Nigerian Brigade, who knew nothing of our arrival at Mahiwa and were expecting to smash General Wahle's force by an attack on his left flank and rear, while his front, facing east, was vigorously attacked by a division.[10]

Göring's recollection of that afternoon was, not surprisingly, far more descriptive. He wrote,

> In the blazing midday heat, I and my detachment crossed a sunny patch that separated us from the enemy-occupied heights. Already on the other bank we came under enemy fire. I informed the brave Lt. Brucker, who was soon seriously wounded, of his objective and gave him the order to attack head on and to conceal the encirclement I proposed. With the remaining 3 companies I marched along the slopes of the flat hill occupied by the enemy to the northwest in order to advance even farther. To the left of the 13th Field Company, I first had the 8th Rifle Company under Oblt. Meyer turn around and tried to advance even farther with the 4th and 17th Field Companies in order to get into the enemy's flank and rear. In the light forest we suddenly received heavy artillery fire. As we advanced into machine gun and rifle fire from the northwest, we looked for the unknown mortars which hurled their thunderous projectiles at us. We had apparently

> encountered an enemy head on. There was no time to think; we had to act immediately. I therefore gave the signal for an assault. Courageous and eager to fight, our brave Askari threw themselves at the new enemy. On the first attempt, a fragment of a mortar shell hit me in the neck and threw me to the ground for a few minutes. I felt as if someone had hit me in the neck with a hard object [causing] a small burn, which I initially felt less in the excitement of the battle. We charged on and put the superior enemy, who was just as surprised by the sudden encounter as we were in the first assault, to flight. The attack by the battle-hardened, brave Askari was so unrelenting that my men managed to capture an entire English field gun. We were able to capture an enemy ammunition column that was brought up by an English officer who mistook our troops for his during the rapidly unfolding battle. For us, who had been dependent on the enemy for weapons and ammunition supplies throughout the war, this was a valuable booty. The enemy left about 100 dead on the battlefield; our losses were insignificant. As it later turned out, the English Nigerian Brigade with several battalions and 2 guns, which had arrived from Namupa, was to attack General Wahle's left flank and thus bring about the destruction of this detachment. At the same time, Wahle's eastward-facing front was energetically attacked by an English division from Lindi. To our right, Lieutenant von Ruckteschell had held his position with the 21st and 13th Field Companies and had thrown back the enemy attacking there. Despite our glorious victory, night arrived. Before darkness fell, I had the valuable booty collected, including the 150,000 rifle cartridges, which were packed in boxes, and reported to the commander. We rested the second night, rifle in arm, with the pleasant feeling of having done our duty successfully. When I returned to the command with my detachment the next morning, Lettow greeted me and expressed his appreciation. Such moments are among the most beautiful in the eventful lives of soldiers, where recognition and condemnation are often so close together.[11]

As Göring intimated, the initial German successes were impressive, but the battle itself did not end on the sixteenth. Instead, it continued on through the eighteenth, with the original aims of the German offensive evolving from a flanking movement, to a defensive reinforcement of General Wahle's positions.

Still, the frequent counterattacks made during these modified tactics continued to inflict significant losses on the British forces. By the end of the battle, which Captain W. D. Downes of the Nigerian Brigade regarded as "one of the biggest engagements ever fought on African soil from the point of view of casualties . . . not excluding the great Boer War, the various campaigns in Egypt and the Sudan, and the Italian Abyssinian campaign,"[12] the British "lost 2,700 casualties out of a total strength of 4,900 infantry employed; thus[,] the British losses were above 50 percent of the number of troops engaged."[13] The Germans casualties, on the other hand, totaled "14 Europeans and 81 Askaris killed, 55 Europeans and 347 Askaris wounded, [and] 1 European and 1 Askari missing."[14] A comparatively small figure compared to the British, but nonetheless a disproportionate one, given that before the battle began, the strength of the German companies in Mahiwa totaled 155 Europeans and 1,088 Askaris—or 39.5 percent of the total complement of *Schutztruppen* fighting in German East Africa.[15] Regardless, and focusing solely on this isolated battle, the outnumbered and ill-equipped Germans still won a lopsided victory. Interestingly, they attributed much of their success to the poor overall command of the battle by the South African brigadier general Beves.

Göring did not mince his words when he criticized the British commander after the battle, claiming that "Beves deployed his troops with great ruthlessness and did not shy away from bringing new troops forward, even if it meant heavy losses."[16] Even the usually deferential Lettow withheld any reservations in admonishing Beves, placing the onus on the British defeat solely on the South African:

> I had learned in the engagement at Reata (March 11, 1916) that General Beves threw his men into action regardless of loss of life and did not hesitate to try for a success, not by skillful handling and small losses, but rather by repeated frontal attacks, which, if the defense held its ground and had anything like adequate forces, led to severe losses for the attack. I guessed that here at Mahiwa he was carrying out the same tactics. I think it was by taking advantage of the enemy leader's mistaken tactics in this way that we were able to win this splendid victory.[17]

Although many British sources remain somewhat mum about the specific tactics of the battle and speak little about Beves's apparent incompetence, Captain Downes does leave us with a rather telling opinion on the matter.

When, following the battle of Mahiwa, General Beves issued orders to have the Nigerian Brigade resume the attack on the Germans at dawn on the nineteenth, he noted that "fortunately for the Brigade, this order was canceled by the G.O.C.-in-C.; otherwise I doubt this book [his memoir] would ever have been written, as it is quite possible that if the Brigade had attacked again they would have suffered extremely heavy casualties."[18] Not surprisingly, Beves was relieved of command shortly thereafter and replaced by General Frederick Cunliffe.

Despite the significant losses of manpower and equipment among the British colonial forces, which according to Lettow consisted of a field gun, six heavy and three light machine guns, and 200,000 rounds of ammunition,[19] when looking at the bigger picture, the defeat at Mahiwa could be regarded as a Pyrrhic, tactical victory for the Allies. As Lettow soon came to realize, even with the capture of significant ammunition dumps and artillery, he could not afford to have the *Schutztruppe* continue to suffer casualties, which, unlike the British, Belgian, and Portuguese forces, could not be replenished from back home or the colonies. Even small numbers of casualties, such as those incurred at Mahiwa, represented a significant portion of his overall forces, and under no conditions could more conventionally fought battles continue to be waged in the future.

From a standpoint of materiel, Lettow estimated that his forces had only 500,000 kg of supplies remaining, which would last only about six more weeks, assuming the various insects suddenly ceased consuming the sacks of grain.[20] Attempts to "live off the land" also began to prove difficult as the native tribes began to realize the British had the upper hand, and soon became hostile to the Germans. In many cases, they too were near starvation. As the cavalryman Alfred Schöffler recalled,

> Patrols were sent out daily to get food from the surrounding villages. Before long there was little left. What millet they were able to get wasn't enough to go around. As a result[,] we had to let many of our porters go. There was no food to feed them.[21]

There was also the problem of a nonexistent means of procuring medical supplies to treat the wounded and diseased. At this point, the lack of facilities and medication meant that as the *Schutztruppe* withdrew southward, hospitals and dressing stations had to be abandoned, along with their patients and wards, in hopes that they would be given care by the advancing Allied armies.

Regarding the ammunition supplies, the 200,000 rounds of ammunition captured at Mahiwa did little to replace the over 850,000 rounds fired during the course of the four days of fighting.[22] All the aforementioned factors subsequently began to break the typically high morale of the Askaris and their retinues, and thus desertion became an additional issue facing the protection forces.

On October 24, after conferring with Schnee, now disparagingly regarded to as the "governor of Chiwata"—after the new center of administration—Lettow made the difficult decision to depart German East Africa and enter Portuguese East Africa. In Mozambique, he expected to meet less resistance, find greater supply stores to capture, and reorganize his forces to again go on the offensive. Specifically, by relocating to Mozambique, Lettow thought,

> In the unlimited territory at our disposal[,] it would be possible to withdraw from unfavorable positions. The enemy would be compelled to keep an enormous number of men and material continually on the move, and to exhaust his strength to a greater extent proportionally than ourselves. There was also the prospect of tying down strong enemy forces and protracting the operations indefinitely if—my forecast proved correct.[23]

All present at the conference still agreed that it was imperative for the war against the Allies to continue, but crossing the Rovuma into Mozambique would still take weeks. At the end of October, the *Schutztruppe* still held 100 square miles of German East Africa in the southeast, including the fortified Boma[24] complex in Newala, in the Makonde plateau.

Back at home, none of Lettow's plans were known by the RKA or the RMA, nor had any additional Allied reports reached Germany to indicate that what little area was held by the *Schutztruppe* in East Africa was being abandoned in favor of Mozambique. Instead, their most pressing concern was an earthquake that occurred in Bulgaria just as the battle of Mahiwa was concluding on October 18. Fortunately for the *China-Sache* operation, the tremors did not cause any additional damage to the Yambol base beyond what was already known to the RMA. All lifting equipment and rail systems were tested on the nineteenth and still proved functional. Additionally, many of the special toolboxes and equipment were still in the process of being transported to Yambol on express trains and were similarly unaffected. This, however, should not imply that there weren't any other difficulties with preparing the base for the arrival of *L 59* or getting the airship there in the first place.

While the report to the chief of the Admiralty on October 15 outlined that Bulgarians would comprise the ground crews for the landing and ascent of *L 59*, they still had to be trained—a task proving easier said than done. As historian Wolfgang Meighörner-Schardt noted, "Of the 450 men promised, 100 men (mostly people who only understood Turkish) were distributed to cordon off the landing area and the rest to fill the holding crews. The Bulgarians and the German army soldiers were first informed, with the help of interpreters, about the nature of airship maneuvers in general and the Germans were given special instructions about the maneuver regulations introduced in the navy."[25] Making matters worse, nearly all the men selected for the teams were fresh recruits, since the more experienced personnel were already required in the front lines. A repeat of the events at Jüterbog certainly must have been in the back of everyone's mind at the RMA and RKA.

The costs and scarcity of supplies to replenish what was lost with *L 57* were additional complications, but owing to the RMA anticipating the resumption of the African mission in the next new-moon phase in November, this could be overcome in the allotted time. As a telegram from October 16 revealed, ammunition could be procured and packaged "in such a way that the airship crew only has to arrange the accommodation in the ship" at the base in Staaken by October 25.[26] Fuel and lifting gas, similarly difficult to source, could be made available by the anticipated transfer date of *L 59* to Yambol, but in the weeks leading up to that point, it impeded the acceptance trials of the airship. When the factory trial flight took place on October 30, much like it had been with *L 57*, the twelve-hour assessment was shortened to less than six hours and the high-altitude test had to be abandoned entirely, both due to not having the required fuel and hydrogen at that point in time. In fact, *L 59* had achieved a height of only 3,700 meters (12,139 feet), or 300 meters less than *L 57*'s factory trial.[27]

Although this was less than ideal, an important distinction from this flight compared to *L 57*'s earlier tests was that most of the nearly 14 tons of cargo was already on board. While the Zeppelin works utilized another one of their tests pilots for the trial, Anton Friedrich Heinen[28]—with Bockholt and his crew again present as observers, *L 59*'s behavior under load could be gauged prior to the transfer to Yambol. Deemed acceptable, November 3 was decided upon as the date that *L 59* would be flown to Bulgaria; however, this too would be slightly different in execution than *L 57*'s planned transfer from Jüterbog.

Perhaps hedging their bets to ensure the success of the mission, or at a minimum providing Bockholt with additional expertise in weather and technical matters, Hugo Eckener would accompany the airship to Yambol, along with experts from the RMA and DELAG (including the Zeppelin works' Captain Lau).[29] Also on board, but continuing onward to Africa, was Dr. Zupitza, who, due to legal constraints as a repatriated POW, had no direct role in the mission except for lending his expertise on medical concerns and imparting his knowledge about local ground conditions in GEA.[30] A memo sent by the *Admiralstab* to Yambol intentionally did not refer to him by name but instead mentioned a "chief medical officer" as "a personality who is familiar with the area."[31] While Dr. Zupitza was essentially a conciliatory inclusion, the former specialists proved to be welcome additions to the flight, since it would be fraught with both familiar and unforeseen difficulties.

When *L 59* took off at 0740 on November 3, poor weather was once again the primary hurdle to success. Much like the conditions on October 7, a low-pressure system was forecasted, and wind speeds of 22 mph were already observed at lower altitudes approaching from the northwest. While this could be beneficial in one way, serving as a tailwind on the journey southeast to Yambol, there was an added problem of visibility. Dense fog at sea level and a low cloud ceiling meant that *L 59*'s ascent from Staaken had the potential to be far more treacherous than *L 57*'s had been in Jüterbog. Dr. Walter Förster, the meteorologist on board the airship, perhaps undersold the situation when he recalled that "it left a lot to be desired."[32] Had it not been for the dire situation facing the *Schutztruppe* in Africa and the optimal lunar and meteorological conditions over southern Europe, the Mediterranean, and Africa, the departure would have been delayed. For the sake of the protection forces, however, *L 59* had to proceed.

Thankfully, the ground crews performed excellently and there were no issues leading *L 59* out of its hangar and into the air, but this did not mean that *L 59* was out of danger yet. In an effort to prevent the Allies from realizing that the flight took place, triangulation by radio telegraphy, the means by which Zeppelins raiding England adjusted their courses, was expressly forbidden. As it turned out, the regulation didn't matter. While *L 59* was still above Germany, following the course of the Oder River, the gearbox on the front engine, which also served as a generator for the radio, broke.[33] Whether he wanted to or not, Bockholt would now have to rely solely on his instruments and landmarks on the ground to find his bearings—the latter obviously being impossible if *L 59* flew above the dense cloud cover.

Given that spotting railways, rivers, and cities was still the most accurate means of navigation, Bockholt flew *L 59* at an altitude of only 1,148 feet. Although this was satisfactory for the early part of the voyage, *L 59* would still have to climb much higher in order to successfully negotiate the Balkans.

As an added risk, at this altitude *L 59* was clearly visible from terra firma, and the secrecy surrounding the mission had the potential to be blown by chatty German radio operators and ground forces. For the time being, however, all was more or less still going according to plan, and *L 59* was averaging a speed of nearly 41 mph, even with a disabled front engine. Then, just over 200 miles into the flight, another disaster struck.

Over Silesia, specifically the town of Brzeg in modern-day Poland, the cables used to control the rudder broke. These had been specially made of bronze for *L 59* instead of the more conventional steel, in order not to cause any interference with the magnetic compass on the long flight. Unfortunately, they quickly revealed themselves to be too soft for the task. To prevent *L 59* from continuing off course at speed, Bockholt ordered the engines to be turned off—essentially turning the massive airship into a free-floating balloon, traveling with the whims of the wind currents. Although it isn't mentioned in any imperial naval or Zeppelin factory sources, the failure of the bronze lines was perhaps expected, since, instead of taking along identically fabricated replacements, *L 59*'s reserve supply consisted of the steel ones that all other wartime Zeppelins were equipped with. In a process that lasted over two hours, the defective bronze cables were replaced with the more durable original types. Auspiciously for the Germans, this marked the turning point of the voyage.

Following the repair, the weather noticeably improved as *L 59* entered a high-pressure system, which caused the skies to clear and the wind to die down. Now, *L 59* was able to ascend to an altitude of just under 3,000 feet and continue southward unimpeded. By the time night fell, a dark ridge observed on the horizon indicated that the Little Carpathians (a mountain range in modern-day Slovakia) were ahead, and searchlights far aft of *L 59* illuminated the large bridges of Vienna. The beams also reflected off the rippling surface of the Danube—Bockholt's next landmark—which provided him with a guiding path onward toward Budapest, Belgrade, and eventually Bulgaria.

After the airship followed the easterly turns of the Danube overnight, the northern Bulgarian town of Nikopol greeted the Germans at dawn. Here Bockholt changed course to the southeast and prepared for the most difficult leg of the flight—crossing the Balkans. Upon reaching the historic, fortified, former capital city of Veliko Tarnovo just over an hour later, Bockholt ordered the release of 1,500 kg (3,307 lbs.) of water ballast to bring *L 59* to an altitude of 5,250 feet (1,600 meters), easily overcoming the 3,904-foot peak of the Shipka Pass.[34] With that final obstacle cleared, Bockholt straddled *L 59* between the Stara Zagora–Yambol railroad on his starboard side and the Tundzha River to port, reaching Yambol at 1250.[35] The flight lasted a total of twenty-eight hours and ten minutes, beating the estimated time of arrival by nearly two hours. No issues were reported involving the inexperienced, four-hundred-man, German/Bulgarian landing crew.

Upon arriving in Yambol, the RMA expected *L 59* to remain for "approximately 2–3 days, to do the final overhaul, outfitting, and loading" of the airship and then, immediately depart for German East Africa, crossing "the Aegean Sea or along the west coast of Anatolia, depending on the conditions encountered, and then across the Mediterranean Sea and mainland Africa"[36]—a journey of four days. This did not occur.

For one, the broken gearbox from the front engine could not be repaired with spares at Yambol, and another had to be sent from Germany via rail. Next, weather interfered, and conditions were so poor that the expected departure had to be pushed back over a week to November 13. While the delay was agonizing, given the hurried nature of the mission, it proved auspicious as the additional time allowed for the RMA and RKA to catch up on intelligence reports from Africa and revise the location of the landing zone in GEA.

On November 6, while *L 59* was still in the process of being prepped for departure in Yambol, the *Reichskolonialamt* forwarded a telegram in cipher to Bockholt, advising him of the current situation of the *Schutztruppe*, or at least the conditions on the ground as best as it could be ascertained from intercepted Allied transmissions. As usual, it was already weeks late and referred to the battle of Mahiwa back in October. It read as follows:

> In the western area, smaller German reconnaissance detachments [this refers to the remaining forces being driven from Mahenge, the *Westtruppen*, or western troops, led by *Hauptmann* Theodor Tafel] were driven eastward by a combined operation of British and Belgian army units. In the Mtama our troops [led by Lettow] are in contact with the main enemy force between Mahiwa, 3.5 miles southwest of Nyangao and Lukuledi. A Belgian army detachment from the direction of Kilwa has reached Liwale.
>
> Thereafter, the main division was not in the Mahenge district, as assumed, but in the Lindi district. Therefore, going to the Makonde plateau north of Rowuma is recommended.[37]

Although the news arrived late, it was accurate. The main concentration of the *Schutztruppe* was indeed now in the Makonde plateau instead of Mahenge. The RKA was so certain of this, and concerned that the message reached Yambol successfully, that they sent another telegram on the tenth to confirm that Bockholt was aware of the new landing zone.[38]

To ensure that Bockholt was able to identify Lettow, Governor Schnee, and Dr. Hugo Meixner (the chief medical officer in German East Africa) upon arriving in East Africa, they also wired their names, birthdays, and birthplaces[39]—information of debatable usefulness and far less practical than a period photograph or postcard, both of which existed and were sold throughout the German Empire for propaganda purposes and donation drives. Even stranger, in order to identify the nationalities of any unidentifiable troops on the ground in Africa, helmsman Grussendorf later volunteered himself to parachute out of *L 59* and approach them and signal back to the airship.[40] Since there was no means of getting back on the Zeppelin or escaping on foot should they have proven to be hostile forces, Grussendorf would essentially be taking a risky "leap of faith." Again, neither the RKA nor RMA was yet aware of Lettow's plans to withdraw to Mozambique, or the accelerated time frame required for *L 59* to still reach the *Schutztruppe* near the Rovuma.

Irrespective of the actual movements of the *Schutztruppe* within German East Africa, the RMA and RKA also remained appallingly ignorant of the actual needs of the colonial forces at this point in the campaign; namely, food and manpower. Although the 383,400 rounds of ammunition, rifles, and machine guns to be transported on *L 59* were far from insignificant, the battle of Mahiwa demonstrated that such quantities would be useful only for continued, small, guerrilla attacks—still important in tying down Allied resources, but otherwise not enough to resume any large-scale, decisive offensives. The medical supplies too, though sizable, would be of little use considering that Lettow was being forced to abandon his established hospitals and dressing stations.

Given that the food and water supplies on *L 59* were intended to be consumed only by the crew during the trip, a successful landing would do little to prevent continued desertion of the native troops. Additionally, the small number of crewmen on board *L 59,* who were to be absorbed into the *Schutztruppe* upon landing, was far too few to replace those who had already absconded or were lost as casualties. If anything, they would only add to the strain of having to feed and supply the colonial forces. Had this been known back in Berlin, it is questionable whether the RMA would have thought the massive investment in continuing the mission was worth it after the loss of *L 57*. However, owing to the importance of improving morale and supporting German forces abroad as long as resistance continued to exist, which the RMA emphasized in its appeal to the Kaiser, it is probable it still may have proceeded as planned. Nonetheless, on November 13, when *L 59* officially set off for its journey to German East Africa, the feasibility of the endeavor was once again cast into doubt.

When *L 59* ascended from Yambol at 0720 that day, weather conditions in Bulgaria were far from prime but were still considered acceptable following a consultation among the local weather station, Hugo Eckener, and Bockholt. Yet again, heavy fog existed at low altitudes, and a temperature inversion, in which air temperature increases with height, was expected due to prevailing warm winds originating in the Aegean Sea and Asia Minor.[41] Despite an officer already stationed in Yambol for over a year advising against taking off, particularly so close to the hangar,[42] *L 59* still made it off the ground safely. Of the twenty-two men on board, the only person listed as a "person not part of the crew" was Dr. Zupitza.

In the control car were *Kapitänleutnant* Ludwig Bockholt in command, *Leutnant zur See* Heinrich Maas as the watch officer, *Feldwebelleutnant* Emil Grussendorf, assisted by *Obersignalmaat* Albert Nolte, manning the elevator controls, and *Steuermann* Emil Wald, assisted by *Bootsmannsmaat* Bernhardt Wiesemann and *Obermatrose* (chief petty officer) Adolf Fuchs at the rudder controls. Noticeably absent from the former crew of *L 23* was *Obersteuermannsmaat* Ernst Fegert, the man who led the boarding party on the *Royal*, who was removed from the crew list while still in Jüterbog to mourn since his wife of just six weeks had died.[43] This was perhaps fortunate, since his replacement, Emil Wald, had been selected for the job due to his experience on board the battle cruiser SMS *Goeben*, which had been serving under the Ottoman flag as the *Yavuz Sultan Selim* in the Mediterranean since August 1914.[44] It was felt that his intimate knowledge of Asia Minor and the Mediterranean would be useful to assist with navigation.[45]

Also deviating from the original specifications of *L 57* was the payload. While in Yambol, the contents of *L 59* had been increased by over 2,200 kg (4,850 lbs.), which included an additional 1,138 kg (2,509 lbs.) of fuel, 194 kg (428 lbs.) of oil, 75 kg (165 lbs.) of water ballast, 550 kg (1,213 lbs.) of cargo (mainly ammunition), and 260 kg (574 lbs.) of provisions and drinking water, allowing for just 500 kg (1,102 lbs.) of free buoyancy within the hangar.[46] While of marginal benefit both to the mission and the relief of the *Schutztruppe*, it had very serious consequences for *L 59*'s static lift shortly after the airship ascended.

At just under 100 ft. of altitude, Bockholt found *L 59* to be "stuck," since warmer temperatures in the air were essentially making the Zeppelin heavier. To free the airship, Bockholt ordered 3,000 kg (6,614 lbs.) of water ballast to be released, along with 250 kg (551 lbs.) of ammunition (which equated to about 9,900 rounds), all of which landed on the roof of the hangar.[47] While successful in "freeing" the airship, he had already sacrificed three-quarters of his available water ballast. At an altitude of 1,476 feet, a further temperature increase of more than 13°F from the ground temperature of 50°F made *L 59* another 800 kg (1,764 lbs.) heavier.[48] At this point he had no choice but to land and reassess. *L 59* had been in flight for only two hours.

Bockholt's report back to Berlin the following day showed a complete reevaluation of the expected temperatures at altitude and the payload. It read:

> Yesterday's experience showed that the temperature conditions of +10°[C] on the ground, +6°[C] at 1,000 meters, based on the original report by *Kapitänleutnant* Sommerfeld, do not apply in any way to the current weather conditions. The voyage has a chance of success only if the abovementioned temperature conditions are approximately extant (i.e., with a high [pressure system] over the Balkans and low in SE Asia Minor and Palestine, with NNE winds over the Aegean and near Smyrna). To increase the static lift[,] I have expended
>
> 600 kg of petrol
> 100 kg oil
> 100 kg provisions
> 2,400 kg transport load
> ------------
> 3,200 kg
>
> Since the ship has been loaded with more ammunition from the outset than the *L 57*, there are still around 420,000 cartridges remaining in the payload.
>
> Both on the way across Asia Minor and on the way across the Aegean Sea, I have to assume an air temperature of 20° [68°F] at an altitude of 500 meters under the current weather conditions. After the additional removal of cargo on the ground, the ship carries 6,000 kg of water ballast at 10° [50°F] air temperature. This would just be enough to lift the ship statically to 500 meters at 20° without

> taking into account the expected increase of temperature of the gas 12°+[C] during the day and nighttime lowering of the temperature of −3°[C]. I consider a reserve gas load of at least 2,000 kg to be necessary when flying in tropical areas that are not yet known in terms of airmanship. Therefore, I have no choice but to add another 2,000 kg [of gas] or wait for cold air to arrive. Since, being that the current weather conditions have existed for six days [and] a change will soon be forthcoming . . . I have decided to wait for this change, in order not to reduce the cargo to be transported by too much.[49]

Unfortunately, time was in and of itself the most pressing factor to the success of the mission and the war in East Africa.

By November 15, Bockholt had a change of heart and decided he couldn't delay any longer, "because it could not be underestimated how every lost day could be of significance for Lettow-Vorbeck's troops."[50] Despite the previous day's weather reports indicating that "strong south-south-westerly winds with a strength of more than 15 m/s prevailed up to high altitudes of more than 3,000 meters"[51] and, on the fifteenth, "mostly cloudy with precipitation, surface winds gradually turning to the west, upper winds south to southwest over ten m/s"[52]—regarded by Dr, Förster and the weather stations at Sofia and Constantinople as being "the exact opposite of what could be described as particularly favorable for the undertaking of such a large and difficult task as the Africa expedition"[53]—Bockholt sent a telegram to the *Admiralstab* in Berlin announcing his intentions.

The message was succinct, stating only that "according to weather conditions [the] ship is being prepared to sail."[54] He felt that despite the risks, the critical situation in East Africa necessitated the flight to take place, regardless of the challenging circumstances. For their part, the RMA did not offer any dissenting opinions. Another attempt at reaching German East Africa was to take place the following morning.

6

The Next Attempt

NOVEMBER 16, 1917. As a new day dawns in the requisitioned army airship base in Yambol, the cool and cloudy conditions that existed the following two days continue to prevail. Despite the loss of *L 57* being attributed to taking off in bad weather, and the initial attempt at reaching East Africa having been aborted three days prior under similar circumstances, Bockholt and his crew are obstinate in their belief that this morning's ascent will prove successful. They don their flight uniforms while the ground crews begin the process of weighing off *L 59* within the hangar. This time, the "Africa ship" has a reduced payload of 13.7 metric tons of ammunition and medical supplies and an increased supply of water ballast equating to about 7,000 kg.[1] When preparations are complete, *L 59* is buoyant enough that just a single man would be capable of supporting the massive airship, hovering just feet above the ground. Before *L 59* is walked out of the shed, Bockholt assembles his officers for a final preflight conference in the control car.

"Men, the weather has hardly improved from earlier this week, but I am certain we can utilize it to our advantage. Instead of proceeding southward over the Aegean Sea, where we are certain to meet Allied patrol planes, we'll take advantage of the westerly headwinds and head east to Burgas [a Bulgarian port city on the Black Sea], then southeast over Asia Minor. This should not only conserve ballast but also keep us from revealing our presence from British naval forces near Greece. Agreed?"

The naval officers and Emil Grussendorf, the army representative, let out a resounding "*Jawohl, Herr Kaleu!*" Dr. Walter Förster, however, is visibly less enthused and remains silent.

"Everything all right, *Herr Doktor*?" inquires Bockholt.

Dr. Förster, stepping out in front of his combat hardened colleagues, opines.

"*Kapitänleutnant*, I firmly believe that the current forecast is reason enough not to warrant risking the airship again. As the meteorological expert on board, I have repeatedly expressed my concerns this week about wind speeds at high altitudes and storms in the eastern Mediterranean. The latest report from Constantinople . . ."

Bockholt cuts him off.

"Doctor, you are no doubt the authority on weather-related matters, and if this were peacetime, I would agree wholeheartedly that conditions are less than optimal for a long-distance airship flight. Myself and most of the men that surround you, however, are officers of the *Kaiserliche Marine*, and the Admiralty has raised no objections to our attempt this morning. Will it be challenging? Certainly, but no more perilous than a bombing raid over England. Think of the brave *Schutztruppen* dying right now because we haven't delivered the means to continue their struggle. They have gone without adequate arms and medications for over three years now and don't have the luxury of waiting things out. Your opinion has been noted, but we simply can't wait any longer."

Dr. Förster appears ready to make a counterargument, but, as he looks around and meets the disparaging glances of the other officers in the hanger, merely puts his head down and utters, "Yes, yes, of course, *Kapitänleutnant*," and backs away into the assemblage.

Contented, Bockholt looks over his men and asks, "Any other concerns before we get underway?"

Lt. Maas steps forward and clears his throat in a poor attempt at disguising his smirk left over from the previous exchange.

"*Herr Kaleu*, although in all probability we won't encounter any enemy patrols in the air, *L 59* now hardly resembles a combat airship anymore. With no machine guns mounted, or bombs on board, what shall we do if we happen to come across any British seaplanes or surface vessels along the way?"

Bockholt, instead of being argumentative, can offer only a sober response.

"Our only hope is to remain unobserved. Thankfully, our undertaking up to this point has progressed in utmost secrecy. In fact, after the loss of *L 57* the Admiralstab even went through the trouble of openly broadcasting that the enterprise was completely abandoned. We have the advantage that no one is expecting us, not even our own people or the Bulgarians, Austro-Hungarians, or Ottomans."

Satisfied, Maas returns to his place in the group.

"Now, if there's nothing else, let's get underway!"

The men then break away and simultaneously proceed to their respective stations on board the Zeppelin. Only then is *L 59* walked out of its cavernous shed and onto the field.

At 0808, *L 59* makes its ascent from Yambol and begins heading east toward Burgas, a distance of approximately 50 miles. Analogous to his strategy during *L 59*'s transfer from Staaken to Yambol, Bockholt opts to maintain radio silence and navigate using landmarks. Similarly, he must fly his airship at a low altitude to keep below the cloud ceiling. For the time being, *L 59* can proceed at a height of only 400 meters (1,312 feet). Although over friendly territory, Bockholt warns his watch officer to keep a sharp eye out; after all, the British had proven repeatedly since 1914 that they could extend the range of their airplanes into enemy territory by transporting them on rudimentary aircraft carriers or by utilizing seaplanes.[2] His premonition was almost immediately proven correct.

Just as *L 59* reaches the Black Sea, *Leutnant* Maas excitedly reports, "Aircraft spotted, approaching quickly. Appears to be a seaplane, others are taking off below."

Bockholt immediately rushes to the window of the control car and strains through his binoculars, trying to identify the intercepting aircraft. Thankfully for *L 59*, he can make out black crosses painted on their upper wings—they are German.

"Well, they're our planes. They must be from our base in Varna, but they are certainly approaching quickly. Surely they can see our markings;[3] why do they continue toward us?"

In what seemed to take an eternity, the leading seaplane turns parallel to the airship and, while attempting to overtake it, surveys it, then turns away, rocking the seaplane's wings back and forth in a wave of recognition; the rest of the flight group then follows suit and returns to their base. Letting out a collective gasp, the officers on board *L 59* relax slightly as the Zeppelin then continues onward toward Asia Minor. With one crisis averted, however, another was literally looming on the horizon.

Upon turning south-southeast over the Black Sea, Dr. Förster once again makes his presence known. "*Kapitänleutnant*, I don't like the look of the cloud formations ahead. Do you see how they are layered, and their edges appear frayed? Not only does this indicate a storm forming, but also that we should anticipate powerful winds very shortly."[4]

Bockholt, remaining unfazed, barks out an order: "Ascend to 650 meters [2,133 feet], using dynamic lift. We will try to keep above the storm, but I must be able to spot our next landmark, the Panderma[modern-day Bandirma]–Smyrna [now Izmir] railway. That is our southerly guide toward the Mediterranean."

By the time *L 59* reaches Panderma at nightfall, the airship is enveloped by cloud cover and winds. This is treacherous in and of itself, but Bockholt is forced to navigate the giant airship in darkness, while thick cumulus clouds continue to obscure his hampered view. In order to maintain contact with the railway, Bockholt eventually has to bring *L 59* down to a height of 550 meters (1,804 feet), but this results only in further dangers, this time emanating from the ground.

At 0400, approximately at the halfway point of the railway, sharp cracks echo in the forward gondola. The officers look at each other and then to Bockholt, who orders a check of the controls, fearing that cables may have snapped again. The rudder and elevator, however, are working perfectly. Then *Leutnant* Maas calls out, "*Herr Kaleu*, we're being fired upon!"

When the men peer out of the window of the control car, rifle flashes are observed from the ground. Apparently, the Ottoman troops guarding the railway interpret the German airship as an Allied one, flying at low altitude to bomb the tracks. "Send for *Obersegelmachermaat* Schulz!" commands Bockholt.

When the sailmaker, responsible for repairing the airship's envelope and gas bags, arrives in the control car, Bockholt sends him to inspect the hydrogen cells and report back on any damage from the rifle shots. His findings are surprising, but it's not yet critical: "Five bullet holes discovered in the gas bags, sir. Hydrogen is leaking slowly, but it can probably be repaired."

"Good, see to it that it's done; we still have a long way to go yet, and every cubic centimeter of gas is critical."

Incredibly, as *L 59* proceeds onward, above the railway line, she manages to escape further damage despite the best efforts of Turkish ground troops. Sporadic rifle fire at the airship is repeatedly heard from the ground while the airship continues on its course toward to Soma, Türkiye. Here,

L 59 must navigate the most dangerous leg of its journey over Asia Minor—a narrow valley surrounded by mountains with peaks of nearly 4,000 feet.[5] The weather only continues to worsen.

What had previously been heavy clouds and winds has now evolved into a full-fledged thunderstorm, soaking the airship with rain and hammering it with lateral and vertical drafts. At one point, *L 59* is thrown upward to an altitude of 950 meters (3,117 feet) and begins to turn horizontally. Having flashbacks of *L 57*'s disaster, Bockholt orders the engines throttled to maximum power and for the rudder to be turned fully in the direction opposite of the gusts. The rudder men exert all their strength at the controls, but it is to no avail. *L 59* continues to turn several times on its axis. Snaps and creaking can be heard within the airship's hull as several strut crosses on the gangway near ring 145, the support ring at the side gondolas, break, and fourteen wire stays in the middle of the airship tear.[6]

Making matters worse, the heavy rains that saturated the airship make their way through an open window and leak into the radio room. The radio-telegraph machine's transmitter, not insulated from the elements, shorts out when its socket is exposed to the pervading moisture. Although it is repaired with onboard spares, its subsequent operation is uncertain, and Bockholt is unsure whether any of his signals will actually reach base.[7] Still, none of these issues change Bockholt's mind about carrying on with the mission. When the rain abates somewhat in the afternoon, *L 59* continues onward toward Hisar—a southwestern port in Türkiye, approximately 150 miles north-northeast of Crete. However, as evening changes into night, cooler temperatures make the already waterlogged airship even heavier. *L 59*'s stern begins to sink, and Bockholt must make a crucial decision.

Fearing losing any more altitude in his already precarious situation in the foggy valley, Bockholt knows that *L 59*'s chances of reaching German East Africa have greatly diminished. Looking around the control car and meeting the worried, exhausted faces of his officers and men, he makes a painful but necessary decision—he aborts the flight. First, all 7 metric tons of water ballast are ordered to be jettisoned, along with an additional 1,000 kg of cargo. When this fails to make an appreciable change in *L 59*'s buoyancy, he has his crew push fourteen barrels of gasoline overboard.[8] The shedding of the fuel has the intended effect. The airship, now an additional 2 tons lighter, rises to an altitude of 2,200 meters (7,218 feet)[9] and begins its ascent over the surrounding mountains, easily overcoming their tall peaks. A course is then plotted for the Black Sea, and Bockholt has his radio operator wire a signal back to Yambol, informing the base of their imminent return. Although it was seemingly successfully transmitted, there is no response.

By 1930, *L 59* reaches Constantinople in heavy rain and with 20 mph winds blowing from the southwest. Even at the much-lower altitude of 700 meters (2,297 feet), conditions are so poor that Bockholt can orient himself only with the city lights shining faintly beneath the airship—he has no idea if he is north of the city, over the Black Sea, or south of the isthmus on which the capital lies, above the Sea of Marmara. Given that the functionality of *L 59*'s radiotelegraph is uncertain, Bockholt doesn't send any further wireless messages back to Yambol or request any assistance in the form of escorts. Instead, he utilizes the airship's searchlights in an attempt at signaling the Ottoman military authorities and surface vessels below—it is to no avail. Thunderstorms once again develop, and no one at ground level can make out the Zeppelin's light beams. Rather than traveling blindly, Bockholt orders *L 59* to remain in its current position to await daybreak, keeping the lights of Constantinople in full view overnight. He was, in actuality, south of Constantinople, over the Sea of Marmara.

When dawn arrives the following morning, conditions have barely improved. Although Bockholt attempts to get *L 59* above the dense cloud cover, it is soon discovered that the ceiling is over 2,400 meters (7,874 feet)—an impossible altitude for *L 59* to reach in its current state. Therefore, in order to get his bearings, Bockholt navigates *L 59* on a course to the northwest at a height varying between 300 and 500 meters in order to re-orient himself. When Medea (now Kıyıköy), a port on the southwestern extremity of the Black Sea, is reached at 1000, Bockholt adjusts *L 59*'s course northward, along the coast back toward Burgas. Fighting through the storm, which is only increasing in strength, *L 59* reaches the Bulgarian port city four hours later and then turns west, landing at Yambol at 1630.

In thirty-two hours, *L 59* had traveled just under 900 miles (1,434 km) at an average speed of 27.5 mph (44.3 km/h).[10] Other than the slight damage to the airship's frame, envelope, and gas bags, the only other notable mechanical issue discovered on *L 59* was burnt valves in the port engine.[11] All these issues could be repaired within a matter of days, and the mission could be resumed; however, the clock remained ticking on all the other factors outside the RMA's control—namely, the weather and the *Schutztruppe*'s disintegrating hold in German East Africa.

Regarding the former, just three days after *L 59* made her inglorious return back to Yambol, the weather conditions over the Aegean and Mediterranean Seas made a remarkable improvement. The depression that had doomed the second attempt at reaching East Africa was proceeded by a high-pressure system, pushing "polar air masses" from the northwest. Additionally, winds of 22 mph were recorded at high-altitude measuring stations in Macedonia, the Balkans, and northern Türkiye.[12] According to Göbel, Dr. Förster felt that "this was finally the situation that [he] . . . had been waiting for."[13] If the forecast held, by November 20, *L 59* could expect not only cloudless skies, but also strong and consistent tailwinds that would carry the airship along its currents and save valuable fuel. Upon presenting this information to Bockholt, it was decided that both lunar and meteorological conditions favored taking off the following week, and a tentative departure date for the morning of November 21 was set. Unfortunately, the good news regarding the weather didn't extend to the *Schutztruppe*'s situation in German East Africa.

On November 19, the *Reichskolonialamt* notified the RMA of an official British report published the previous day that claimed that, on November 14, German troops had "finally [been] expelled from all Mahenge area," with disastrous losses.[14] This was referring to the *Westtruppen*, composed of *Hauptmann* Theodor Tafel, *Korvettenkapitän* Werner Schönfeld, and *Hauptmann* Ernst Otto's detachments, which had been the sole remaining army groups holding and, slowly but steadily, retreating from the Mahenge district. More worryingly, it stated that British troops had occupied Mwiti within the northern area of the Makonde plateau—near *L 59*'s new landing zone. Yet again, the intelligence gleaned from intercepted Allied reports was mostly accurate,[15] but with no news from German personnel on the ground, the RKA was skeptical and came to a conclusion quite divorced from reality.

In their instructions regarding what information should be released to the German press, they noted,

> After their report on the fighting that took place from the 6th to the 8th of the month, the English claimed to have been close to Chiwata and Mwiti. The fact that they were only able to occupy both points on the 14th and 15th proves that the resistance they encountered could not have been so weak. Still, this does not mean that the Makonde plateau has been reached, as the English would have us believe. Therefore, in regard to the military situation, no essential change has occurred. The figures for German losses in men and material cannot, of course, be verified here. In general, such reports have proven to be exaggerated on previous occasions.
>
> There has[,] therefore[,] been no significant change in the military situation.[15]

Interestingly, the RKA did not deny that Mahenge had now been completely overrun, only that the resistance from the *Schutztruppe* was, in all likelihood (and in actuality), greater than what was being reported. It is also unclear how they were able to prove that previous stories had been exaggerated, considering that no recent news from German forces within the colony had been forthcoming.

Indeed, it is exceedingly difficult to understand the mentality of the RMA and RKA when looking at the desperate situation in East Africa through a modern, omniscient lens. Certainly, they must have been aware that German East Africa was now more than 80 percent occupied by enemy forces and that the materiel to be transported to the combat zone by *L 59* would do little in shifting the fortunes of war; however, as both earlier and future memos indicated, they felt that any signs of German resistance in the colony, regardless of how meager, justified the relief mission. The British report, like all the preceding ones, had no impact on operation *China-Sache*. If anything, it seemed to only strengthen their resolve. Although there were no signs of changing plans, there were slight changes to the undertaking's policies in order to avoid further incidents with friendly forces. While the secrecy of the "China matter" had been closely guarded up to this point, with neither the Ottomans, Austro-Hungarians, Bulgarians, nor other German forces aware of *L 59*'s mission, the events involving German seaplanes over the Black Sea and Turkish ground fire over the Panderma–Smyrna railway made the RMA reevaluate this strategy, largely due to concerns raised by Bockholt.

In his postmission report concerning the aborted second flight, he requested in writing that the navy's Mediterranean Division notify the Ottoman "railway guards" of *L 59* in order to prevent further attacks from the ground. This was followed up with a phone conversation between Bockholt and *Kapitänleutnant* Hans Humann, the German naval attaché in Constantinople, after which the latter wired Berlin assuring the RMA that the Mediterranean Division would "get in touch" with the Turkish general headquarters, and the response would be wired both to Bockholt and the *Admiralstab*.[16] Although Bockholt made no mention of the earlier, uneventful encounter with the German seaplanes in his commentary, a telegram received the same day as his phone call with Humann reiterated the importance of sharing *L 59*'s presence with additional forces.

Arriving in Berlin just three hours after Humann's transmission, a telegram sent by Arnim, the naval attaché in Sofia, conveyed the problems with having a mysterious Zeppelin suddenly appear in the German navy's Black Sea patrol zone completely unannounced. It noted that on the morning of November 16, Bulgarian coastal posts had observed four enemy surface vessels approximately 25 nautical miles distant and scrambled reconnaissance seaplanes to scout the area. While none of the enemy warships were positively located, an unidentified airship *was* spotted in "square 67." Although it is difficult to infer emotions through brief telegrams, you can sense both frustration and the impression that the situation may have turned out much worse had the naval airmen taken the initiative to attack before realizing that *L 59* was German. The second half of the message read:

> Nothing is known about the arrival of a naval airship in Yambol. Only [the] knowledge of the intention to transfer [it]. In order to exclude any doubts in the future that would lead to renewed air reconnaissance due to incoming reports, please order that the naval departments in Constanța and Varna are informed in good time about the relocation and long-distance flights of our own airship from Yambol to the coast.[17]

The message appeared to have hit home. At 0130 on November 20, or twelve hours before Bockholt wired the Admiralty that *L 59* was resupplied and ready to fly, the navy's Mediterranean Division sent a telegram (through Humann) requesting the postponement of the departure until confirmation from all parties about *L 59*'s presence in the area was received. Specifically,

> Turkish General Headquarters will notify Mediterranean Division when all offices, including inland offices, have been informed. The message will then be forwarded immediately to *L 59*. German naval offices have been instructed to pay more attention to signals. Recommend postponing the trip until the above message from General Headquarters arrives.[18]

Thankfully for the *China-Sache* mission, the requested confirmation arrived that same evening.

Finally, to rule out any further confusion about *L 59*'s allegiance, in addition to the already extant German crosses and naval ensigns (with the colonial flag of GEA replacing the *Reichsflagge* in the corner quadrant), large German and Ottoman flags were painted on the airship's hull[19] on the bottom of the bow, in front of the forward gondola. They were added in pairs to the port and starboard nose sections of the Zeppelin's underside and would be unmistakable national identifiers to troops located on the ground. Between this and the radio notifications to the Turkish headquarters, if any further rifle fire originated from the ground, it would be attributed only to a significant lapse in discipline on the part of the Ottoman troops.

With the repairs completed, the weather conditions ideal, and all other concerns addressed, *L 59* was set to take off from Yambol on the morning of the twenty-first. Since the giant Zeppelin had not yet reached the arid deserts and subtropical climates of the African continent on its previous flight, no one was quite sure what to expect of their airship, or themselves. *L 59* would be crossing a new frontier in aerial travel if it were successful, but would its mission be enough to turn the tide in German East Africa? Would it make it there at all?

7

Into the Winds of Destiny

AT DAWN ON NOVEMBER 21, 1917, the anticipated polar air mass had indeed arrived in Yambol from the north. The winds were light, the sky was overcast, and the ground temperature was at the freezing point. True to Dr. Förster's forecast, a weak high-pressure system near the Balkans and a similarly weak low-pressure system over Asia Minor suggested that this third attempt at reaching German East Africa would be a much-smoother journey.

Building on the experiences of the prior, aborted flight, where all of *L 59*'s water ballast had to be dumped to gain altitude following the storm, Bockholt once again made changes to the airship's weight. For this attempt, the water ballast on board was increased from 7,000 kg to just over 9,000 kg (19,842 lbs.),[1] and an additional 200 kg (441 lbs.) of cargo was added to the payload, equating it to the 13.9 metric tons (30,644 lbs.) originally specified for *L 57*.[2] He also modified the course. Now, *L 59* would skip the journey eastward over the Black Sea and instead proceed directly southward toward Adrianople (modern-day Edirne, Türkiye). Only then would the Zeppelin turn east over the Sea of Marmara to once again pick up the trail of the Panderma–Smyrna railway over the northern coast of Asia Minor.

Although the Aegean Sea would almost entirely be bypassed, Bockholt was concerned about British air and sea patrols upon his approach to

Adrianople, since the Gallipoli (now Gelibolu) Peninsula, some 85 miles south, was still swarming with Royal Navy surface vessels and aircraft. To alleviate this threat, the navy's Mediterranean Division was instructed to make feinting sorties in the area following *L 59*'s ascent, while simultaneously scouting for enemy planes and warships as they flew defensive patrols. This combined with the pledge from the Turkish headquarters that no Ottoman troops would fire at the Zeppelin over the railway line provided assurance that *L 59* would no longer be misidentified as a hostile airship. The lessons of the prior flight had been well learned.

Despite the airship being slated to take off at 0500, the frenetic preparations for the flight pushed back *L 59*'s departure for just over three and a half hours. On the basis of what Göbel personally observed in the Bulgarian hangar that morning, it appeared that all involved in the operation were either ensuring that no stone was left unturned in readying the giant airship, or, as he more cynically put it, "Everyone was despairing in coping with the overwhelming number of their duties."[3] Even after the hangar doors were slid open, the hydrogen cells were still being filled, fuel was being pumped into the gas tanks, the engines were being run and tested, and maps were laid out in the forward gondola in preparation for the journey. When the command to march the airship out of the hangar was given, the German-Bulgarian ground crew had to be roused from their relaxed state—they had gotten bored sitting idly since dawn.

With just two aft engines running, *L 59* is slowly led out of its shed. Then, at 0835, the command "Ascend!" is given. The aft engines are throttled up to their maximum rpms, and the holding crews at the airship's extremities are commanded to let go of their tethers. Those grabbing on to the forward gondola give the Zeppelin a final push upward. As the "Africa ship" climbs, Bockholt orders all engines to be run at full speed ahead. This is the prompt for *Leutnant* Maas to move all the arms of the engine telegraph in the control car, each representing an individual engine location on the Zeppelin, to "A.K"—*alle Kräfte*, or maximum power—at the four o'clock position on the dial. Utilizing dynamic lift against the northerly headwinds, Bockholt brings *L 59* to an altitude of 700 meters (2,300 feet). Although this is only 300 meters higher than the height that *L 59* climbed to on the sixteenth, this time flying at such a low altitude has nothing to do with the cloudy weather conditions.

While Bockholt still has to remain below the cloud cover, which would otherwise obscure the navigational landmarks on the ground, today the ceiling is much higher than it had been on the previous attempt. Instead of climbing in order to reach the lower edges of the clouds, Bockholt wants to keep *L 59* below the airship's pressure height and avoid venting any precious hydrogen. Given that his purpose-built Zeppelin isn't armed with any machine guns for the trip, whose flashes could potentially ignite the flammable gas, it isn't imperative to reach such a high elevation at the outset of the voyage.

Despite being easily visible from the ground, for the time being the mood inside the Zeppelin is more relaxed than the previous flight. Even the ever-alert Dr. Förster can remark only on the beauty of the sights observed below, noting in his and Göbel's memoir the historical significance of towns, fortresses, and temples from antiquity and their surrounding mythology as the airship soars above them.

At 0945, *L 59* is above Adrianople, and, after turning east, the source of the Panderma–Smyrna railway is once again reached at 1145. Opting for radio silence, Bockholt takes advantage of the opportunity above Panderma to drop messages to the Ottoman forces below so that they could be forwarded on, via telegraph, to: the *Admiralstab*, the Yambol airship base, the naval Mediterranean Division, and FdL Strasser.[4] With no threats from any friendly Ottoman ground fire this time around, *L 59* continues onward at the same low altitude of 700 meters.

As an early indication that the British weren't aware of the resumption of the *China-Sache* mission through any intercepted radio signals between the RMA, the Mediterranean Division, or Constantinople leading up to the voyage, when the German scouting seaplanes fly over the Royal Navy airbase in Mytilene (located on the island of Lesbos in the Aegean Sea) that morning, they note no unusual activity. Additionally, all British aircraft already observed in the air are not proceeding on any courses that would lead them to intercept *L 59*.[5] When *L 59* reaches Soma at 1400 that day—the point at which Bockholt had to abort the last flight—the officers in the forward gondola look at each other and smile. They are certain that if the weather continues to cooperate, their mission will be successful. Unfortunately, back home in Germany, a feeling of dread and panic has set in.

At 0510 that day, or just ten minutes after *L 59*'s original slated departure time, *Korvettenkapitän* Knorr's[6] telephone rings in Berlin—it is an urgent call from the *Reichskolonialamt* for the RMA concerning an intercepted British report from East Africa. The news is disconcerting; it reads:

> Our [the British] troops, continuing the pursuit of the enemy on the Makonde Plateau, occupied Lusonje, four miles south-east of Chiwata, on November 17; in passing through difficult terrain[,]

> they encountered considerable resistance. 172 undamaged rifles were collected. On November 18, our columns occupied a large enemy camp near Nambindinga, five miles north-west of [the] Kitangari Mission Station, where twenty German officers, two hundred and forty-two other German combatants, fourteen German non-combatants, and seven hundred Askari surrendered. Twenty-five English, two Belgian, and five Portuguese prisoners of war were liberated. The remainder of the enemy force was driven into the Aj Valley.
>
> Portuguese troops approach the vicinity of Newala from the south. The last of the enemy's 4.5-inch field howitzers was discovered intact on the Mahiwa-Ndanda road, where it was left on the 9th or 10th of November. Near Handebe [this area was questioned by the Germans, since nothing exists with a similar name in the location], 38 miles south-west of Liwale, English and Belgian columns engaged on the 15th and 16th of November with enemy forces attempting to break through from Mahenge territory to the south. In addition to the enemy's losses at Nandete, which have not yet been reported, 798 German Europeans have been killed or captured by our various columns since the 1st of November.[7]

Although this news could not be substantiated by German colonial forces, who had no means of sending radio signals back home, it prompted an immediate discussion at the RMA. If the news were true, even though it did not claim that Lettow had capitulated, it meant that the combined Allied forces were now occupying *L 59*'s new landing zone and making an encircling assault from the south. With no further viable areas to touch down within German East Africa, and the *Schutztruppe*'s foothold in the colony itself being put into doubt, the entire relief mission was now in jeopardy.

By noon, the *Admiralstab* concluded that the *China-Sache* operation would have to be abandoned.[8] Three hours later, a simple wireless message was sent from Berlin to Yambol to be forwarded on to *L 59*; it read: "Abort the mission. Return to Germany."[9] Unfortunately, at this point, with *L 59* already over Asia Minor, flying south over the Panderma–Smyrna railway, the airship was out of range of the small wireless transmitter at Yambol and continued on with the flight. When the response from the Naval Special Command in Yambol arrived in Berlin at 1820 that day, it advised, "*L 59* can no longer be reached from here; please call back through Nauen."[10] This meant that the RMA would have to rely on the massive wireless station in Nauen (in Brandenburg), already being utilized by the *Kaiserliche Marine* to communicate with long-range U-boats, to reach the "Africa ship." Its range of nearly 9,000 km (5,592 miles)[11] ensured that not only would the message reach *L 59*, but that the whole world, from Los Angeles to the west and to Tokyo to the east, could potentially listen in on the broadcast.

At nearly same time the *Admiralstab* was being advised to try other means at reaching *L 59*, darkness began to descend upon Bockholt and his crew. Navigating by moonlight through the valleys that surround the railway, they have just reached Smyrna. With the railway terminating at the coastline, Bockholt's next navigational landmarks—the Dodecanese Islands—are obscured by the commanding height of Mount Nif, rising nearly 5,000 feet above sea level.[12] Instead of immediately heading west toward the Icarian Sea, where *L 59* would surely encounter enemy aircraft based on the Greek island of Chios, Bockholt keeps the mountain to his starboard side and commands his airship southward over Smyrna's suburbs, providing his meteorologist with another sightseeing spectacle. Perhaps with a sense of foreboding, after observing various mosques, minarets, ruins, and even a monastery belonging to the Sufi "dancing Dervishes," Förster focuses on cemeteries lined with cypress trees, which remind him of "eternity."[13] Bockholt, after studying the engrossed doctor from within the control car, snaps him out of his awestruck trance.

"Men, we'll soon be approaching the 'danger zone' in the Mediterranean. We shouldn't encounter any seaplanes, but we must be mindful of British surface vessels. Besides enemy ships, stay alert for lit beacons on the small islands in the Aegean; they'll be our guide to Crete."

With Maas once again replacing Förster at the windows of the forward gondola, *L 59* continues over the remainder of the railway line under cloudy skies. At 1940 she reaches the Bay of Akbük on Türkiye's southern coast and then steers west toward the Greek island of Kos, the first of the Dodecanese Islands that *L 59* would traverse. Keeping to the north of the island, Bockholt changes the airship's course to south-southwest upon crossing the Strait of Leipsoi at 2010. At 2200, shortly after crossing the Strait of Karpathos, Cape Sideros—the northeastern extremity of Crete—is spotted and *L 59* once again turns south-southeast toward the Egyptian coast. This, however, isn't a cause for celebration within the control car.

Förster is the first to sense that something is amiss, noting that the "strange flickering of stars" on the horizon isn't a good omen but instead signals an approaching monsoon.[14] As the wind rapidly begins to pick up, *Funkmaat* Kettner notifies Bockholt of strong electrical interference affecting the airship's wireless telegraphy equipment. *Feldwebelleutnant* Grussendorf is next to chime in, suddenly exclaiming, "There's lightning over there! Lightning from cloud to cloud just observed."[15]

Bockholt, remaining calm, instructs his helmsman to track the storm's direction. Grussendorf replies, "Storm heading northwest, directly toward us."

Pausing to assess the situation, and in all likelihood replaying in his mind his disastrous experiences with storms thus far, Bockholt opts for boldness. "We have to go through, one way or another; if we turn back the storm would overtake us."[16]

As the wind speed continues to increase, *L 59* can barely make any headway on her southerly course. Making matters worse, *Leutnant* Maas spots enemy warships through a hole in the clouds below. Their funnels, when viewed directly from above, lead down to their boilers and the coal fires burning within, making the vessels appear as though they are constellations, floating on an otherwise impenetrably jet-black sea. Although the ships are sailing on an opposite heading, *L 59* is moving so slowly against the forthcoming winds that for a moment, they appear to be still; yet, they show no signs of engaging the airship.

"Don't worry about them, *Leutnant*," advises Bockholt. "They can't see us, and in weather like this, the last place they'll be looking is up." Given the situation, the advice offers little in the way of consolation.

As Grussendorf continues to note unrelenting lightning flashes approaching, Kettner informs Bockholt that the electrical interference has now rendered his equipment unusable. With no means of sending any wireless signals, and its antenna (essentially just a thin, braided wire with a weight on the end, spooled onto a winch) acting as a lightning rod suspended from the airship's gondola, Bockholt orders it reeled in. For the duration of the storm, and several hours later, *L 59* is unable to transmit or receive any radio communication. Coincidentally, it was shortly after this point that Nauen began broadcasting the recall message. It fell on deaf ears.

Continuing onward on a south-southeasterly course, at 2225, at coordinates of 34°N, 30°E—approximately the center of the Mediterranean Sea, 150 miles south of Asia Minor and 200 miles north of Alexandria—*L 59* enters the monsoon. Lt. Maas begins to lose his composure.

"*Herr Kaleu*, we can't get through; we have to try to circumnavigate this cliff of storm clouds!"[18]

Rain begins to soak *L 59*'s canvas shell, and the intense winds whip the airship upward and downward at altitudes ranging from 500 to 1,200 meters (1,640–3,937 feet).[19]

Bockholt remains steadfast: "Continue on course; the only way out of this witch's cauldron is through it!"

As *L 59* pushes forward, there is a frantic call heard from the back of the control car: "We've been hit by lightning; the airship is on fire!"[20]

Indeed, it appears that a varying blue-and-purple plasma has enveloped the forward gondola, accompanied by a buzzing sound seeming to emanate from the duralumin girders within the airship. For the more experienced airship men on board, it is not a cause for alarm, but a premonition that the worst is behind them.

"St. Elmo's fire," explains Bockholt. "The surfaces of our airship are causing the electrical field from the storm to fluoresce. It happens on ships at sea as well, and other Zeppelins have experienced it during raids on England. Perhaps our patron saint is giving us his blessing for our mission."[21]

Reflecting Bockholt's assuredness that the storm was nothing but a minor inconvenience on the flight, both his war diary and mission report note only the presence of "widespread thunderstorms and rain showers,"[22] and none of the accompanying drama. Surely enough, the optical phenomenon soon subsides, and the rain and wind similarly begin to die down. While stars can occasionally be seen through breaks in the overcast sky, given that *L 59* is now flying over an area in the Mediterranean where there aren't any islands, neither celestial navigation nor the use of landmarks can be utilized. Although the magnetic compass is functional, Bockholt orders *Peilbomben*, or "bearing bombs,"[23] to be dropped from the control car to determine the speed and direction of both the airship and the wind. For the remainder of the nighttime hours, *L 59* continues steadily on a course due south at an altitude of 700 meters.

At 0515 on the twenty-second, *L 59* arrives on the North African coast at Ras Bulau, Egypt—just over 180 miles west of Alexandria. While Bockholt's version of the event notes that "the African coast, which could already be recognized from the side by the clearing sky, was crossed exactly at the points headed for,"[24] Förster's account is a poetic masterpiece. In describing reaching the continent at dawn, he recalls that "silver streaks line the horizon, soon turning to dull gold. The crimson light shoots across the dome of heaven, a flicker twitches on the eastern horizon, and in boastful splendor the glowing orb of the sun rises from the dark, mysterious waters."[25] For a man who previously placed such emphasis on the significance of graveyards, his words, perhaps, divulge a gratefulness for surviving the night.

Although *L 59* had escaped the storm and British naval forces over the Mediterranean, her arrival in Egypt did not signify the end of her difficulties. In fact, the subtropical climate over the North African deserts brought complications completely unforeseen by airship men accustomed to flying over temperate, north-central Europe.

Upon first entering the airspace over Egypt, with sunny skies and a temperature of 10°C (50°F) at 700 meters in altitude, the water-saturated airship begins to dry and thus becomes lighter. Taking advantage of the buoyancy, Bockholt orders *L 59* to an altitude of 1,000 meters (3,281 feet). Unfortunately, this has an unintended effect. Unlike in Europe, where higher altitudes bring cooler temperatures, the inverse appears to be true in Africa.

At 0700, with *L 59* now 100 miles inland from the Egyptian coast at coordinates of 30°N, 27°E, the temperature rises to 12°C (54°F), causing the hydrogen in the gas bags to warm, expand, and then vent—subsequently necessitating the release of about 100 kg of water ballast.[26] By 1030, although the outside air temperature remains the same, the lifting gas, continuously baking in the intense heat of the sun, climbs to 20°C (68°F), and then 22.5°C (72.5°F) at 1100, and ultimately peaks at 25°C (77°F) around 1430.[27] As *L 59* soars over the seemingly endless ocean of desert dunes, the airship becomes so hot and dry that the gas bags "crackle" when touched[28] and continue to expel their precious hydrogen through venting. To maintain altitude, water ballast must be continuously released from the airship.[29] According to Göbel and Förster,

> As soon as it gets warmer, the gas in the individual cells expands considerably as a result of the higher temperature. Next the ballonets fill to the brim and the excess gas then finds its way out through the relief valves. The ship then buzzes like an angry bee. This approving humming—which of course can only be heard when the engines are switched off—makes the airship almost like a living being that one grows fond of. Only now this phenomenon was considered less pleasant, today more than ever it was important to keep the gas losses to a minimum. But the atmosphere cannot be dictated.[30]

Besides the problem of the gas expansion, the higher altitude also brings stronger wind gusts, which, as *L 59* continues farther inland toward the Farafra oasis, increase from force 1–2 (4–7 mph), experienced near the coastline, to 4 (13–18 mph).[31] This, combined with thermal currents rising from the hot sands below, buffets *L 59*, causing the airship to repeatedly pitch and for several of the crewmen to get seasickness—specifically experiencing headaches, vomiting, and insomnia.[32]

In order to counter this effect, Bockholt orders *L 59* down to an altitude of 600 meters (1,969 feet), which could be sustained only by having helmsman Grussendorf position the elevators downward, working against "the tendency [for the airship] to climb higher"[33] and by adjusting the trim of the airship by 750 kg.[34] This too, however, changes once *L 59* reaches the Farafra oasis at 1230. Here, the air temperature sinks to 3°C (37.4°F), and ballast must once again be released to compensate for the condensing of the hydrogen in the gas cells.

Making matters worse, it is also at this point that the Zeppelin's front engine, located in the rear of the control car, becomes inoperable due to a fracture in the gearbox (transmission) housing. This was likely caused by overheating due to the increased atmospheric heat over the desert, combined with the strain of having to utilize the engines both for dynamic lift in cooler temperatures and to fight against static lift from the airship lightening in warm currents. For the time being, a temporary repair is made to the gearbox, but it is uncertain how long it will last.[35] Given that this engine also spins the generator's armature, which in turn powers the wireless transmitter, if it stops running, *L 59* will only be able to receive wireless messages, but not send any. To prevent further failures with the remaining engines and gearboxes, Bockholt must keep *L 59* "out of the dangerous air zone"[36] and shut down an engine every eight hours to allow it to cool and to be serviced.[37]

While Bockholt and his crew continued to make difficult headway toward East Africa, back in Germany the *Admiralstab* had the uncomfortable task of informing Kaiser Wilhelm II that the operation was in the process of being aborted. They opted to break the news via a telegram, which read:

> "*L 59*" started its journey to East Africa yesterday, Wednesday 21 November at 8:30 a.m. Based on the news that the *Reichs-Kolonialamt* received on the same morning about the further advance of the English troops against the rest of the *Schutztruppe* on the Makonde plateau, the office declared at noon that it could no longer take responsibility for the operation. As a result, an attempt was made to recall "*L 59*" via Nauen using a radio telegraph. —Chief of the Admiralty staff[38]

Nonetheless, with *L 59*'s antenna still reeled in, the "Africa ship" continued onward, completely oblivious to the evolving situation back home and on the ground in East Africa.

At 1515, *L 59* reaches the Dachel oasis, and Bockholt adjusts the airship's course south-southeastward toward the Nile River. At this point, the wireless cable-antenna was once again lowered from the control car, and various weather reports from north of the Suez Canal are received, along with news from home announcing German and Austrian advances in the Piave, on the Italian front.[39] However, just over an hour later, at 1620, the temporary repair on the front engine fails and puts it, and its associated wireless transmitter, out of commission.[40] From this point on, the radio operator has to rely on the fickle whims of the air flow around the gondola to naturally turn the propeller and the attached generator, hoping that just enough current could be produced in order to send a signal out.[41]

Later that evening, at 2145, *L 59* reaches the Nile, immediately south of the border of Egypt and the Sudan, and the skies become clear. Over the invariable desert during the day, Bockholt relied upon the position of the sun and his magnetic compass for navigation, but now there was a tangible guide southward toward his destination. Additionally, the bright moonlight allows Bockholt to utilize the shadows on the ground to further orient his airship.[42] Similar to nearly all favorable occurrences on the journey thus far, serious complications soon arose.

As the high temperatures of the daytime begin to cool with the oncoming evening, so do the gas bags of the "Africa ship." With the subtropical sun now set, the temperature quickly begins to drop to 5°C (41°F), and *L 59* starts to fall.

Bockholt orders, "Release 500 kg of ballast. All engines ahead full. *Feldwebelleutnant* Grussendorf, keep us at a 4-degree pitch."[43]

With difficulty, *L 59* maintains altitude and continues southward, keeping the Nile to her port side. Creating further obstacles, the previous terrain of sandy dunes over Egypt on the north of Sudan evolves to rocky crags and plateaus, with elevations approaching 600 meters (1,969 feet), and the temperature once again begins to rise. By midnight, at 18°N, 30°E, a further 1,500 kg (3,307 lbs.) of water ballast has to be dumped. Still, *L 59* is now nearly at the midpoint of her journey, and with only twenty-four hours remaining on the flight, her crewmen who are "off shift" find they are unable to sleep—excitement over reaching German East Africa and completing a record-breaking voyage has overtaken them.[44] Their high spirits were about to suffer a devastating blow.

At 0045 on November 23, approximately 125 miles west of Khartoum, the wireless receiver in *L 59*'s radio room comes to life. *Funkmaat* Kettner immediately begins recording the various dots and dashes. He then races to *Leutnant* Maas, whose duty it is to decipher the message.[45] It reads: "Abort the operation, return. The enemy has occupied most of the Makonde highlands, is already at Kitangari; the Portuguese are attacking the rest of the *Schutztruppe* from the south."[46] The radioman and watch officer are dumbfounded. Confirming that the message was no fluke, it repeats again on the wireless receiver, followed by an additional signal from the radio station in Damascus, similarly advising, "Abandon the undertaking!"[47] With a heavy heart, Maas delivers the deciphered messages to his commander, who is likewise utterly devastated.

Lowering the paper transcriptions in silence, Bockholt turns to his officers in the control and breaks the bad news. "Men, it appears the situation regarding our brave *Schutztruppen* has become hopeless. The British have overrun our landing zone and are pushing our troops out of the colony; we have to turn back."

This elicits loud protestations from the men in the gondola, urging Bockholt to ignore the message and press on. Dr. Zupitza too opines.

"*Kapitänleutnant*, I understand that as an officer you must comply with orders you've received, and, given the circumstances, our mission seems bleak, but we've already come so far! Even if we are captured by the British in East Africa, don't you see what the effect of our arrival would have on morale and the greater war effort? This feat would far exceed the exploits of the *U-Deutschland*[48] in reaching the United States!"[49]

Bockholt, putting aside the maps he picked up from the table, is visibly disheartened but remains resolute. He retorts, "Dear Professor, I understand your position and share it wholeheartedly, but what do you want me to do? As an officer I have only one task, which is to follow orders! I'm not the Prince of Homburg!"[50]

Even so, the arguing continues for more than an hour. By 0250, at coordinates of 16°30'N, 30°E, Bockholt finally has enough. "Orders are orders! Set a course north-northwest; we are returning to Yambol!" According to Göbel and Förster, Bockholt was simply "too much of a soldier to act against the order to turn back, a virtue which later became his undoing."[51] The situation in the control car would quickly develop from bad to worse.

As *L 59* changes direction to proceed on an opposite course, back toward the Dachel oasis, the Zeppelin now has to fight against the wind currents that had previously acted as tailwinds, pushing the airship toward its destination. Additionally, the heat radiating off the mountainous terrain causes dangerous updrafts, which, besides warming the gas bags to 77°F, results in severe turbulence. Indeed, just a half hour after turning back, *L 59* suddenly plummets from a height of 950 meters (3,117 feet) to 400 meters (1,312 feet) over the Gebel al-Ain plateau.[52] A noticeable jarring is felt throughout the control car, and it is believed that the gondola has actually touched down on the peak of a mountain. In reality, this was caused by the weight of the wireless antenna dragging along the rapidly approaching jagged rock formations below, and tearing away from the cable.

To regain altitude, Bockholt must act immediately. He orders, "Stop all engines and release water ballast!" The airship, however, continues to fall. Given that additional ballast cables leading to the control car had been omitted to save weight when the extended airship was designed, the crewmen have to climb into the Zeppelin's hull, run along the walkway to the ballast tanks, and manually release water[53]—it is taking too long. With the mountain crags drawing ever nearer, he then commands some of the ammunition intended for the *Schutztruppe* to be dumped. After discharging a combined 3,800 kg (8,378 lbs.)[54] of ballast and cartridges, *L 59* finally begins to regain altitude.

As the airship continues to climb, utilizing static lift, Bockholt waits until a height of 2,000 meters (6,562 feet) is reached before ordering the engines to be restarted. *L 59* will maintain this altitude for much of the remainder of the journey. Interestingly, and auspiciously, at the higher elevation, *L 59* encounters wind currents running opposite to those in the lower atmosphere. Instead of fighting against a headwind, a weak "southerly to westerly" current now assists in propelling the "Africa ship" back home.[55]

In an act of hammering the final "nail in the coffin" for the *China-Sache* operation, at noon on the twenty-third, Bockholt destroys his orders at 22°N, 29°20'E—almost precisely over the northern border of Egypt and Sudan.[56] At 1800, *L 59* once again crosses the Dachel oasis, and at 2030 it reaches Farafra oasis. With the evening temperatures once again cooling the gas bags, Bockholt has to drop more ballast in the form of the ammunition intended for the *Schutztruppe*, some of which exploded upon impact with the sands below.[57] With no intended recipients, this cargo could now be discarded often and without regret. Continuing onward at a sustained altitude of 2,000 meters (6,652 feet), *L 59*'s progress back to the Mediterranean Sea is speedy (now averaging about 90 kph / 56 mph)[58] and largely uneventful.

At 0300 on November 24, the "Africa ship" crosses the northwestern Egyptian coast at the Gulf of Sallum and reenters the Mediterranean, but the prospect of returning home only casts gloom over the crew. According to Göbel and Förster, the feeling throughout the airship was akin to "falling down before the finish line with the best racehorse."[59] Adding insult to injury, at 1000, off the eastern approach of Crete (about 60 nautical miles south of Karpathos), the watches in the forward gondola spot, through heavy cumulus cloud cover, a convoy of two steamships and two steam trawlers on a westerly course. Bockholt curses out loud.

"*Verdammt!* If only we had bombs on board, we might be able to salvage something from this cursed trip!"

After checking with *Funkmaat* Kettner to confirm that the merchant ships haven't spotted the airship and telegraphed their coordinates, he orders *L 59* to an altitude of 3,000 meters (9,843 feet) to ensure the Zeppelin stays out of sight. Three hours later, nearing Cape Gelidonya on the southern coast of Asia Minor, another steamship—this time identified as being Italian and also not spotting the Zeppelin—must also be let go due to a lack of offensive capabilities.[60]

Unfortunately, avoiding detection comes at an unintended cost. Now nearing the European continent, such a high altitude brings temperatures within the airship down to between −1°C and −3°C (30°F–26.5°F), and, given that the crew is wearing only tropical uniforms under their flight gear, they suffer from the effects of the cold.[61] Additionally, more ballast has to be released, which, given that Bockholt wanted to save the remaining 2,440 liters of water for his landing in Yambol, again consists of the cargo intended for the *Schutztruppe*.[62] The high elevation does, however, provide a benefit. The airflow around the forward gondola at this height is able to turn the propeller of the disabled engine in the control car enough to generate current, and at 1946, Kettner is able to send a signal back to Yambol advising of the mission's status and their current surface contacts. It reads:

> Thursday 5 AM African coast / Friday 2 AM desert edge west of Khartoum according to orders have turned back / Saturday 3 AM in the area of Sallum / Adalia 4 PM / [estimated time of arrival] 10:30 PM Constantinople / Sunday 7:30 AM landing [at] Yambol. Engines held out, front gearbox bearing block broken Thursday 3 PM, repaired in a makeshift manner, engine no longer used. Navigation over sea and land astronomical. Saturday 10 AM 60 nm south of Karpathos 2 steamers with convoy heading west sighted.
> —*L 59*[63]

Prior to the radio update, the imperial navy's Mediterranean Division had been desperately trying to reach *L 59* by utilizing wireless stations in Damascus and Osmaniye. Garbled telegrams received by the RMA referred to the initial arriving of the "Africa ship" over Panderma on the twenty-first, but by the twenty-third, *Kapitänleutnant* Hans Humann in Constantinople could advise only that "nothing else is known about its whereabouts; further investigations have been initiated."[64] When *L 59*'s signal reached Berlin, the Admiralty surely must have been relieved. Unfortunately, Bockholt and his men were still far from arriving home safely.

Now in the center of Asia Minor, over the mountainous region north of Uşak, Türkiye, Bockholt orders *L 59* to an altitude of 3,900 meters (12,795 feet) while nightfall cools and, yet again, shrinks the volume of hydrogen in the airship's gas bags. Much like the situation in the Gebel al-Ain plateau, *L 59* is precariously flying just 400 meters (1,312 feet) above the numerous steep peaks. Despite running all engines at full power and Grussendorf keeping the airship's upward angle at an incline of 5°–6°, the Zeppelin struggles to maintain altitude and begins to sink. Still wishing to conserve water ballast, Bockholt orders more ammunition to be thrown from the airship and this time also allows 900 kg (1,984 lbs.) of fuel to be dispensed with. After sacrificing a total of 3,000 kg of weight (6,614 lbs.), the airship regains buoyancy and continues onward, reaching Constantinople by 2220.[65]

Perhaps in a rush to get back to Yambol as soon as possible, Bockholt opts for a course divergent from his previous return leg on November 17. As Dr. Förster later recalled, when Bockholt was pressed about once again turning north over the Turkish isthmus before steering west to Bulgaria, he quipped, "I don't want to have anything more to do with the Black Sea. All engines full ahead."[66] Indeed, by heading west-northwest from Constantinople, Bockholt trims hours off his estimated time of arrival. At 0300 on November 25, Adrianople is reached, and at 0305, with Bulgaria now in sight, Bockholt, empathizing with his exhausted and downcast crew, orders a simple wireless message to be transmitted to the airship base. It reads:

> Request a warm bath for the crew immediately after landing. [Airship's] spotlights will be on from 3:00 a.m.; the ship will be in the vicinity [of the base] tonight.[67]

Yambol's response, arriving at 0400, is concise, stating only that "everything is arranged."[68] Unfortunately, the requested baths were likely cold by the time Bockholt and his men actually disembarked from their airship.

Although Yambol had been forewarned of *L 59*'s early arrival—with *L 59* actually arriving over the base at 0430—and had given the approval for landing twenty-eight minutes later, the inexperienced Bulgarian holding teams on the ground struggled with their task of securing the airship, and *L 59* wouldn't actually touch down until 0730. For the highly strung crew of the "Africa ship," the gravity of their record-breaking journey hit them quite literally. The sudden release of their pent-up, nervous tension, coupled with the effects of seasickness and bouts of insomnia experienced on the trip, caused some crew members to collapse upon setting foot on terra firma.[69] Those who remained upright were utterly dejected and hardly in the mood to speak about their monumental, albeit anticlimactic, voyage.

While German East Africa *had not* been reached, *L 59* traveled a total of 6,757 km (4,199 miles) in ninety-five hours, averaging a speed of 71 km/h (44 mph), primarily utilizing just three or four of its five engines.[70] Although it was six hours shy of *LZ 120*'s endurance trial, the distance covered by *L 59* was nearly four times that of *LZ 120*'s estimated patrol and round-trip flight.[71] True to the article read by Dr. Zupitza in the *Wilnaer Zeitung*, the third attempt at reaching German East Africa proved that the New World could easily be reached by a German Zeppelin, without even having to double the size of the existing airships. In fact, *L 59*'s flight crushed the newspaper's estimate of reaching North America in one hundred hours, since the distance flown in ninety-five hours would have been enough for the airship to travel from Berlin to Washington, DC (a distance of about 4,170 miles). Additionally, when *L 59* landed in Yambol, despite dumping 900 liters (238 gallons) of gasoline on its return leg of the journey, it was found that there was still enough fuel to fly for an additional two and a half days, allowing further penetration into the North American continent, potentially as far as San Francisco![72]

This fact must have loomed in the back of Bockholt's mind when, shortly after landing in Yambol, he was handed the transcript of another intercepted British report from East Africa, this time originating from a station in Malta. It read:

> East Africa: Left column of our force which had traversed Makonde plateau entered Simbas and Kitangari valley 7 miles northeast of Kitangari mission station, 52 German Europeans and 75 Askaris surrendered. On same day, our right column entered Newala[,] where 126 German troops and 78 Askaris were captured. In action near Mandebe 38 miles SSW of Liwale on Nov. 16, our small

> forces were opposed by enemy troops in considerably superior numbers and put up a most gallant fight[,] in fact causing greater losses than they themselves suffered and captured 5 German troops and 59 Askaris.[73]

Although it was not drastically different in content from the news the *Reichskolonialamt* shared with the *Admiralstab* on November 21, Bockholt interpreted its meaning in an entirely different manner.

Whereas the *Reichsmarineamt* deduced that the earlier telegram indicated a collapsing German foothold in the colony, Bockholt reasoned that by "reading between the lines," the intercepted telegram from the twenty-fifth actually meant that "even-stronger German detachments" stood north of the Makonde Highlands.[74] As Bockholt later confided with *Korvettenkapitän* Knorr on the twenty-sixth, had he been aware of this telegram while still in the air, he would have immediately turned around and headed back toward East Africa.[75] At the very least, he felt that the message constituted a cause for the resumption of the relief mission.

The RMA, justifiably, was not willing to rush to any conclusions. First, they requested a complete statement, including a synopsis of the journey and Bockholt's experiences with handling the extended airship, as well as technical concerns for future flights to East Africa (or other distant locations, since other parties were interested in utilizing the W-class airship), to be prepared. Next, they had to sort through the various intercepted Allied intelligence reports in order to ascertain a true picture of the *Schutztruppe*'s position within the colony. Only then, after consulting with FdL Peter Strasser, would they submit a report to the Kaiser for the future use of *L 59*. Just as it was with *L 57*'s inception, the future of *L 59* rested on technicalities, suppositions, and conflicting egos.

8

Confusion, Disinformation, and Decision-Making

A DAY AFTER RETURNING TO THE YAMBOL BASE, *Kapitänleutnant* Ludwig Bockholt began preparing the first draft of his report on the long-distance flight of *L 59.* He also sat down with *Korvettenkapitän* Knorr on the twenty-seventh for a personal interview concerning the resumption of the *China-Sache* mission. Since the former involved facts about the trip and technical matters, and the latter was a largely hypothetical conversation, Bockholt's assessment of the flight will be investigated first.

Concerning the flying characteristics of *L 59*, Bockholt reported:

> The 68,400 [volume in cubic meters] type [W class] responds well to the elevator and rudder in a balanced ship. With a light ship, the tendency to be nose-heavy is far more noticeable than with the 55,000 [m^3] type [R-class]. The dynamic stern-heaviness of a heavy ship is significantly greater than that of the 55,000 type. How much the ship can carry at each degree of banking has not yet been evaluated exactly due to a lack of test flights. On the last long-distance voyage, the approx. 2,500 kg heavy ship[,] with a 6° incline and four engines [running] with 1,260 revolutions [per minute][,] just stayed at an altitude of 3,000 meters with an enormous drop in

> speed and almost complete failure of the rudder ability. At a 7° incline, it slowly sank. In my opinion, the [W] type should not be flown at more than 3° of incline in the long term.
>
> With a very unladen ship, when descending below 1,200 meters, the center of gravity in the 15-meter gas cells was pushed backward, which had a very disruptive effect.
>
> On all long-distance voyages, the lack of enough water ballast cables makes itself felt in an unpleasant way. Jettisoning ballast from the walkway [inside the hull] takes too long and can easily become catastrophic with sudden temperature increases and a heavy ship (the Gebel al-Ain mountain incident). The additional weight of 1 kg per ballast cable is no problem.
>
> I did not allow the RMA's proposal of lightening the ship by removing buffers, gondola support struts, and anchor cables to be carried out. Without these aids it would have been impossible to land after returning from Asia Minor on November 17, with 10 m/s [22 mph] winds.[1]

Besides the aforementioned, Bockholt again reevaluated how much ballast and cargo should be taken on a future flight to Africa.

Had *L 59* actually made it to German East Africa on the third attempt, Bockholt estimated that only 7–8 metric tons of the 13.9 tons of cargo would have remained upon reaching the destination, since the difference would have been dumped as ballast.[2] Given the wild temperature swings over the desert, which caused the hydrogen to vent during the day and condense in the evening, a future flight would require more water ballast and less cargo—specifically 12,000 kg (26,455 lbs.) of the former (an increase of 3,000 kg), and 10,000 kg of the latter (22,046 lbs., a reduction of 3,900 kg).[3] Given that the weather and temperature conditions experienced over Africa dictated that *L 59* could not approach an altitude of 4,500 meters (14,764 feet), as originally predicted by the RMA and the Zeppelin factory engineers, Bockholt suggested that *L 59* should instead remain at the 700-meter altitude the airship actually flew at for most of the flight. Despite the stronger wind conditions at that elevation, the initial complement of fuel would still be more than adequate to "comfortably reach German East Africa in four days" by utilizing the original route through Asia Minor.[4] With this in mind, when Bockholt spoke with Knorr on the twenty-seventh, he was very optimistic about resuming the operation by the end of the week. Knorr, too, was also extremely enthusiastic.

After questioning Bockholt about the "good news" he heard from East Africa—the intercepted broadcast from Malta—and also interpreting the message in the same vein that Bockholt had, Knorr promised to get in touch with the *Reichskolonialamt* immediately. Additionally, he imparted that 20,000 liters of fuel had been already been ordered but may take up to eight days to arrive, during which "the military and weather conditions" may become less favorable.[5] This was actually a response to a telegram sent by Bockholt to the Admiralty on the previous day, which, going over the head of FdL Strasser, read:

> Last message from German East Africa very favorable. Based on experience, delivery of 10 tons of ammunition guaranteed. May I repeat or complete Yemen task? If so, send 20 tons of gasoline immediately. —*L 59*[6]

In the interest of resupplying sooner, Knorr inquired if Bockholt could instead utilize "Eastern stocks" from Bulgaria to accelerate the process.

Bockholt had, in fact, already spoken with Arnim in Sofia and confirmed that 10,000 liters could be delivered by the end of the week (Friday, November 30), but also that "in the most extreme emergency, I [Bockholt]can even do without a replenishment [of fuel] since only about half of the estimated petrol had been consumed [on the last flight]."[7] Additionally, a spare gearbox was also slated to arrive with the fuel delivery. According to Bockholt, if the replacement gearbox and fuel arrived on time, small engine repairs were completed (replacing four burned intake valves and one burned exhaust valve), a test flight proved successful, and his men remained healthy, the "China matter" could resume on Saturday, December 1.[8]

Should the mission get delayed, or scrapped entirely, Bockholt intimated to Knorr that *L 59* could be utilized for a mission to Yemen, as alluded to in his previous telegram, or that the "Africa ship," essentially being a cargo Zeppelin without any offensive capabilities, could be used for reconnoitering minefields in the Bosphorus and the Black Sea to allow for more shipping to reach the Ottoman forces.[9] It is unclear how Bockholt arrived at any of these possibilities, since no archival evidence exists that shows such eventualities were ever discussed before this point.

Regarding the ambiguously worded flight to Yemen, while no telegrams or reports prior to *L 59*'s return to Yambol can be found in any sources, it was obvious that Bockholt had been informed about the task earlier on. Indeed, while the paper trail is cold before November 25, it is repeatedly mentioned afterward, with telegrams between the RMA, the Mediterranean Division, Yambol, and the Germania *Ettappendienst*[10] in Constantinople becoming quite frequent. Even the Kaiser, on November 28, was informed of the possibility of flying *L 59* to Yemen or for minesweeping purposes in the region.[11] In all likelihood, *Kapitänleutnant* Hans Humann, a personal friend of Enver Pasha,[12] had been communicating behind the scenes to the various parties involved.

What he had apparently been discussing was utilizing *L 59* for shipments of gold/currency, personnel, and equipment to Yemen in the service of the Ottoman Empire. Various telegrams from November 28 between the RMA and Constantinople indicate that Enver Pasha had been requesting support, seemingly from any available airship, for the Yemen mission, since his lines of communication to the region had been essentially cut off by Bedouin forces in support of the British Empire. As a telegram to the *Admiralstab* on the twenty-eighth implies, the landing of *L 59* on the twenty-fifth was a matter of convenience, since it was located at a base in the vicinity of the Ottoman Empire, was modified for transporting cargo, and was designed for long-range operations, but other options were likely previously studied. According to *Kapitänleutnant* Arthur von Haas, an intelligence officer in the Mediterranean Division, corresponding with the *Admiralstab* in Berlin,

> The military authorities had a lengthy meeting with Enver Pasha today, during which the question of the airship was proposed to be discussed with Enver. . . . Admiralty wires whether Enver Pasha wants an airship for transporting money etc. to Yemen? I asked Enver and told him that it was probably the airship that we wanted to bring machine guns, medicines, etc. to East Africa, and that it was specifically built for this special purpose. Enver is very desirous for airship for shipments to Yemen. He primarily wants to send hard currency, some officers[,] and a radiotelegraph station there. If it is possible, should the airship come back, to repeat the route to Yemen from time to time? Enver is working on further communication, also as to whether a short stopover at Constantinople is possible in order to take over the cargo destined for Yemen. If a stopover is not possible, he will send personnel and material to Yambol. —Haas[13]

Despite the possible diplomatic benefits, and potential impact on the war on the Middle Eastern front, both Strasser and the *Admiralstab* were completely against this idea. Responding first to Bockholt's telegram from the twenty-sixth, on the twenty-eighth the Admiralty telexed Strasser advising the FdL that the navy wasn't prepared to rush into another mission with the "Africa ship," warning, "Further use of *L 59* not decided . . . malaria danger [in Yambol] immediate. Bockholt will be given immediate report when available."[14] Then, on the twenty-ninth, Strasser gave his verdict on both a return to East Africa and the Yemen mission, reporting to the *Admiralstab*:

> Referring to today's telephone conversation between *Korvettenkapitän* von Knorr and FdL. First, we advise against repeating heading to Khartoum with *L 59*. Given the current military situation in East Africa, the airship would most likely fall into enemy hands. Second, advise against doing Yemen [mission] under the assumption that the airship can return from there. It is not accurate as the route is too far. The airship will fail on landing in tropical heat and, since there is no brake ballast, will certainly be so damaged that it will be impossible to climb again. Consider the use of an airship with a crew to be too costly for the questionable Arab purpose. —Chief, FdL[15]

Notwithstanding the damning conclusion reached by Strasser, the Ottomans, using the navy's Mediterranean Division as an intermediary, began to word their cause more desperately and in the tone that the RKA had used for the *Schutztruppe*'s relief mission, even after Strasser had given his final word. As a telegram from December 2 reveals,

> Enver Pasha has been trying to safely send money to the Yemen troops for a year and a half, with very little success in all of the ways attempted thus far and at great expense. The perseverance of the Turkish troops would be increased to the greatest possible extent through the safe transfer of money. Enver Pasha therefore places the greatest worth on sending an airship on a one-way flight, taking money, two radiotelegraphy stations, a few officers[,] and, as far as it is known, machine guns, ammunition, medicines [the cargo originally intended for the *Schutztruppe*].
>
> Please consider whether an existing airship might be suitable for the undertaking or whether a new build (?)[*sic*] is possible[.] If affirmative[,] message back with requested manufacturing time, cost. A successful enterprise would make great and important political gains in Arabia. —[Mediterranean] Division Chief, through Haas[16]

Enver's concerns weren't without precedent. As early as 1908, in much less dire circumstances, Ottoman forces in Macedonia revolted and deserted largely due to an "irregular disbursement of pay."[17]

Strasser's mind, however, had already been made up by the end of November. Although the Schütte Lanz airship, *SL 21*, which had been ceded to the navy while still under construction after the army abandoned airship operations in February, was ready by November 26 and could have fulfilled the purpose outlined by Enver Pasha, Strasser still didn't trust the wooden frames of the Schütte Lanz ships for naval service and utilized *SL 21* only for static testing in its hangar in Zeesen.[18] There would be no flight to Yemen, with *L 59* or a substitute airship, and minesweeping operations in the area were also cast into doubt.

As telegrams reveal, Strasser was also against both retaining *L 59* in Bulgaria for an extended period of time or utilizing it for scouting in the Bosphorus and Black Sea. Writing to the *Admiralstab* and the Office of Naval Aviation on November 27, he raised numerous valid concerns about *L 59*'s future use in these respects. First, he felt that "only questionable results can be expected from mine searches, since such mines can be found only when the sea is very calm, the lighting conditions are particularly favorable and the tide is low."[19] Second, he felt both that Yambol was undermanned and that its Bulgarian ground crews stationed there were too inexperienced for any task other than "an exceptional trip in ideal weather conditions." Further utilization of the large airship required retention of the trained German naval personnel, who were, unfortunately, more urgently required for airship operations back in Germany and would soon be recalled. Adding to this issue, he felt that the preventive maintenance and minor repairs that would persistently have to be carried out on the airship with regular use would be able to be executed only with "great difficulty." Last, due to Bulgaria's geographic location, repairs that required shipyard assistance would become extremely lengthy due to transport and personnel difficulties, "new raw materials for gas production" were "scarcely obtainable," and resupplying them after the existing raw materials had been used up would be "very difficult" and would place "a heavy burden on the railways, [which] would have to be carried out by tank wagons from Germany."[20]

Ultimately, Strasser concluded that the best future role for *L 59* would be for it to be further converted into a seven-engine, high-speed, high-altitude reconnaissance airship for use in the North Sea.[21] Whatever option would be decided upon, crucially, there would be no flight back to East Africa to resume the relief mission.

Interestingly, the rationale behind Strasser's and the RMA's decision to first call back *L 59* during its flight and subsequently abandon the *China-Sache* operation entirely has led to considerable debate in the postwar years—largely due to rumors, propaganda, and poor scholarship over the course of many decades. Although the RMA, making use of only British wireless reports, had unwittingly made the correct decision in scrapping the "China matter," the various conjectures are worth exploring before establishing the exact situation in East Africa that Lettow and the *Schutztruppe* were facing in late November 1917.

One of the most prevalent myths is that the recall message sent to *L 59* was a British ruse designed to prevent supplies from reaching the *Schutztruppe*. Not surprisingly, this theory appears to originate in British memoirs and books and is oft repeated in lesser-researched English-language histories relating both to *L 59* and the greater war in Africa that rely heavily on secondary sources.

The earliest version of this legend appears in 1925's *Spies of the Great War*, by Edwin T. Woodhall, who already contributed other fantastic stories regarding *L 59*'s mission (see chapter 4). In his account, British forces in Africa had observed *L 59* "15 miles south of Khartoum," a location never actually reached by the airship, and then wirelessed "a bogus message . . . purporting to originate from von Lettow[-]Vorbeck" advising Berlin that "his position was desperate and that help[,] if now sent[,] would arrive too late."[22] It is a curious claim, especially considering that Woodhall makes a contradictory statement on the previous page that asserts that "at about this time [when *L 59* was approaching German East Africa] Lettow[-]Vorbeck had broken through into Portuguese East Africa."[23] If his statement about the radio signal were true, the British were actually precluding the Germans from following through on a hopeless effort, and sabotaging their own chances of potentially shooting down the Zeppelin with their aircraft based in East Africa, thus robbing themselves of a significant propaganda victory.

Perhaps reading Woodhall's book, Richard Meinertzhagen (a British intelligence officer stationed in Africa and the Middle East during World War I) made revisions to his wartime army diaries in 1926. His modified, unpublished typescript was subsequently unearthed and given credibility by Michael Occleshaw in his book *Armour Against Fate: British Military Intelligence in the First World War, and the Secret Rescue from Russia of the Grand Duchess Tatiana*, published in 1989. In this reimagined version of the diary, Meinertzhagen claims to have heard about the "China matter" mission through intercepted and deciphered German wireless signals and, after personally witnessing *L 59* near the Gulf of Sallum, sent a fake, encrypted message to the airship, recalling it with a signal advising about the capitulation of Lettow and the *Schutztruppe*—single-handedly ending the *China-Sache* operation. The author Brian Garfield, in *The Meinertzhagen Mystery: The Life and Legend of a Colossal Fraud*, successfully debunks this mendacity but also makes an error of his own by claiming that the British report intercepted from the RKA was actually a legitimate signal from Lettow that was "amplified and forwarded by neutral stations in a few towns friendly to Lettow," reaching German naval command "after some hours."[24]

Leonard Mosley's *Duel for Kilimanjaro, Africa, 1914–1918: The Dramatic Story of an Unconventional War* (1964) discredits both Woodhall and Meinertzhagen's accounts but also contributes to the spread of disinformation by supplying additional falsehoods. While admitting that Lettow couldn't have sent a wireless signal of his own, due to the *Schutztruppe*'s sole remaining, weak wireless antenna at Newala being dismantled prior to their retreat toward the Rovuma (and itself being capable only of receiving messages, not transmitting them), he echoes the sentiment that the recall message was all a British trick. In his book, while correctly noting that *L 59* was approaching Khartoum on November 23 at 0250, he claims that the British, after setting up their own wireless station in Africa and being in possession of German codes, transmitted a message directly to *L 59*, saying, "Go back. Newala has been taken. The war is over and the *Schutztruppe* has been defeated."[25]

Interestingly, German sources also participated in the same dissemination of mistruths, perhaps trying to salvage some prestige by blaming the British for the anticlimactic end of the *China-Sache* operation. Göbel and Förster, who otherwise present a *mostly* reliable account of the flight, were the first Germans to give credibility to the concept of the British being aware of the mission beforehand. They claimed that *L 59*, upon returning to the Mediterranean after heading back to Yambol, was greeted by searchlights from British warships intending to locate and shoot down the airship.[26] As mentioned in the previous chapter, Bockholt's log and postmission report indicate that these were not naval vessels, but instead innocuous merchants (without searchlights) whom he regretted not being able to attack.

Rolf Marben, in his 1931 compilation of narratives allegedly sourced from Zeppelin veterans, goes even further in recognizing the British as having advanced knowledge of the undertaking. Seemingly never having actually read the "famous, secret files" to which he refers, he states that

> to this day it has not been clarified who actually gave the order to turn back. There is no mention of this in the famous secret file "China matter," under which the African flight of *L 59* was recorded during the war. . . . There is a theory that has some probability in its favor: that the radio message giving the order to return was sent from England. Thanks to the excellent espionage organization of the English, they were probably informed about the African flight of the German airship and perhaps took a clever countermeasure with the radio message.[27]

Other German works, while not outwardly accusing the British of devising a plan to undermine the mission or asserting that they had previous knowledge of it, hinted that the Allies embellished their news reports from the African front, which inadvertently caused the Germans to abandon the mission. They seemed to believe that, like Bockholt, contrary to the RKA's intercepted reports, the *Schutztruppe* was actually still in control of the Makonde plateau and actively engaging the enemy.

Buttlar-Brandenfels, in his 1932 memoir, wrote that the reports from East Africa that reached Germany and "led the authorities to order" *L 59*'s return were "as it was afterward discovered, all false."[28] Ernst Lehmann, too, while not outright claiming that the British reports describing the situation in East Africa were fabricated, did feel that the "semiofficial" reports, particularly the one originating in Malta, "had falsified and exaggerated the situation."[29] Perhaps both read Marben's book before making their determinations, since he also wrote that "the fact is that Lettow-Vorbeck was not in any difficulties at the time the radio message was sent; on the contrary, he had just had new military successes in the Makonde highlands, and he and his brave troops remained undefeated."[30]

In reality, the British reports from both the twenty-first and the twenty-fifth reflected actual conditions on the ground in German East Africa. By November 17, after retreating to Nambindinga, Lettow made the decision to withdraw farther southward toward the Rovuma and enter Portuguese East Africa, where he expected to find, and capture, significant supply stores.[31] He also reduced the size of his forces in order to extend the provisions, ammunition, and medications they were already in possession of, willingly giving up both healthy and wounded/sick Europeans and Askari into the care of the enemy. According to Lettow,

> Our large force with little ammunition was of less value in the field than a smaller number of picked men with plenty of ammunition. It amounted to the reduction of our strength to about 2,000 rifles, including not more than 2,000 Europeans. All above this number had to be left behind. It could not be helped that among the several hundred Europeans and 600 Askari that we were compelled to leave behind in the hospital at Nambindinga, there were men who would have liked to go on fighting and were physically fit to do so.[32]

The estimates given by Lettow are not unlike the figures noted in the British report that reached Berlin on the twenty-first, which claimed that 20 German officers, 242 other German combatants, 14 German noncombatants, and 700 Askari were captured at a "large enemy camp near Nambindinga."[33]

Indeed, just as *L 59* was taking off on its journey to East Africa on the twenty-first, Lettow further trimmed down his forces, which excluded Captain Tafel's fourteen companies of *Westtruppen* that were similarly retreating, and began a march toward the Rovuma River. He and his main complement reached the bank of the river at Mpili the same day,[34] with 38 officers, 12 medical officers, a veterinary officer, 3 military officials, 214 noncommissioned officers and men, just over 1,700 Askari, around 3,900 porters, and 470 boys.[35] This was followed by an entourage consisting of six hundred women and children, and an additional seven hundred Askari boys.[36] Whereas *L 59* was making its way across the Asia Minor, the Mediterranean, and North Africa, the *Schutztruppen* were not in the Makonde plateau, but instead as far south as they could travel while remaining in German East Africa, proceeding along the northern banks of the Rovuma in search of Portuguese camps and supply depots lying across the natural border.

When *L 59* landed in Yambol on the morning of the twenty-fifth, Lettow and his army were concentrated just over 60 miles southwest of Newala, at the confluence of the Rovuma and Lugenda Rivers, near the modern-day Mtambaswala border post. They were preparing to split up, with the main group under Lettow set to cross the river to attack a Portuguese outpost in Negomano, and Göring's detachment traveling farther upriver to invade Mozambique near Nazombe. Tafel's *Westtruppen* still hadn't located the main body of the *Schutztruppe* but had themselves already crossed the Rovuma farther west.[37]

Almost precisely when *L 59* touched down in Yambol, Lettow's forces initiated a barrage with their limited artillery against the Portuguese garrison while simultaneously making a flanking movement with six field companies to attack the Portuguese from the south. Although the Portuguese had been tipped off by a British intelligence officer[38] that an attack was imminent that morning, they were still unprepared and were easily outflanked. In one fell swoop, Lettow's troops captured the fort in just two hours, inflicting devastating losses on the Portuguese while suffering only four killed and a few wounded on their side. In doing so, the *Schutztruppe* seized six heavy machine guns, six hundred rifles, 250,000 cartridges, thirty horses, uniforms, medical supplies, and European provisions.[39]

More succinctly, Lettow had secured what amounted to the entire complement of machine guns being transported by *L 59*, exponentially more rifles (which according to Lettow were enough to replace the ancient Gewehr 71/84 rifles that half of his troops were still armed with),[40] 65 percent of the ammunition, and literally tons more medical supplies and provisions. Still, while satisfying immediate needs, it wasn't enough to sustain the *Schutztruppe* for an extended campaign.

As an indication of the futility of the airship relief mission, despite its best intentions and potential moral effect, the *Schutztruppe* were forced to remain in Portuguese East Africa, and later Nyasaland (now Malawi) and eventually British Northern Rhodesia (now Zambia), searching for food stocks to feed themselves and additional forts and camps to replenish their ammunition and food stocks. They did not return to German East Africa until September 1918.

Obviously, neither the RMA nor the RKA could have foreseen this on November 21, 1917, when the decision was made to recall *L 59*. Although they had to rely solely on the various intercepted Allied reports from Africa to determine the situation facing the *Schutztruppe*, they correctly interpreted the pattern of reported Allied advances in the colony throughout the month. Contrary to what other authors have concluded over the years, it was not a British ruse that returned *L 59* to Yambol, but the RMA's and RKA's prudence in assessing the mission's chances for success. The fact that they had accurately judged the situation was further cemented when another British wireless report was intercepted on November 29—a day after a report about *China-Sache* was presented to the Kaiser. It stated,

> The course of operations since November 21 has been as follows: The German forces driven out of Simbas in the Kitangari valley are said to be near the Rovuma River with little food and ammunition.
>
> The German force under Captain Tafel, mentioned in the reports of November 20 and 23, which, as reported, moved southwards from the area of Mahenge and had been involved in a battle

> near Nandebe, thirty-eight miles southwest of Liwale by a small, detached English force engaged in combat on November 15 and 16, was quickly pushed in a south-easterly direction towards Newala. Apparently, they didn't know that this place was already in our [British] hands.
>
> On November 27, Captain Tafel surrendered with 12 officers, 6 medical officers, 92 Germans of other ranks, 1,212 Askaris and 2,200 other natives.[41]

Although further proving the soundness in scrapping *China-Sache*, this must have brought little in the way of relief to the RMA, who, in their missive to the Kaiser on the twenty-eighth (regarding the flight), lamented that

> from these reports and from the course of the voyage, it can be anticipated that the technical considerations that preceded the decision to undertake the operation turned out to be essentially correct and that the efficiency of the airship would have enabled it to reach the set goal. And it is therefore permissible to express the immediate regret that the fire accident, which 6 weeks earlier sacrificed the first airship intended for the undertaking, resulted in such a loss of time, despite the exertion of all forces, that the change in the military situation has rendered the enterprise obsolete and thus thwarted an outward success which in every respect could have rendered excellent use to other military-political interests such as our technical reputation in the world.[42]

Certainly, if *L 57* had not been destroyed back in October, the undertaking would have likely been a success—at least from the standpoint of having an airship actually reach German East Africa and enhancing Germany's "technical reputation in the world." As can be discerned from the numerous memoirs and histories written by members of the *Schutztruppe* after the war, whose experiences were completely unknown to the *Reichskolonialamt* in late 1917, *L 57*'s arrival would have been a significant morale booster but would have been of only a marginal benefit to the war on the ground, since the supplies, although welcome, would have been exhausted almost immediately. The additional twenty-three men of the airship's crew who would have been absorbed into the colonial forces would also have resulted in even more heads to feed, with completely inadequate food stocks being available.

Unfortunately, since *L 59* returned to Bulgaria, the *Reichsmarineamt* now had a purpose-built airship that no longer had a function, and were struggling to figure out what to do with it. As a result, they presented all the discussed options[43] to Kaiser Wilhelm II, including those they had already privately decided against. Yet again, heads would butt over *L 59*'s next role.

In the days immediately after *L 59*'s return to Yambol until November 29, the airship remained in its hangar as its engines were being overhauled.[44] Apparently still awaiting a decision from the *Admiralstab* on what to do with the "Africa ship," at 0800 on December 1, Bockholt and his crew took off on an all-day flight from Yambol toward the Black Sea. His war diary notes two purposes for the patrol—blowing out gas (essentially climbing to the pressure height and venting out the old hydrogen from the flight to Africa) and searching for mines. After reaching Varna at 1037, *L 59* spent nearly five hours over the Black Sea, with Bockholt's only notation in his war diary from that period reading, "Searched for mines, blockade identified."[45] At 1535 he headed for home and landed back at Yambol at 1705.

Instead of waiting for additional orders to arrive from Germany, on December 4, Bockholt prepared a report for the *Admiralstab* wherein, apparently at the behest of the navy's Mediterranean Division,[46] he proposed returning to Germany, converting *L 59* to a bomber, and then returning to Bulgaria indefinitely, retaining the airship in Yambol for attacks on Italy, the Middle East, and North Africa. His argument was reminiscent of Strasser's justification for bombing raids on Britain (i.e., diversionary attacks that would draw resources away from the Western Front). According to Bockholt,

> This proposal offers many advantages, both in terms of the location of the Yambol airship base and the effect of airship attacks on remote places that have not previously been subject to aerial bombardment.
>
> From a purely aeronautical point of view, the Yambol base is very conveniently located in the wide, wind-protected valley between the Balkans and the Rhodope Mountains. During *L 59*'s stay in November, there were good opportunities to enter and exit the base on almost every day. The wind strengths relevant here are significantly lower than in the North Sea bases, even at high altitudes.
>
> The strategic location of Yambol as a source of attacks against more remote targets is also very favorable. Most of the approach could be made during the day, hidden from the enemy, over friendly territory or the very little-traveled Mediterranean.[47]

Appealing to Strasser, Bockholt—in noting the deficiencies of remaining in Yambol (namely, malaria and the warm weather and daily temperature fluctuations having an "extremely unfavorable effect" on the airship's gas cells)—suggested that in the period between July and September, when weather conditions were the worst, "the ship could be transferred for reconnaissance purposes and an overhaul in a North Sea base, with a simultaneous reduction in the number of troops [stationed at Yambol] during this extremely unfavorable time for malaria."[48] Additionally, "the hangar's irrigation system, which was started when the site was occupied by an army ship, could also be completed."

Concerning viable bombing targets, Bockholt proposed attacking Valona (now Vlorë, Albania, which had been occupied by the Italians since 1914), Brindisi, Malta, and Naples west of Yambol; Tripoli to the southwest; Alexandria, Cairo, Port Said, the Suez Canal, and Aswan to the south; and the "English ammunition depots near Baghdad" to the east.[49] Bockholt felt that "attacks on these places will be significantly less dangerous than attacks on well-defended London and the English coast" and would have the following immediate effects:

> (1) A major military effect through the immediate construction of air defense systems and thus indirect relief of our own front
>
> (2) A disruption of enemy trade (e.g., by attacking port facilities near Port Said and Alexandria)
>
> (3) A major political impact. The appearance of a bomb-dropping airship over Cairo or Aswan would be seen by the inhabitants of North Africa as proof of Germany's greatness and power.
>
> (4) A great moral success for the airship force, given that attacks from Europe could be carried out on foreign continents that are currently inaccessible to aircraft[50]

While these points certainly echoed objectives already established by Strasser for utilizing airships for offensive purposes against Britain, Bockholt argued against Strasser's plans for having *L 59* converted to a seven-engine airship. Although he admitted that if *L 59* was going to be used for attacking England, the conversion to a seven-engine airship would have to take place, because *L 59*, in its current configuration, "hardly had the speed" to be successful, it would, by simply reinstalling the bomb bays and related equipment, otherwise be suitable for the long-range Mediterranean missions with the five-engine layout.

Finally, Bockholt "twisted the knife" in his superior by suggesting not only that experienced German ground crews be retained in Bulgaria, but that considerable investment should be made in the existing silicon plant in the area, which would be responsible for supplying the hydrogen to the base at a rate of 800 cubic meters per hour. He further suggested that two mobile plants, outputting 400 cbm/hour, also be procured by the RMA for a reserve hydrogen supply. The reaction from Strasser was just as one would have expected.

Responding on December 20 (he received a modified report from Bockholt on December 16; see chapter 9), Strasser did not spare any criticism about the proposal or about Bockholt. In fact, he attacked each point systematically.

Beginning with the strategic basis behind Bockholt's report, Strasser gave credit to its "compelling features" but felt that Bockholt was under a false impression that continuous long-distance missions could be feasible just because *L 59* successfully returned from Khartoum. For one, he felt that the risks involved in executing the *China-Sache* operation were taken only in light of the much "greater purpose" of resupplying the *Schutztruppe*. Due to the engine failure, which Strasser pointed out is common on long-distance voyages, he felt that "the fact that the ship returned must be considered an extraordinary stroke of luck, which [was] primarily due to the fact that the airship encountered southerly winds at 2,000 m and above on the return journey."[51] For Strasser, *L 59*'s record-breaking flight was an exception, not the rule. Putting it rather bluntly, Strasser maintained

> from experience that the planned attack flights of 50 to 70 hours in duration can be carried out only in exceptional cases; that is to say, almost never. In theory, the matter can be easily achieved; in practice, my feeling tells me that it will not work, and if it does succeed, it will be an exception. Let me remind you of [St.]Petersburg. We wanted to attack this target for two years, and it never became practicable, and there we were talking about distances of only 1,300 km and a return leg. It is an outmoded sentiment that, on the basis of individual successful long-distance flights, the greatest hopes are always placed on regular, gigantic airship operations. The hopes have always been and always will be deceptive. The airship is and remains an exceptional weapon, which can achieve extraordinary things when the right opportunities are taken advantage of[,] but as soon as such achievements are taken as a basis for the general

> and regular use [of airships], one experiences the greatest disappointments, which then tend to damage the [reputation of the] weapon even where its uses are really advantageous.[52]

Next, he reiterated all the downfalls of retaining Yambol as an airship base that he made in his earlier telegram.

Seizing on Bockholt's comment about the weather conditions, Strasser noted that due to the rising ground temperatures in the spring and summer, on landings "damage to the large airship will occur much more frequently than with the airships on the North Sea front."[53] As such, repairing the airship and supplying it with new equipment would be time consuming and put further strain on the already overwhelmed railways. Additionally, while the fickle weather would allow for missions to take place only infrequently and in ideal conditions, four hundred experienced naval personnel would be required to serve at the base at all times, along with numerous replacement crews due to the persistent outbreaks of malaria—men whom Strasser was not willing to give up to serve on what he considered to be a minor theater of operations. Becoming more vitriolic, Strasser then criticized the significance of the Mediterranean theater as a whole, noting that

> if, by some exception, such an attack does take place [against targets in Italy, North Africa, or the Middle East], I do not expect any particular success from it. England will at least be pleased that this airship is being kept away from [attacking] her.
>
> Airship missions have never and will never be worthwhile anywhere else in the world, except in the North Sea theater of war for the purposes of reconnaissance for the [High Seas] fleet and for attacks against England.[54]

Finally, Strasser reserved his last words for the censuring of Bockholt himself.

After somewhat softening the impending blow by claiming Bockholt was "a capable airship commander and a daring officer," he then dropped the hammer by stating that his proposals were "doomed to failure, even if large amounts of money [were] spent and considerable effort [was] exerted."[55] The rationale for his judgment was, for the most part, sound, even if it was written with a tinge of umbrage.

What Bockholt was essentially requesting in remaining in Yambol was to be his own FdL, carrying out missions independently in his own personal theater of war. However, as Strasser was eager to point out, Bockholt didn't have "enough experience with the possible uses of airships." Up to the point of the "China matter" operation, Bockholt and his crew had flown only reconnaissance flights over the North Sea, a task Strasser openly admitted Bockholt performed well. Nevertheless, for each of those thirty-odd missions, Strasser assigned the objectives for him and the courses flown, and even had the final say in deciding whether or not flights would go forward with regard to the weather. If Bockholt and *L 59* were to remain in Bulgaria, all these were tasks that Bockholt would have to perform autonomously, since Strasser, remaining in Ahlhorn, was far too removed from the Mediterranean theater to effectively pass judgment. Then, saving what he felt was his best argument for last, Strasser made one final reproach against Bockholt—he hadn't carried out any attacks whatsoever against ground targets during any of his previous combat missions.[56] This crucial point, however, actually negated Strasser's previous arguments and, when scrutinized, went a long way in justifying Bockholt's desire to operate in the Mediterranean.

While there can be no arguing against veracity of the claim that Bockholt hadn't participated in any bombing raids in the war thus far, Strasser's final statement actually made a case for *L 59* remaining in Yambol. Prior to being assigned to *L 57*, Bockholt was given command of *L 54,* a U-class Zeppelin that would almost certainly have destined Bockholt for the skies over England. In fact, following Bockholt's transfer of the airship's command to Buttlar in September 1917, it flew on a mission with exactly that purpose—a catastrophic bombing raid on October 19, 1917, that would become the last major raid over Britain for the remainder of the war.[57]

During this mission, *L 54*, *L 42*, *L 51*, *L 53*, *L 45*, *L 41*, *L 46*, *L 47*, *L 50*, *L 55*, *L 49*, and *L 52* departed their bases in Nordholz, Tondern, Ahlhorn, and Wittmundhaven to bomb targets in central England; namely, the "industrial region of Sheffield, Manchester, Liverpool, etc."[58] Although Strasser predicted good weather conditions from his headquarters in Ahlhorn, an unforeseen depression making its way over Great Britain brought gale-force winds and thunderstorms that disrupted the raid and scattered the twelve Zeppelins taking part in it. Buttlar, commanding the new *L 54,* correctly assessed the changing weather conditions and gave up on attacking his original targets and opted for Nottingham and Derby, farther southeast—in actuality dropping all his bombs in an open field over 100 miles closer to the coast. He was subsequently chased away by an intercepting B.E.2c that ultimately couldn't catch up to the fleeing airship. Others weren't so lucky.

L 23, as viewed from the surface, taking part in a mine-searching mission. Given that the upper machine gun platform is clearly visible, it is likely that Bockholt was at the helm during the flight. *Author's collection*

An artist's rendition of *L 23* capturing the *Royal* as it appeared in a Norwegian newspaper on June 5, 1917. While the barque is shown in detail, expressing the artist's familiarity with sailing ships, the Zeppelin is drawn crudely and out of proportion. *Morgenbladet* (Oslo)

L 23 pictured in her usual role of assisting minesweepers. *Author's collection*

A propaganda photo of the *Royal*'s prize crew. Wiesemann is pictured to the left, Engelke to the right, and Fegert in the center, seated. *Courtesy of the Tobias Weber Collection—www.buddecke.de*

Führer der Luftschiffe, Korvettenkapitän Peter Strasser. *Author's collection*

A sketch of Paul von Lettow-Vorbeck. *Author's collection*

Naval airship *L 3* being led back into its hangar. Note the driveshaft connecting the laterally mounted propeller to the engine within the forward gondola. *Author's collection*

Artist's rendition of *LZ 17* bombing Antwerp in August 1914. *Author's collection*

Official British press photo alleging to show an airship lit up by searchlights and surrounded by circling, intercepting aircraft. Unfortunately, the aircraft appear to have been added to the photo and are so disproportionate to the airship that if they were actually present, they would be far too low to possibly reach the airship's altitude. *Author's collection*

Dr. Ludwig Dürr. *Author's collection*

Dar es Salaam as it appeared to the painter Willy Stöwer before the outbreak of war. This image was sold during the war to raise funds for the colonial troops. The stripes on the steamer's stack indicate it was probably the *Kronprinz* of the Deutsch Ost-Afrika Linie (German East Africa Line). *Author's collection*

Lettow-Vorbeck as depicted in a postcard sold to benefit the *Schutztruppe*. His Askaris are clearly visible marching in the background. *Author's collection*

The SMS *Königsberg. Author's collection*

The *Feldmarschall* of the Deutsch Ost-Afrika Linie. During the British blockade of German East Africa, on August 17, 1915, the *Feldmarschall* was fired upon and damaged by the HMS *Hyacinth*. The British subsequently repaired her and put her into service as the *Field Marshall. Author's collection*

Max Zupitza. *From Langsdorff,* Deutsche Flagge über Sand und Palmen, *copy in author's collection*

Carl Christiansen. *From Langsdorff,* Deutsche Flagge über Sand und Palmen, *copy in author's collection*

A patriotic postcard featuring a painting by Willy Stöwer titled *Durch Kampf zum Sieg* ("through struggle to victory"). It depicts the army, navy, and *Schutztruppe* embracing over a portrait of the Kaiser. Another example of a card sold to benefit the *Kolonialkriegerdank* (colonial war effort), this one was mailed in 1918. The late sale of the card and mailing indicates that those at home didn't forget that the *Schutztruppe* was still fighting in East Africa, even late in the war. *Author's collection.*

L 59 under construction in Staaken. The design of the frame rings and supports is clearly visible. *From Göbel,* Afrika zu unsern Füßen, *copy in author's collection*

Another photo of *L 59*'s frame, this time viewed from within the zeppelin. *From Göbel,* Afrika zu unsern Füßen, *copy in author's collection*

The R-class "super-Zeppelin," *L 30*, commanded by Buttlar-Brandenfels. *Author's collection*

An R-class Zeppelin (likely *L 30*, *L 31*, or *L 32*) flying above the High Seas Fleet as Richard Stumpf would have observed it from his battleship. *Author's collection*

Kapitänleutnant Ludwig Bockholt.
Author's collection

L 57 over Friedrichshafen. *Author's collection*

Hugo Eckener. *Author's collection*

Hauptmann Karl Ernst Göring. *From Langsdorff,* Deutsche Flagge über Sand und Palmen, *copy in author's collection*

Artist's rendition of a wounded German officer being led away from the field of battle by two Askari. *Author's collection*

Askari machine gun crew and German officer. *From Langsdorff,* Deutsche Flagge über Sand und Palmen, *copy in author's collection*

L 59 being led out of the airship hangar in Yambol. A painted imperial war ensign is visible near the Zeppelin's stern. *From Göbel,* Afrika zu unsern Füßen, *copy in author's collection*

The control car of *L 59* being supported by the Bulgarian ground crew in Yambol. *From Göbel,* Afrika zu unsern Füßen, *copy in author's collection*

L 59 ascends off the landing field in Yambol. *From Göbel,* Afrika zu unsern Füßen, *copy in author's collection*

A fantastic photo clearly depicting the portside imperial German and Turkish flags painted below *L 59*'s nose in order to identify the German Zeppelin as being friendly. *From Göbel,* Afrika zu unsern Füßen, *copy in author's collection*

The crew of *L 59* in their flight gear, prior to taking off toward East Africa. Bockholt is pictured standing in his leather jacket and officer's cap (*center*); to his right is *Obermaschinistenmaat* Engelke, followed by *Leutnant* Maas. To his left, in the visibly distinct army uniform, is *Feldwebelleutnant* Grussendorf. *Courtesy of the Tobias Weber Collection—www.buddecke.de*

The tropical *Schutztruppe* uniforms as worn by the crew of *L 59* under their flight gear. These were required, since the men were expected to be absorbed into the colonial army after landing. *Courtesy of the Tobias Weber Collection—www.buddecke.de*

The holding teams and ground crew as seen from *L 59*'s control car. *From Göbel,* Afrika zu unsern Füßen, *copy in author's collection*

L 59's forward gondola as viewed from the ground. *From Göbel,* Afrika zu unsern Füßen, *copy in author's collection*

L 59 on the field as viewed from the inside of the cavernous airship hangar in Yambol. *From Göbel,* Afrika zu unsern Füßen, *copy in author's collection*

Artist's depiction of an Askari artillery team in German East Africa. *Author's collection*

Part of the *Schutztruppe*'s supply train and retinue, following closely behind the Askari. *From Langsdorff,* Deutsche Flagge über Sand und Palmen, *copy in author's collection*

Kapitänleutnant Franz Stabbert. *Author's collection*

MG 08 machine gun equipped to a Zeppelin. In this case, it's mounted in the forward gondola of *L 49* and pictured on the ground during a benefit for wounded soldiers in Paris. *Author's collection*

A stamp printed by the Red Cross to raise funds for the victims of *L 59*'s bombardment of Naples. Unlike actual events, it depicts a daytime or afternoon raid, with Mt. Vesuvius billowing smoke in the background. The text roughly translates to "in memory of the barbaric outrage of the night of March 10–11, 1918, against the city of Naples." *Author's collection*

SM *UB-53* moored in Beirut during the spring of 1918. *Courtesy of Simon Schnetzke*

Bockholt, in *L 59*'s control car, with Maas and Grussendorf to his left and right, respectively. The crew is once again wearing their naval uniforms instead of the tropical, colonial attire. *Courtesy of the Tobias Weber Collection—www.buddecke.de*

A close-up photo of *L 53*'s streamlined rear gondola, clearly showing the various exhaust pipes and mufflers to which Bockholt was referring. *Author's collection*

View of *L 47* (*left*) and *L 46* (*right*) in the "Alrun" hangar in Ahlhorn during the busy, raiding times under Strasser. The hoses to fill the gas bags with hydrogen are clearly observed on the floor of the shed, as are the Iron Cross markings atop the Zeppelins. Both airships were lost in an explosion at Ahlhorn on January 5, 1918. *Author's collection*

The memorial at the Yambol airship base for the fallen crew of *L 59*. *From Göbel*, Afrika zu unsern Füßen, *copy in author's collection*

Kapitänleutnant Franz Stabbert was killed when *L 44* was shot down by French antiaircraft fire over Lunéville while trying to make his way back to Germany. Likewise, *Kapitänleutnant* Hans-Karl Gayer and *Kapitänleutnant* Roderich Schwonder (commanding *L 49* and *L 50,* respectively), who were relying on Stabbert to guide them back home, were forced to crash-land in France following *L 44*'s destruction. Even *Kapitänleutnant* Waldemar Kölle in *L 45*, whose later experiences in captivity are described in chapter 4, was forced to crash-land in Sisteron, France, after suffering from multiple engine failures and drifting helplessly to the south. In his analysis of the failed "silent raid"[59] in which one-third of the Zeppelins taking part were lost, Douglas Robinson noted that had Strasser been on board an airship participating in the raid, as he often was, he would have become aware of the evolving weather conditions and aborted the mission. Since he was at headquarters in Ahlhorn, the commanders in the air had to rely on their own initiatives. Robinson concluded that while "certain experienced commanders such as von Buttlar . . . could diagnose the unusual conditions and take appropriate measures," others, "such as Gayer and Schwonder, could only have been saved by direct orders" from Strasser.[60]

It is uncertain if Bockholt would have fallen in the latter category had he remained in command of *L 54* and taken part in the raid. Regardless, if Bockholt was to become a successful Zeppelin bomber commander, the weaker anti-airship defenses and better weather conditions over the Mediterranean could ease him into the job instead of immediately throwing him at London and suffering the fate of those who took part in the October raid. The *Admiralstab*, seemingly growing tired of Strasser's emphasis on costly raids over England, appeared hesitant to immediately acquiesce to Strasser's conversion plans for *L 59* and saw value in Bockholt and the Mediterranean Division's proposals. Nonetheless, while the *Admiralstab* agreed with both men that a conversion of *L 59* had to take place in any event, Holtzendorff continued to leave all options open. As his report to the Kaiser concluded,

> Should a use in the Balkans be abandoned after all circumstances have been evaluated, the intention is to call the ship back to Germany and to convert it into a particularly fast reconnaissance vehicle after installing 2 new engines (the 6th and 7th).[61]

Thus, when *L 59* was ordered back to Germany for the conversion to a bomber and refitting at the beginning of December 1917, the airship's fate remained largely undecided.

While some historians have suggested that Bockholt's alleged connections with higher-ups in the Admiralty had guaranteed the endorsements of his interests up to this point, a theory that Wolfgang Meighörner-Schardt claimed could not "be definitively determined from the available sources,"[62] one piece of archival evidence suggests that Bockholt may not have been the darling of the Admiralty he was purported to have been. When it came time to award decorations for the *China-Sache* operation, Bockholt was denied the "appropriate decoration" of the Knight's Cross with Swords of the House of Hohenzollern[63] "because the operation did not reach the intended military conclusion and this was partly caused by the loss of '*L 57*. . . ,' which could have been avoided had the prevailing weather conditions been assessed more carefully."[64] He had to settle with a letter of recognition from the Kaiser, forwarded by the chief of the Naval Cabinet, Georg Alexander von Müller, on December 29.[65] Meanwhile, Bockholt's recommendations for the Iron Cross 2nd class to be awarded to ten members of his crew[66] were bestowed on his men wholesale.[67]

Indeed, much discussion, both technical and political, was to take place in the coming month concerning *L 59*'s future role both before and during its conversion process. Like the resumption of *China-Sache* after *L 57*'s loss, the ultimate decision regarding the giant airship appeared to rest outside the dominion of the FdL.

9

Relighting Vulcan's Forge

AFTER POOR WEATHER CONDITIONS PREVENTED *L 59* from returning to Germany from December 2 through 10, the giant airship finally made its flight toward Ahlhorn on the morning of December 11. "Hall" II at the Zeppelin factory in Friedrichshafen would be its ultimate destination; however, due to another airship, *L 61*, still being under construction in the hangar, *L 59* was required to make the stopover to await her berth.[1] Although not mentioned in the airship's war diary, a memo on the dissolution of the "China matter" from December 12 indicates that her cargo now consisted only of a telescope, reading and sewing equipment, maps, and radio-telegraphic material that were to be returned to the *Reichskolonialamt*. All the weapons, ammunition, and medicines intended for the *Schutztruppe* would remain in Yambol to be transferred onward to the Mediterranean Division.[2] The voyage confirmed much of Strasser's trepidations about continuous, long-distance flights.

Shortly after *L 59*'s ascent at 0843, the portside elevator became unresponsive (possibly due to icing up) and was freed only hours later, when the airship reached Philippopolis (now Plovdiv, Bulgaria), approximately 100 miles west.[3] Then, in the evening hours as *L 59* crossed Belgrade en route to Vienna, dense cloud cover arrived, and Bockholt, no longer being able to observe any landmarks on the ground, had to rely on radio triangulation to plot his position. Although the Zeppelin made continuous progress on a north-northwest course, conditions were about to get much worse.

After crossing Vienna at 2230, *L 59*—now flying at an altitude of 300 meters (984 feet) in heavy cloud cover—encountered "occasional snow storms," which coated the shell of the Zeppelin and soon turned into a thin layer of ice. Besides adding additional weight to the airship, the ice nearly proved to be fatal when fragments of it broke off and came into contact with *L 59*'s propellers—subsequently redirecting the icy shards into the airship's hull. Although no crewmen were injured by the high-speed projectiles, they succeeded in penetrating "cell 11," the gas bag located immediately above the lateral engine nacelles in the forward third of the airship. The resultant leak emptied the cell of its hydrogen by midnight and jeopardized the structural integrity of the airship, given the gas bag's central location.[4] Now in serious danger and still blinded by the heavy cloud cover, Bockholt had his radioman make attempts at establishing "radiotelegraphy contact with the fleet" every half hour in order to keep his course toward Ahlhorn.[5] Mercifully, shortly after *L 59* reached Torgau around 0420 (just under 50 miles northwest of Dresden), wireless bearings were received from Ahlhorn and orientation was reestablished. Still, *L 59* was not yet "out of the woods."

Due to the prevailing foggy conditions over Germany, when Bockholt passed over Bad Belzig at 0615, still over 300 km (190 miles) from Ahlhorn, he decided to go no farther. Feeling that "a longer journey would have compromised the damaged ship,"[6] he ordered *L 59* on a southeast course to make an emergency landing at the airship base in Niedergörsdorf (Jüterbog), only 32 km (20 miles) away. *L 59* would remain there until the twentieth, when, following the repairs to the gas cell between the thirteenth and the seventeenth, she was finally flown directly to Friedrichshafen—landing there at 1647 after completing an uneventful flight of eight hours and thirty-five minutes.[7]

While still in Niedergörsdorf, Bockholt made another appeal to FdL Strasser and the *Admiralstab* for the continued use of *L 59* at the Yambol base. He wanted a quick decision to be made before the personnel there were recalled and the process of dismantling the former army airship base could take place. Although much of his report was a reiteration of his previous statement from December 4, he now gave detailed timetables and routes for arriving at, and returning from, the various targets. He also added two bullets justifying the airship's proposed new role. Concerning the former,

For the targets west of Yambol:

Valona (would be reached in 24 hours), Brindisi (28), and Naples (54). Approach would be made during the night over the Adriatic Sea, and the return would be made during the day by flying south of Greece and over Asia Minor.

To the southwest:

Messina and other ports in Sicily (52–56). Approach and return would be made during the day flying south of Greece.

Malta (56), same course.

Tripoli (72) same course.

To the south:

Alexandria and Port Said (48). Approach and return would be made over Asia Minor.

Suez (60–66). Approach would be made by flying over the North African coast west of Alexandria and making a surprise attack from the desert. The return leg would proceed over the Sinai Peninsula and Damascus.

Aswan (68–72), same course as the Suez.[8]

As far as the additional benefits for remaining in Bulgaria, Bockholt "promised" he could inflict "serious damage to enemy trade by destroying port facilities at Naples, Port Said, Alexandria, [and] Suez" and provide "valuable support of the U-boat war by determining enemy steamer routes in the Mediterranean."[9]

While Strasser remained unmoved, for the reasons outlined in the previous chapter, the Admiralty's interests were piqued. Thus, when *L 59* landed in Friedrichshafen on December 20, it was not immediately apparent how the conversion was going to proceed. Delays in acquiring Strasser's envisioned engines, however, may have helped tip the scales in Bockholt's favor.

Although the RMA initially entertained Strasser's high-speed reconnaissance airship concept as a possibility, the required seven Maybach Mb.IVa high-compression, high-altitude engines[10] were not yet available. Despite having been installed on the recently completed *L 61* Zeppelin, future deliveries were being prioritized for the army's *Riesenflugzeug* strategic bomber aircraft. Therefore, on December 26, the RMA advised the following:

> Conversion to a 7-engine ship is to be considered, but only when H.L.[*Hochluft* or "high-air/altitude" Mb.IVa] engines are available. Until then, FdL will use the ship at its own discretion, or lay it up until then.[11]

However, just a day later they did a complete about-face, now declaring,

> Everything has been revised. Ship is going back to Yambol as a 5-engine [airship]. Nothing further needs to be done here.[12]

Certainly, the delay in engine availability played a role in this decision, but given that *L 59* still required other structural changes prior to going back into service, it seems curious that the navy wasn't willing to wait for them, particularly when there was no longer a time-sensitive mission anticipated for the airship, such as *China-Sache*. Indeed, other interservice communications behind the scenes, combined with Bockholt's proposal and the demands of the Mediterranean Division, may have effectively forced the RMA's hand and led to the abrupt change in direction.

As Bockholt mentioned in his report from the sixteenth, the army was eager to withdraw their personnel from Bulgaria and station them at more-critical fronts. This was, no doubt, largely due to the armistice on the Eastern Front being signed on December 15, 1917, wherein Russia essentially ceased combat operations against the Germans, Austro-Hungarians, and Ottomans on an indefinite basis.[13] On December 24 the general department of the *Kriegsministerium* (the "War Ministry") advised the RMA that at the beginning of the new year, the army airship troops "currently stationed in Yambol, consisting of 6 noncommissioned officers and 50 men," would be recalled, and noted that "if it is important to keep the Yambol airship base with its hydrogen gas plant ready for any purposes there, then the facility would have to be taken over by the naval administration."[14]

While the navy made an attempt at delaying the inevitable by stating that negotiations were still ongoing with the OHL (*Obersten Heeresleitung*, or "Supreme Army Command"), General Ludendorff, the army's chief of staff, pressed the issue, writing on December 29 that it would be impossible to retain army airship crews in Yambol since they were required for the formation of new balloon units elsewhere. All army airship staff would have to be replaced by naval personnel if Yambol was to remain in operation.[15]

This was a quandary for the RMA, since, although the army was essentially without an enemy in the east at this point in the war and was primarily focused on the Western Front and, to a lesser degree, the southern front, the *Kaiserliche Marine* still had to deal with Britain's Royal Navy, Italy's *Regia Marina*, France's *Marine Nationale*, and even the 2nd Special Squadron of the Imperial Japanese Navy in the Mediterranean Sea. As Bockholt pointed out, an airship would be an essential tool in supporting the Mediterranean Division and the German and Austro-Hungarian U-boat bases in Pola (now in Croatia)[16] and Cattaro (now Kotor, Montenegro), respectively, besides diverting resources from the main theater of war—the point that Strasser had so successfully argued for continued raids against England.

Certainly, while the *Kaiserliche Marine*'s surface vessels and submarines were afforded airship support for escort, reconnaissance, mine-searching, and bombing operations in the North Sea, the Baltic, the English Channel, Flanders, and the German coastline, no Zeppelins existed for this purpose in the Mediterranean, Adriatic, and Aegean Seas or the Dardanelles Strait. *L 59* would essentially be putting the southern naval assets on an equal footing as their colleagues in the north by remaining in Yambol, but only if the navy acted quickly in preventing the dismantling of the base and transferring of its resources.

On the basis of archival evidence,[17] it appears that it was the navy's, or more specifically the Mediterranean Division's—which had been operating with a high degree of autonomy since 1914 due to its distance from Berlin—desire for airship support in what Strasser considered an inconsequential theater of war that trumped the FdL's wishes, not because of any particular favoritism afforded to Bockholt. This is further reinforced by a top-secret memo from January 29, 1918, in which the state secretary of the RMA, submitting a report on naval troop strength required to man the Yambol base,[18] critically advised that only for "training and personnel matters are the troops subordinate to the FdL; otherwise [they are subordinate] to the Mediterranean Division, and in administrative matters [namely, food supplies and equipment] to the commissariat in Wilhelmshaven."[19] Another telegram from April 8 further committed *L 59* to the Mediterranean Division by placing the "crew of the airship . . . and the naval airship troops stationed in Yambol under the [legal] jurisdiction of the judicial lord and commander of [the] SMS *Goeben*."[20] Strasser was essentially being muscled out of making any future tactical decisions in the Mediterranean theater and was instead confined to his *Marine Luftschiff Abteilung* fiefdom in northern Germany, a sentence, given his statements regarding the triviality of the former, he was likely more than content with.

With the future of *L 59* having been decided on by December 27, the only changes that would have to be made to the airship were (1) the addition of two bomb bays, installation of the associated weapons systems for dropping ordnance (i.e., the bomb racks and electric bomb releases in the control car), and machine gun platforms; (2) the relocation of the rear gondola 15 meters forward from ring 55 to ring 70, and the two lateral engine nacelles 15 meters aft from ring 145 to ring 130; and (3) another overhaul of the five Maybach HS-Lu engines.[21] After the modifications were completed, *L 59* gained an additional 1,000 cubic meters of gas volume, increasing from 67,500 m^3 to 68,500. Given that the initial, much more labor-intensive, lengthening of *L 59* by two frame rings was accomplished in a matter of two weeks, the second conversion of *L 59* should have been completed by mid-January—it wasn't. Instead, the process dragged out for nearly a month and a half.

Much of this had to do with the fact that the engine work was carried out by the Maybach factory instead of the Zeppelin works, which necessitated the removal of the engines from the airship and their transport within Friedrichshafen to the Zeppelin subsidiary. Additionally, previous field maintenance on the engines appeared to have been completed in a haphazard manner, which, as the Maybach technicians soon uncovered, resulted in more refurbishment work than expected. A particularly heinous example of a lack of care concerning frontline upkeep was discovered in engine #931[22] in the form of a piece of *Putzwolle* (literally "cleaning wool," or the steel wool still used today) being stuck on the engine's camshaft.[23]

Adding insult to injury, when all the necessary tasks to convert and service *L 59* had been completed, there was trouble procuring the necessary hydrogen to fill the gas bags, which pushed the factory acceptance flights back into the first week of February. This delay, however, was perhaps welcome, given that Strasser and the RMA spent nearly the entire month of January and much of February rushing personnel and provisions to Yambol while simultaneously bickering with the Bulgarian authorities regarding accessible food stocks.[24]

Upon the required lifting gas becoming available on February 4 and 5, the first factory test flight, once again piloted by Captain Lau with Bockholt and his crew also present, took place on the sixth. Unfortunately, this was aborted after an hour due to poor visibility—an altitude of a mere 250 meters (820 feet) was reached in that time frame. A second flight the following day was more successful despite being two hours shorter in duration than *L 59*'s similarly swift trial on October 30. On this occasion, *L 59* realized a respectable maximum speed of 28.16 m/sec. (63 mph) and a cruising speed of 24.05 m/sec. (54 mph).[25] Additionally, the relocation of the lateral engine gondolas 15 meters aft seemed to solve the problem of the airship being tail heavy, while at the same time making the airship much more manageable with a light payload than it had been in its previous configuration—both being issues that Bockholt reported on his return from the African voyage. Still, *L 59* was able to reach a height of only 2,900 meters (9,514 feet) during the four-hour duration of the test, which was far lower than what both *L 57* and *L 59* achieved during their previous trials.

An altitude of 6,900 meters (22,638 feet)[26] was eventually reached on February 9, which allowed for Bockholt and his crew to experience firsthand the extreme cold and lack of oxygen their colleagues had been suffering through during their latest raids on England. Although Bockholt's proposal to serve in the Mediterranean theater alluded to a lack of anti-Zeppelin countermeasures, the war had proven that the best method of surviving missions, regardless of enemy airship defenses, was flying bombing runs well above the range of intercepting aircraft and artillery. It was better to understand one's behavior in those conditions during trials than over a battle zone. With this final test deemed satisfactory, and the other conversions for combat use having already been completed, the transfer of *L 59* back to Yambol was scheduled for February 12. Poor weather conditions, Yambol not yet being fit for occupancy,[27] and another "in-flight" accident involving *L 59*'s wireless antenna,[28] however, pushed the ultimate departure date back to the twentieth. This too was not without incident and again exhibited the difficulties with flying long-distance missions.

Taking off at 0900 on the twentieth, the transfer of *L 59* to Yambol initially began swimmingly. Low cloud cover experienced over Lake Constance[29] immediately dissipated upon passing the body of water, and *L 59* encountered good weather and favorable wind conditions for much of the morning and early afternoon. By 1400 the Zeppelin had reached Vienna. Fifteen minutes later, inquisitive Austrian pilots even circled *L 59*, casting curious glances at the giant airship on an easterly course toward Budapest.[30] However, upon reaching Belgrade at 2000 that day, snow showers developed, causing *L 59* to "lose its orientation" and unknowingly pass over the Danube—Bockholt's guide back to Bulgaria. As such, the next six hours were spent confusedly wandering the skies looking for landmarks. According to the airship's war diary,

> When searching for the ground, we found mountains. Following the commander's instructions to search for the Danube, we took

> alternating courses, sometimes flying in clouds at 1,500 meters [4,921 feet] due to the proximity of the mountains, with slight ice [accumulating on the hull].
>
> Upon breaking through a gap [in the clouds] a fortified plain with trenches [was observed]; we first took a southerly course, the area gradually became mountainous; then, assuming we were south of the Danube, we headed north.[31]

The Danube was finally located at 0200 on the twenty-first, 20 km (12 miles) west of Lom, Bulgaria, in the northwest corner of the country. Since the cloud cover was now below *L 59*, at an altitude of 250 meters (820 feet), Bockholt wanted to be sure of *L 59*'s position and ordered the airship eastward, with the intention of following the Danube all the way to its terminus in the Black Sea—a vast, unmistakable landmark.

At 0539, *L 59* once again descended below the clouds, and Bockholt still found himself over land. Then, at 0600, when the clouds finally broke up completely, the watches on board *L 59* spotted Cape Kaliakra (approximately 30 miles east-northeast of Varna on the Black Sea).[32] Now certain of their bearing, Bockholt commanded *L 59* on a course to the southwest, landing in Yambol at 0825. Bockholt and the Mediterranean Division were about to open up an entirely new front in the Zeppelin war against the Allies, albeit not immediately. Following *L 59*'s arrival on the twenty-first, the period between the twenty-second and twenty-sixth was spent overhauling the airship's engines. Then, bad weather between February 27 and March 2 yet again grounded *L 59* and its eager crew. Finally, at 0625 on March 3, 1918, *L 59* took off for a long-awaited "attack on southern Italy."[33]

Although the wind and weather conditions that morning were favorable, with "a light breeze from the southern quadrants and mostly clear skies over the Balkans" being recorded in the airship's log,[34] *L 59* wasn't able to escape the bad luck that had plagued her over the last three months. After crossing Philippopolis and Somokov in Bulgaria; Pirot, Niš, and Novi Pazar in Serbia; and Lake Skadar (on the border of Albania and Montenegro, less than 20 miles from the Adriatic Sea) without incident, at 1630 *L 59* had to descend to a lower altitude in order to thaw the frozen radiator on her starboard engine.[35] Having disregarded Strasser's maxims on flying bombing raids in new-moon lunar phases, Bockholt now found himself exposed both by his low altitude and "unfavorable moonlight" and thus opted for the "shortest route over the Adriatic and Italy."[36] Unfortunately, the situation was about to get much worse.

After returning to an altitude of 3,000 meters (9,843 feet), Bockholt ordered *L 59* on a course to the northwest toward the island of Lesina in Dalmatia, then west-northwest into the Adriatic, with a rapidly increasing wind from the southeast. This weather system subsequently brought light snowfall, which obscured the visibility of the ground from the airship. Upon turning south at 1730, *L 59* encountered "strong hail and wind gusts of 20 m/s [45 mph] from the southeast,"[37] which then resulted in Bockholt and his crew completely losing their orientation. With the situation now appearing hopeless, Bockholt made the decision to turn back.

Bockholt didn't reestablish his bearings until 2300 that night over Šabac, Serbia, but he quickly lost them again in dense cloud cover around midnight. Eventually, when the skies began to clear for good, the Danube was spotted, and the river, yet again, guided *L 59* back to Yambol. Even though *L 59* arrived at the base at 1215 on March 4, "strong gusty winds"[38] prevented a landing from taking place. As a result, Bockholt was forced to keep *L 59* hovering over the landing field until 1807 before he, and his exhausted crew, finally touched down. Strasser's earlier points about Bockholt being successful only in missions in which the FdL made the critical decisions for his subordinates must have loomed in the back of the young commander's mind, but Bockholt remained undeterred. As his war diary indicates, in the period between March 5 and the 7, *L 59* was already being prepared for the next voyage.[39]

This arrived on March 10, with another "attack on southern Italy." This time the target was definitively Naples, and, as the airship's log and ballast chart indicated, 6,400 kg (14,110 lbs.) of bombs and 150 kg (331 lbs.) of machine gun ammunition were taken on board.[40] It would prove to be *L 59*'s most tactically successful mission thus far. After ascending from Yambol at 0630 that day in "clear weather and light winds," *L 59* made steady progress back to Lake Skadar, where it remained from 1420 to 1930 "at a low altitude, [going] up and down" awaiting the evening's darkness. Bockholt also took this opportunity to "give all engines a rest for several hours, one after the other."[41]

When nightfall arrived, Bockholt commanded *L 59* to an altitude of 2,000 meters (6,652 feet) and turned west on a course for Manfredonia, a town on the eastern coast of Italy, about 60 miles north of Bari—arriving at 2215. Upon making landfall over the Italian peninsula, Bockholt then ordered *L 59* to an altitude of 3,000 meters (9,843 feet) and headed for Naples. He noted that, unlike in England, "on the [Italian] mainland, all towns except the coast are brightly lit."[42] Even more fortuitously, *L 59* was able to utilize cloud cover until just before arriving at its objective. The people of Naples, quite literally, had no idea what was about to hit them.

At 0055 on March 11, *L 59* reached Naples and, continuing westward at altitudes between 3,650 and 4,850 meters (11,975–15,912 feet), set a course to attack the city's gasworks, the steel refinery at Bagnoli, and, eventually, the Armstrong naval shipyard and munitions factory in Pozzuoli. After dropping all 6,400 kg of his bombs in a period of just twenty minutes, Bockholt recorded in his log, "Harbor facilities and industrial plants bombarded, no resistance. [Bombs had a] very good effect, observed fires and thick clouds of smoke."[43] With all his ordnance expended, Bockholt then ordered *L 59* on a course to the northeast in order to head home. Incredibly, it was at this point that the crew of *L 59* experienced their first casualties, which occurred despite the total absence of any defensive actions on the part of the enemy.

Immediately following Bockholt's log entry about the bombardment, he noted, "Shortly after the attack, all personnel within the rear gondola were rendered unconscious by gasoline fumes; engines I and II out of action for 2 hours."[44] His postmission technical report expanded on the incident and also acted as a formal complaint about the rations in Yambol. It read:

> At an altitude of 4,300 meters, gasoline fumes accumulated [in the gondola] which caused the crew and both engines to be out of action for 2 hours. I attribute this to the contamination of the exhaust collector screens [mufflers] and the simultaneous heavy oil-fouling of the spark plugs of the rear engine. The harmful gases first appeared near engine I, whose installation location was[,] to a certain extent[,] isolated from that of engine II by the lowered radiators, and one after the other they incapacitated the two mates located there. By the time this was noticed in the darkness by the two mates of engine II, the entire gondola area had been poisoned as a result of the oil-fouling of the spark plugs of engine I, which had been running unattended for quite a long time.
>
> [The] No. 1 [mate] of engine I, who passed out first, complained of digestive problems and general physical discomfort even before the attack. I attribute this and thus his reduced physical stamina solely to the completely inadequate nutrition that the people receive [in Yambol]. A good diet, such as that which the airship crews receive at home, is an absolute necessity for this operation, where the demands placed on the personnel are far greater on 2–3-day trips.[45]

Besides the crew, the airship itself suffered damage on its homeward leg, again completely unrelated to the attack. A structural break at "ring 50 on the longitudinal beam 11" occurred due to stress on the frame member being exacerbated by preexisting "considerable oxidation." Since this location in the airship was near the water ballast release points, Bockholt advised that "anti-rust paint, which was ordered a long time ago, has not yet arrived, and a new order has been placed urgently."[46] Neither this nor the incident with the engine crews, however, were life threatening and did not impede *L 59*'s journey home in the slightest.

At 0220, flying at an altitude of 1,500 meters (4,921 feet) in "partially broken cloud cover," *L 59* reached Termoli, just over 50 miles northwest of Manfredonia, and continued eastward toward Lake Skadar, arriving there at 0820. While above the lake, just as he had over Asia Minor in November, Bockholt took the opportunity to drop a message bag containing his attack report to the Austro-Hungarian *K.u.K*[47] naval forces below for forwarding onward via telegraph to the *Admiralstab*, the Mediterranean Division, and FdL Strasser. Apparently, due to having to maintain radio silence, he simply couldn't wait until he arrived back in Yambol to share his good news. Indeed, it wasn't until 1942 that *L 59* eventually landed at the Bulgarian airship base. The entire journey lasted an incredible thirty-seven hours and seventeen minutes,[48] far shorter than Bockholt's earlier estimate of fifty-four hours mentioned in his proposal to Strasser and the Admiralty.[49]

On March 12, Bockholt sat down with representatives from the *Admiralstab* (Hagen and Eichel) in Yambol to discuss the mission. Both parties considered it a resounding success. Interestingly, Bockholt opened up the meeting by once again complaining about his crew's rations, stating,

> I apologize if I bother you again about the food. The strain on the personnel during the voyages over very steep[,] rocky mountains is extraordinarily great. The strain becomes greater on longer trips as the personnel are poorly fed. One day after the next they eat rice or poultry with tough canned meat without any variety. In frontline bases, the crew have special kitchens with special food and extra allowances before each mission to keep them strong for the high-altitude flights. On the last attack flight, 3 people passed out. The enterprise stands or falls with good food, just like it is with the submarine crews . . . Up to now, the crew's wages have mostly been spent on buying allowances privately, which they get for free and of better quality in Ahlhorn. Strasser has been informed by me;

> please get his opinion by phone from the *Admiralstab*. I request that double food allowances for the troops' food, i.e., 4 marks, be paid out until the decision is made on the outgoing written application. Then people can buy some allowances themselves.[50]

Then, regarding the attack on Naples, Bockholt rather candidly remarked, "Yesterday's attack went well. If I were to get married, I would probably never be allowed to go to Naples on my honeymoon."[51]

After congratulating Bockholt on his "splendid voyage and . . . great successes," Hagen and Eichel informed the commander that the Italians thought the attack was carried out by airplanes. They then asked Bockholt if he was of the opinion that they should allow the Italians to continue to think that, or if he had any ideas on how they could exploit the narrative. Although not explicitly stated, it appeared that they weren't yet keen on making the Allies aware that a German Zeppelin was operating in the Mediterranean theater. Interestingly, Bockholt was not eager either to claim credit for the attack or disguise it as originating from bombing aircraft. Instead, he suggested "using the expression 'air force,'" further suggesting that "the Austrians can publish it [the news], but we can't deny it completely."[52] More important to Bockholt at this meeting was whether or not the Italian media was reporting the deaths of women and children—casualties the *Marine Luftschiff Abteilung* had attempted to minimize throughout the war. He was informed that newspapers were claiming that *L 59*'s bombs almost all fell within the city's center, without causing any damage to military targets, and instead resulted in numerous civilian casualties.[53] Bockholt was dumbstruck.

Countering the Italian reports, Bockholt attested,

> I was able to watch the Venetian festival lights [Bockholt is referring to the Carnevale celebrations that preceded Easter on March 31 that year] up close and can swear that the bombs all fell close to the harbor. The third bomb also hit the gasworks between the train station and the harbor. It was a colossal explosion, and in some parts of the inner city the lights went out. While the electric street lights still continued to burn[,] I wanted to lob the remaining ordnance at Armstrong [the naval yard], which had previously been fully lit, but when Armstrong suddenly dimmed [the lights], I dropped them [the bombs] at Bagnoli, where there were very good impacts and large fires.[54]

This seemed to have placated the naval representatives, who were pleased that Bockholt had apparently taken out the "largest ironworks in Italy before the war." Before parting ways, they promised Bockholt that he would receive a response concerning the rations as soon as possible, but in the meantime they would attempt to provide him and his crew with "wine and cigars as gifts of appreciation."[55] Unfortunately, much like the Zeppelin attacks over England, there seemed to be more truth in the news reports from the ground than the purported eyewitness accounts from thousands of meters above sea level.

True to what the *Admiralstab* imparted to Bockholt, Italian newspapers were, in fact, claiming that an attack was carried out by aircraft and that the assault was of no significance to the war effort. Instead, they referred to it not as a legitimate military undertaking, but an act of terrorism. On the morning after the bombardment, *La Stampa* reported:

> Last night around 11:00 [CET] there was an aerial attack on the city of Naples. A total of about twenty bombs were dropped and almost all of them hit the center of the city, causing no military damage. . . . The Teutonic rage wanted to vent itself against our beautiful city. Its objective was twofold: military and moral, in the sense of alarming and demoralizing the public spirit. However, no damage was caused to the military operations and auxiliary establishments. The victims mentioned in the press release[56] were among the civilian population struck by the bombing while sleeping. . . . Yet another episode of barbarism. . . . German airplanes bombed the center of Naples, not the ships and buildings of its port. There is therefore only one explanation: the purpose of terrorizing the population, a purpose that a thousand examples have now shown to be vain. It is therefore indisputably an act of simple brutality, which can have no other effect than that of attracting the curses of the citizens toward those who committed it and increasingly exacerbating the character of the war. The Austrian and German aviators can boast of it. . . . For those gentlemen, killing women, old people, and children is a chivalrous means to break the resistance of the population and force it to accept German peace; that is, German slavery. Where the German cannon does not reach, where the mephitic moral gases of defeatism fail to dent the steel of popular strength, the two pious emperors resort to bombings and assassinations by means of aerial machines.[57]

In total, twenty civilian deaths and over a hundred injuries were attributed to *L 59*'s bombs.[58] Given the details noted in the press release concerning the victims, it certainly didn't appear that the Italian news sources were lying in this regard. This shouldn't imply, however, that the rest of the newspaper stories weren't embellished or oozing with Allied propaganda.

La Stampa, in an attempt to alleviate the worries of the civilian population, also made the claim in the article that

> the anti-aircraft defense systems worked well. The defense system has been improved even further today and made more efficient so that, in the event that other attacks should occur, the citizens can be at peace.[59]

This was an outright lie. True to Bockholt's testimony, there was no anti-aircraft response throughout the entirety of the attack. In fact, the authorities in Naples initially suspected that domestic terrorists, in the form of anarchist, anti-war extremists, were responsible for the explosions—believing that they had carried out the bombings on the ground during the Carnevale celebrations. It took only a few more days for both falsehoods to come to light. Indeed, by the fourteenth, it had firmly been established that it was a German airship that conducted the raid, having done so completely unmolested. As *La Stampa* now reported,

> The Hon. Labriola sent the following question to the Presidency of the Chamber [of Deputies, the lower house of the Italian Parliament]: "I query the Minister of War and the Undersecretary of Aviation in order to find out whether the antiaircraft defenses for which so many millions have been spent have a purely decorative purpose and, above all, to find out whether, following a favorable combination of circumstances, an enemy airship was able to travel from the Adriatic to the Tyrrhenian Sea, bomb Naples, and remain in the sky over it for at least twenty minutes after the bombing, all without disruptions or other hindrances in a not excessively advanced hour of the night."[60]

It was certainly a valid question, and, as the probe indicated, it gave credence to Bockholt's intimation that aerial attacks in the Mediterranean theater would draw resources away from the front lines. As the article went on to suggest, if a German airship could strike Naples, Rome too must deal "with the possibility of an incursion" and make the necessary preparations, which included additional anti-airship defenses, alarms, and blackouts.[61] Rome was not, however, the next target in Bockholt's sights. Instead, the Yambol base spent the next week preparing *L 59* to fly even farther, this time setting off with another 6,400 kg of bombs to attack Port Said on March 20.

The bombing mission to northern Egypt should have been one of the easier flights taken by Bockholt and his crew, since the route outlined by Bockholt in December was already familiar to them from their two previous attempts at reaching German East Africa. Instead, it was a comedy of errors. Things got off to a bad start before *L 59* even took off, as one of the hangar door's wires jammed itself on its girder's trolley, preventing *L 59* from being walked out onto the field. This delayed *L 59*'s 0535 departure time by an hour. Next, while flying over Asia Minor toward Antalya, a 110 kg bomb "accidentally" fell off the Zeppelin over Adrianople.[62] Although the incident didn't result in any casualties on the ground, it may have caused the Ottoman troops to question *L 59*'s nationality, as an event that occurred later in the flight suggested.

Flying at the low altitude of 700 meters (2,297 feet) prescribed by Bockholt after returning from the *China-Sache* mission, *L 59* struggled to make headway against strong winds on a southerly course over the Mediterranean throughout the duration of the night. Even after arriving above Damietta, Egypt, at 0400 on the twenty-first, the heavy gusts continued, this time blowing from the southwest, and Bockholt found that it took nearly an hour and a half to approach the vicinity of Port Said despite Damietta being located only 30 miles west. By this time, dawn had already arrived, and the attack had to be abandoned due to the prevailing daylight. Not satisfied with the thought of returning home with most of his bombload, Bockholt ordered *L 59* on a northwest course to attack the Royal Navy base located off Souda Bay on the northern side of Crete. This too resulted in a battle with the elements as opposed to enemy forces.

While en route to the occupied Greek island, an enemy steamship was observed making a zigzag course, but Bockholt felt that it was too small a target to attack. Then, upon climbing to an altitude of 4,000 meters (13,123 feet) over Crete to prepare for the attack on the base, *L 59* was caught up in a snowstorm whose thick clouds prevented the watches in the control car from observing the ground. Additionally, its strong squalls pushed the airship well off course and led to the abandonment of yet another attack.

Continuing to drift farther north over the Aegean Sea, when *L 59* reached the island of Serifos, just under 70 miles south of Athens, searchlights spotted the airship, which then forced *L 59* to an altitude of 5,000 meters (16,404 feet) and, once again, into another heavy snowstorm. This time, the additional snow/ice load on the Zeppelin forced Bockholt to order the release both of 3,000 kg (6,614 lbs.) of water ballast and 1,000 kg (2,205 lbs.) of bombs to lighten the airship and regain buoyancy.[63] With fuel and provisions now running low, Bockholt had no other choice than to give up on any further bombing runs and return back to Yambol. Setting a course for the northeast, *L 59* then continued toward the Dardanelles Strait, arriving there on the morning of the twenty-second. This, however, did not spell the end of Bockholt's difficulties.

Just over an hour prior to reaching Yambol, when *L 59* once again passed over Adrianople, she was greeted by Ottoman anti-aircraft batteries.[64] Although Göbel later asserted that it was standard practice for the Turkish forces to fire upon any aircraft, regardless of allegiance, it seems more than likely that they had mistaken *L 59* for an enemy dirigible due to the German airship having dropped a bomb over the area on the outbound leg of the voyage. Unlike the first attempt at reaching German East Africa, however, this time *L 59* escaped unscathed. She arrived back in Yambol at 0715, having completed a nearly forty-nine-hour journey across a distance of 3,849 km (2,392 miles).[65]

With attacks now having been attempted in the geographic zones west and south of Yambol, it was time for Bockholt to explore the third offensive possibility he recommended—a bombing run to the southwest, in the direction of Sicily, Malta, and Tripoli. After spending another two weeks servicing and repairing the airship and waiting for favorable weather, on the afternoon of April 7, *L 59* was walked out her shed in Yambol to attack the Royal Navy base on Malta. Unlike Bockholt's originally proposed route, a course was plotted to fly over the north of Greece to the Strait of Otranto, then south to the Ionian Sea, and then southwest to Malta. It would be the last flight ever taken by the "Africa ship."

10

The Fall of Icarus

APRIL 7, 1918, CATTARO, THE AUSTRO-HUNGARIAN EMPIRE. *Oberleutnant zur See* Robert Sprenger descends the gangway of the SMS *Cleopatra* and steps onto his U-boat, currently tethered to the towering auxiliary ship. His crew, belonging to the Imperial German Navy's Mediterranean U-boat Flotilla, are already on deck for inspection, impatiently awaiting the prompt to proceed to their stations.

Sprenger's charge is SM *UB-53*, a UB III-type, coastal attack submarine capable of traveling 9,040 nautical miles.[1] It isn't his first command, or his first patrol in the Mediterranean. Taking over *UC-34* at the end of 1916, he had already sunk sixteen ships in the *Mittelmeer*, accounting for a total of 28,393 gross registered tons.[2] By all metrics, the thirty-year-old commander is already a well-experienced hand in the U-boat war. Today, his orders are to sail toward Tripoli to monitor maritime traffic off the North African coast and subsequently wage a trade war in the eastern Mediterranean, focusing on the waters approaching Alexandria and Port Said.[3] With such a great distance to cover, he expects to be at sea for a month.

Looking toward the overcast sky, Sprenger turns to his number one—*Oberleutnant zur See* Joachim Wolfram, the first watch officer. "Looks like a storm is coming. I hope it'll conceal our entry into the Ionian." Then, facing his crew, still standing at attention, he breaks the news about their mission.

"Now men, we have a long trip ahead of us. We're headed toward North Africa. We can be certain to encounter Italian patrols on the surface and in the air before we reach the open sea, and we must stay alert at all times, understood?"

"*Jawohl Herr Oberleutnant!*"

"Good—to your stations!"

As the crewmen release the mooring lines and make their way through the hatches leading into the submarine, Sprenger faces the bow of the U-boat and waves. Two Austrian torpedo boats observe the signal and make steam. They will serve as *UB-53*'s escorts into the Adriatic. Then, at 1400, *UB-53* is pushed off the *Cleopatra* and follows in the wake of the Austrian destroyers. The trio continue southward for approximately two and half hours before the escorts break off and return to Cattaro. Now, *UB-53* is on her own.

At 1820, off Meterizi, Montenegro, Sprenger gives the order for a test dive. After forty minutes of submerged travel, *UB-53* once again comes to the surface. Sprenger, like so many other U-boat commanders, wants to enter the Strait of Otranto, and its deadly nets and mine barrages, in a position that offers some means of escape should the worst scenario unfold.

The overcast conditions have now evolved into thick storm clouds, and it begins to rain.[4] Despite the weather conditions otherwise being favorable for camouflaging the small coastal U-boat, the Adriatic's surface is unusually phosphorescent. It wouldn't be difficult for an enemy warship or seaplane to spot *UB-53*'s luminous wake.

Donning their sou'westers, the crew of the first watch aggressively scan the horizon, occasionally pausing to wipe rain and seawater off the lenses of their binoculars. At 2000, *Oberbootsmann* Friedrich Schuster, positioned on the stern of the conning tower, notices a strange orb in the sky, growing larger. After using his handkerchief to clean the objective lenses again, he takes a second look and immediately snaps back, leaning into the conning tower toward the open hatch. He calls out, "Airship approaching from the stern, heading about 200 degrees; it's closing on us!"[5] Sprenger hurriedly rushes up the ladder and, following his subordinate's hand gestures, peers to the north with his Zeiss 7×50 glasses.

"*Mein Gott*, it's so low! A rifle shot from here would surely hit it. I can even make out the gondolas; nose appears to read '*L 59*.' Either he's one of ours and is significantly underestimating his visibility from the ground, or he's an enemy that sees our wake and is heading in to bomb us."[6] Calling down the open hatch to the radioman, Sprenger inquires if the U-boat has received any signals from Pola about a friendly airship in the area. Unfortunately, the wireless telegraphy equipment is currently malfunctioning.[7]

Oberleutnant Wolfram, now standing next to Sprenger on the conning tower, asks if he should fire a recognition signal to confirm its nationality. Sprenger responds in the negative.

"No, if by some miracle they haven't already spotted us, a flare would surely do the trick. Then we'd have the Italian, French, and British fleets to worry about as well. We'll let him approach us and then change course to throw off his run. Have the crewmen man the deck gun just in case."

The mysterious airship continues toward the U-boat, and, flying at an altitude of only 200 meters (656 feet),[8] all the details of the Zeppelin's underside can be observed by the naked eye. Sprenger takes this moment to act.

"Change course to 90 degrees, all ahead full!"[9]

As the submarine turns on a perpendicular course away from the airship, Sprenger keeps it in his binoculars' focus. Now he can make out the Iron Crosses painted on its hull.

"Thank God! It's one of ours! Both engines, stop!"

The men on the U-boat stare at the behemoth as it passes overhead on a southerly course. Within minutes it is out of sight.

After ordering *UB-53* back on her original heading, Sprenger remains in the tower with his first watch officer. "That was close, I wonder what he was doing so low? Maybe Pola dispatched him to scout ahead for us or . . ." Their conversation is interrupted by another contact.

At 2030, about 12 nautical miles southwest toward the back "heel" of Italy, a vessel is spotted traveling north toward the Bay of Kotor, making continuous light signals. Then the muzzle flashes from several guns are observed.[10] Given that there are no splashes anywhere near the U-boat, it is unclear what the unknown warship is firing at.

"Do you think that could be our Zeppelin?" asks the first watch officer. Sprenger responds, "Couldn't be; that went out of sight a while ago and was on an entirely different heading. No matter; it's about time we made our turn. Adjust course to 170 degrees."

The U-boat turns slightly to port and continues onward in a south-south-east direction. Twenty minutes later, the watches on board *UB-53* alert Sprenger to another phenomenon on the horizon.

"*Herr Oberleutnant*, look over there!"

In the direction of about 200 degrees, approximately 25–30 nautical miles from *UB-53*, two burning dots can be seen in the sky. "Shrapnel, perhaps?" remarks Sprenger.[11] Just as he finishes uttering the words, several powerful detonations are heard and "a huge flame lights up the entire horizon as bright as day and slowly sinks toward the water."[12] He concludes, "It appears that *that* is our Zeppelin. It must have been shot down and crashed into the sea!"

For another twenty minutes the southern skyline continues to glow. After the distant flames diminish, searchlights can be seen scanning the water, apparently looking for the downed dirigible. Soon, they too go dim. Sprenger orders *UB-53* to head to the area to search for debris or survivors.

Upon reaching the expected location of the crash site at 2330, all available men on board *UB-53* strain their eyes trying to find any evidence of *L 59* or her crew. There is no trace of the giant airship—not even a scrap of doped canvas or a sailor's cap. After remaining in the area desperately searching for any sign of wreckage, Sprenger gives up. He notes the time of *L 59*'s destruction as being 2034,[13] and the final resting place of Bockholt, his men,[14] and the "Africa ship" as being 41°2'N, 18°53'E.[15] With the wireless apparatus on board *UB-53* now functioning, Sprenger instructs his radioman to monitor Allied signals for any news on the downing of *L 59*. Unfortunately, in the twenty-nine days remaining in his patrol, *UB-53* intercepts no reports, from land, sea, or air, taking credit for the destruction of an enemy airship. The Germans, too, would initially struggle to explain the loss.

News about *L 59*'s disappearance first reached Germany on April 9, after *UB-53* wired the Mediterranean U-boat Flotilla's base about the sighting. A telegram from the FdU (*Führer der Unterseeboote*, or leader of the U-boats) in Pola, Kurt Graßhoff, succinctly advised the Admiralstab that *L 59* "apparently crashed[,] burning after being hit by enemy artillery."[16] Then, two days later, *Korvettenkapitän* Arnim in Sofia expanded on the event, noting,

> Austrian military personnel have provided me with the following telegram from the *K.u.K* 19th Army Corps in Skadar: "On the 7th of the month at 8:30 p.m. an airship was observed west of Cape Rodon. At about 9:00 p.m., according to several independent reports, a glow of fire was visible about 20 km west of Durazzo [now Durrës, Albania], followed by several cannon-like detonations. One of the reports said, it seemed as if a burning ball was descending into the sea; an aircraft sent out the next day could not find anything except an oil stain and a floating piece of wood.[17]

In actuality, the Austrians dispatched a tender (*Tender IV*) to the area immediately after the explosion was reported. Unfortunately, it was recalled at 2150 due to enemy activity in the vicinity—the sources of the searchlights observed by Sprenger. Then, at 0600 on the eighth, they sent two Hansa-Brandenburg seaplanes, K.177 and K.183, to scout the crash site, subsequently losing the former to engine failure.[18] Although the oil slick and wood fragment mentioned by Arnim were, in fact, discovered shortly after 1100 that morning by K.183, the Austrians identified them as originating from the downed K.177 seaplane.[19]

On the same day that Arnim's telegram arrived, the OHL offered their own intelligence report, which was sourced from witnesses on the Italian mainland and occupied Valona. It indicated that the Italians appeared to be just as surprised at the light show they saw on the seventh and played no role in shooting down *L 59*. It stated,

> AOK [*Armeeoberkommando*, or "Army High Command"] Baden reports: "According to reliable reports from April 8 and 9, a strong fire phenomenon was observed from Brindisi on the night of April 7 and 8. Four enemy seaplanes then reconnoitered the explosion area from Valona. Further details are unknown to the fleet command. The report is probably related to *L 59*, about which no separate report has been received since it passed Dulcigno [now Ulcinj, Montenegro] toward the west on that evening in April."[20]

Given that the fifty-six-hour flight duration estimate for reaching Malta had long expired at this point, FdL Strasser and the Admiralty officially struck *L 59* from the list of active airships. Now, while the investigation into the loss was initiated, they had to ensure that the incident remained a secret.

This process had actually started on the tenth, when the *Marine Luftschiff Abteilung* wired Arnim and the *Admiralstab* to "please arrange for Bulgarian censors to confiscate [any] news about [the] whereabouts of *L 59*."[21] Since no Allied forces took credit for shooting down *L 59*, the Germans wanted to ensure that they remained under the impression that a Zeppelin was operating in the Mediterranean theater. Strasser's next concern was the possibility that various encryption codes may have been captured by the enemy.

Upon first hearing about the crash, he contacted Yambol to see what ciphers were on board *L 59* during the flight. By April 12, he was able to inform the *Admiralstab* that the "radio name list 83, weather key 321, encryption procedure 896, and the switchboard port with [its] corresponding encryption procedure 1496" were missing from *L 59*'s inventory list and were on board on April 7. He concluded that "it can be assumed that these encryption items were destroyed by fire and when the airship crashed into the water, and did not fall into enemy hands."[22] With *L 59*'s codes thus secured, it was time to determine what led to the destruction of the giant airship.

In 1918, as today, there were three main hypotheses surrounding *L 59*'s loss. Either *L 59* was struck by lightning and caught fire, the airship was shot down by enemy aircraft or surface vessels (or both), or it suffered some sort of mechanical malfunction on board that caused the hydrogen to ignite. The only conclusion seriously considered by the RMA, and echoed by Göbel, was the third scenario; however, each conjecture will be summarily investigated here.

The case for a lightning strike was not without precedent. There were at least three noted airship crashes attributed to this occurrence, both before and after the war. *L 10* was the first confirmed instance, having been struck by lightning and lost with all hands near Cuxhaven on September 3, 1915. The loss of *SL 9* followed next, on March 30, 1917; the Schütte-Lanz airship was theorized to have suffered the same fate and crashed in the Baltic. Finally, *L 72*, which was ceded to France after the war and renamed the *Dixmude*, was hit by a lightning bolt over Sicily on December 21, 1923, and crashed, killing all on board. There is, however, evidence that such occurrences were not always fatal. *L 42*, commanded by *Kapitänleutnant* Martin Dietrich in the infamous May 23–24 raid, was struck by lightning twice but still made it back to base. According to Dietrich's report,

> On the way back, "L 42" approached a strong frontal thunderstorm, which had a height of 6,000 to 7,000 meters [19,685–22,966 feet]. Since it was impossible to avoid it, we had to break through the wall of storm clouds. During the hailstorm that ensued, the ship suffered two strong lightning strikes, which, as far as we have established, did not cause any damage. The lightning apparently entered the bow and exited again at the stern.[23]

Incredibly, *L 42* arrived safely in Nordholz later that morning, with six holes in the cotton outer cover at the bow, two melted bracing wires, a "pea-sized" hole in a girder, and burn marks on the port propeller.[24]

While *Oberleutnant* Sprenger did allude to potential stormy conditions in *UB-53*'s war diary, at no point did he note any exceptional weather other than "occasional rain" in the time he left port, even after he witnessed *L 59* crashing from the sky. In fact, the only time he mentioned any noises that could possibly be construed as thunder, or flashes that could have been lightning, was when he described the "detonations" heard when *L 59* was already assumed to be on fire. This matched the summary of events described by the Austro-Hungarian witnesses in Skadar—a glow of fire was observed first, then explosions were heard. Regardless, Sprenger later admitted to FdU Graßhoff that although he originally attributed the bright dots in the sky as being shrapnel, potentially shooting at *L 59*, "he now also consider[ed] destruction by lightning (ball lightning?) [*sic*] to be possible."[25] Given *L 59*'s proximity to the U-boat and the prevailing weather conditions, it should have been quite apparent if lightning were the catalyst for the airship's loss at the time of the incident, but Sprenger didn't think of that prospect until nearly a month afterward. His watch officer, too, recalled that night differently, albeit nearly twenty years later.

Writing to the Zeppelin company in 1937, Oblt. Wolfram decided to share his own experiences on *UB-53* to help solve the mystery of the *Hindenburg*'s explosion in Lakehurst. After reading numerous newspaper articles about the weather conditions in New Jersey, and once again revisiting *L 59*'s loss over the Adriatic in his mind, he now claimed to have seen "a slight flash of lightning" toward the south, followed by another that "suddenly left an intense red dot" in the sky.[26] Going against Sprenger's reports, Wolfram also asserted that when *UB-53* arrived at the crash site, burning gasoline and sections of the airship could still be seen on the water's surface. Given the disparity between Wolfram's recollections and both the U-boat's war diary entries and Sprenger's later reexamination of the event in May 1918, one must cast considerable doubts about the accuracy of his memory.

Indeed, besides Sprenger's, and much later Wolfram's, revelations about the possibility of an electrostatic charge destroying *L 59*, it is never mentioned otherwise during the investigation. Göbel also completely discounted the lightning theory, which, according to him, could be traced back to an Italian eyewitness report from Taranto wherein "sheet lightning" observed in the sky was, in all likelihood, a misinterpretation of the huge flame from *L 59*'s explosion, which lit up the horizon.[27]

The scenario in which *L 59* was shot down is easier to discount. Obviously, the most incriminatory evidence against this supposition is the absence of any Allied claims of responsibility for the attack. Given that the destruction of an airship, either German or Allied, during World War I was a significant propaganda victory, typically lauded in newspapers, war-bond drives, and commemorative postcards, the "Africa ship," whose existence the British asserted they were already well aware of, would have been a monumental prize. The Italians, too, having lost seven airships by April 1918,[28] would have been eager to collect their own Zeppelin trophy, particularly as retribution for the "barbaric" raid on Naples. As it stood, none of the Allied powers took credit for the kill or, as substantiated by the reconnaissance flights and naval vessels that scoured the area of the crash site following the blast, even appeared to be aware of *L 59*'s presence in the Strait of Otranto that night. This fact was further confirmed by Sprenger's war diary entries, wherein no enemy fire was observed in the vicinity of *L 59*. The only vessel noted as appearing to have displayed "muzzle flashes" was located too far to the west and was on a heading completely opposite the Zeppelin. These rationalizations, however, address the incident only from an Allied point of view. What if friendly fire downed *L 59*, and the Central Powers had taken efforts to cover up the disaster?

While the Austro-Hungarian forces stationed in Montenegro and Albania were aware of *L 59*'s mission and tracked the airship's movements through various coastal lookouts, Sprenger and the crew of *UB-53* were surprised by *L 59*'s sudden appearance in the Adriatic. As the *Oberleutnant* admitted, he was initially unsure of the nationality of the airship and its intentions. Is it possible that his crew fired on the airship before realizing *L 59* was a German Zeppelin? On the basis of archival evidence, the answer is no. Although SM *UB-53* was armed with a powerful, long-range 10.5 cm SK L/45 deck gun,[29] its limited firing arc meant it would have been impossible to target an airship flying at an altitude of 200 meters.[30] Additionally, the *Munitionsverbräuche*, or ammunition expenditure, page of *UB-53*'s war diary accounted for every shot taken during the patrol.[31] Sprenger would have had to falsify multiple entries in his log over the period of a month to hide an erroneous attack on a German airship—an extremely unlikely event. The fact that both Austrian and Italian reports claim that flames were observed prior to hearing "cannon-like detonations" also seems to clear Sprenger of any misconduct that April.

This leaves a mechanical failure as being the only remaining scenario for the fire that consumed *L 59*, and the one that has the most tangible evidence. As stated earlier, this was the theory supported by Göbel, and the hypothesis that the Admiralstab, the RMA, and FdL Strasser investigated most deeply.

The basis for their placing such importance on this notion was a second report written by Bockholt on April 3—separate from his earlier technical report from March 16—regarding the gas leak and structural failure that occurred during the March 10–11 raid on Naples. In it, Bockholt noted four specific causes for the incident in the rear gondola, which were as follows:

> (1) As already occurred with *L 53*, the accumulation of combustion gases due to the rear position of the two exhaust pipes and the double exhaust collector screens [mufflers]. (After its landing, the exhaust pipes were taken apart. They showed contamination but no breaks or damage, just like the exhaust pipes in *L 53*.)
> (2) The frequently experienced release of harmful gasoline fumes from the sump during sharp course changes, which, instead of being expelled through the hood, enter the interior of the gondola through the air intake screens and settle there. (This is particularly complained about by the engine crew of engine I, where the issue is most noticeable.)
> (3) Strong heating and, to a certain extent, isolation of the bad air in engine I due to the cranking down [lowering the position] of both radiators. (The radiators of *L 59* are about 20 mm longer than the radiators of the frontline ships.)
> (4) The severe oil fouling of the spark plugs that occurred after the crew was absent from engine I due to its continued operation without maintenance.[32]

A handwritten note in the margin of the report from April 15 initially cast doubt on the clogging of the exhaust screens that occurred on *L 53* having anything to do with the situation on *L 59*, or for the catastrophe that occurred on the seventh. However, another note, this time from April 24, indicated that the report was forwarded on to Zeppelin engineers and given credence.

Certainly, the conditions in the rear gondola described by Bockholt are eerily reminiscent of the accident that occurred on *L 2* in 1913, wherein a magneto failure caused a backfire through the carburetor, resulting in a fire that quickly spread through the airship.[33] If enough flammable vapors accumulated in the confined space of the gondola, it would have taken very little effort for an errant spark to cause ignition, particularly if the engine crew had already been incapacitated by carbon monoxide poisoning from the clogged mufflers. Fires within the rear and forward gondolas, or in combination with the lateral engine nacelles, could also explain why two burning points were observed in the sky by Sprenger, particularly if one assumes that fuel leaks and concentrations of vapors weren't isolated only to the two rearmost engines.

A hint that such leaks may not have been unique to *L 59* exists in a report made by *Kapitänleutnant* Martin Dietrich upon being awarded command of *L 71*, then still under construction. Writing to the Zeppelin factory in June 1918, he requested this: "Please supervise the installation of the engines and the laying of the fuel lines as closely as possible to avoid breaks in the fuel lines due to poor soldering points, as was the case with *L 64*."[34]

When one considers all the mechanical factors involved (namely, the poor engine field maintenance unearthed by the Maybach technicians during *L 59*'s conversion in January; the frequent, rapid overhauling of the engines in Yambol between sequential long-distance combat missions; the potentially poorly soldered fuel lines directly from the factory; and the rushed nature of *L 59*'s construction in the first place), it becomes all the more likely that a mechanical malfunction, leading to a gas leak, started the fire(s) that engulfed *L 59*. Indeed, this may have been the reason that Bockholt was flying at such a low altitude over the Adriatic. While it is possible that he could have been trying to find his bearings—Sprenger doesn't specify how low the cloud cover was that night—it could have also indicated that *L 59* had been in distress, with multiple crewmen already rendered unconscious through carbon monoxide poisoning.

Whatever scenario the reader chooses to accept as true, the fact remains that *L 59* had been destroyed, and there was now a redundant, vacant naval airship base in Yambol.

Incredibly, proposals for the reduction of the forces remaining in Yambol began almost immediately after the RMA learned of *L 59*'s loss, with the complete abandonment of the Bulgarian base also being considered. Calls for the latter were coming mostly from FdL Strasser, who was adamant that all airship troops should be returned to Germany for operations in the North Sea. However, a telegram sent on April 20, from the state secretary of the RMA to Strasser, indicated the *Reichsmarineamt* was not yet willing to give up on the Mediterranean theater. Instead, it suggested, as a means of placating Strasser, that the troops stationed in Yambol would be reduced in size, specifically during the "unhealthy" summer months, when malarial infections were widespread.[35]

Then, on April 22, the RMA recommended that *L 59* be replaced with another airship for continued attacks on Port Said and Alexandria. They were certain that the British were planning offensives for Palestine and the Middle East in the fall and wanted to have an airship available to counter the threat. Strasser, however, successfully quashed such designs by arguing that he had "only 11 airships in the North Sea and none could be spared."[36] For the immediate future, none of the existing Zeppelins, or those still under construction, would be slated for operations in the east or over the Mediterranean.

Still, the navy remained unyielding in their desire to keep Yambol open, with or without an airship. Even after a summer of inactivity, due to following through on their promise to reduce troop strength and not transfer any of Strasser's limited frontline airships, the naval war command advised the following on September 15: "Abandonment of Yambol is not possible. However, it is not planned to maintain Yambol in such a way that an airship can be stationed there at any time. The retention of a guard command in the suggested strength is sufficient."[37]

Arnim, on the other hand, interpreted this austere plan as being hopeless, and argued for the total decommissioning of the base. Perhaps his experience as the naval attaché in Sofia gave him better insight into the wartime state of Bulgaria than the planners had back in Berlin. With the Armistice of Salonica being signed on September 29, effectively taking Bulgaria out of the war, he warned that retaining a largely unmanned, minimally guarded base without airships would likely result in "destruction and looting" and could potentially be used by enemy forces in the future.[38] Instead, he felt that, along with the exodus of the bulk of the airship troops, all immobile facilities should be destroyed, and all inventory that could potentially be transported by truck or rail be transferred back to Germany.[39]

Although there is no archival evidence confirming that such acts took place in the last few months of the war, past practices at the former army airship bases in Kovno and Wainoden (Vaiņode) in occupied Lithuania indicate that this dismantling of the base likely occurred prior to the German forces returning home. In fact, much of the same winding down of operations had been occurring within Germany since the end of the summer following a single, disastrous bombing mission over Great Britain on August 5.

On that evening, the last airship raid against England took place. Taking part in the attack were *L 53*, *L 56*, *L 63*, *L 65*, and, with Strasser on board, *L 70*. Their mission was to bomb either the southern or central zones over England, with London also potentially being a target if the FdL so advised during the flight.[40] *L 70*, which was to be flown in the lead of the group, was the newest airship in the fleet. It was an "X-class" Zeppelin designed for seven Maybach Mb.IVa engines (it ended up being equipped with only six) and was capable of reaching an altitude of 20,300 feet (statically). Strasser had high hopes for *L 70*, since it was the embodiment of everything he wanted *L 59* to be converted to. Yet, flying in the face of his earlier criticisms of Bockholt, he awarded its command to twenty-nine-year-old *Kapitänleutnant* Johannes von Loßnitzer—an officer of limited combat experience.[41] It would prove to be a fateful decision. According to Douglas Robinson,

> With von Loßnitzer in *L 70* was Peter Strasser, leading in person the first raid on England in four months. Strasser, the chief who did not believe that *L 70* could be attacked by British aircraft, and von Loßnitzer, inexperienced, rash, making his first raid on England under the eye of the man who had given him the finest airship in the world as a special favor. Neither man would be restraining influence on the other. It was a bad combination.[42]

Claiming it was a "bad combination" was, perhaps, an understatement.

Taking off from Nordholz and Wittmundhaven between 1355 and 1512 that August day, the quintet of Zeppelins set a course northeast toward England, with *L 53*, *L 65*, and *L 70* composing one attack group and *L 56* and *L 63* following closely behind. Upon reaching the coast off Norfolk at 2010, the leading trio were promptly spotted by sailors on board the Leman Tail Lightship, who then telegraphed their positions to the mainland. The Great Yarmouth air station, heeding the signal, consequently scrambled thirteen aircraft to intercept the raiders, with ten flying inland and three heading north, out to sea. Of the three airplanes flying the actual intercepting course, one was an Airco D.H.4, which, having a service ceiling of 22,000[43] feet, could meet or surpass *L 70*'s cruising altitude. As chance would have it, this single D.H.4 was piloted by Maj. Egbert Cadbury, with Capt. Robert Leckie in the gunner/observation seat—both experienced airmen with previous individual victories over Zeppelins.[44]

After spotting the three Zeppelins flying in a "V" formation, and spending forty minutes climbing to an altitude of 16,500 feet, Cadbury flew head on toward *L 70*, which was then cruising at a height of 17,300 feet.[45] As the D.H.4 passed below the airship, Leckie opened fire vertically into the airship's underside with explosive Pomeroy, anti-Zeppelin ammunition—it had a powerful and immediate effect. According to Cadbury's report, *L 70* "was completely consumed [by fire] in about ¾ of a minute."[46] Upon witnessing the state of the art in Zeppelin design go up in flames with the FdL on board, the remaining two airships in the trio turned east and fled. The other group of two Zeppelins, *L 56* and *L 63*, reached the coast approximately 30 miles south of the leading group and, having seen *L 70* set alight in the distance, continued on with their mission, dropping bombs over England and the sea, with no material effect or casualties. All except *L 70* made it back to Germany safely.

In shooting down *L 70*, Cadbury and Leckie destroyed more than just an airship and its crew—they completely snuffed out the driving force of the *Marine Luftschiff Abteilung* and the greatest advocate for the Zeppelin war, Peter Strasser. His replacement, *Korvettenkapitän* Paul Werther, although a capable leader, was not driven by the same fervor and obsessiveness with airships as a combat arm. As such, when *Vizeadmiral* Franz von Hipper replaced Scheer (a supporter of Strasser and airships) as chief of the High Seas Fleet in August 1918, and long-range reconnaissance became the singular role of Zeppelins in the Great War—the new FdL offered little in the way of resistance.

Although the southern front still appeared to be favorable for offensive airship operations, as Bockholt proved over Naples, and Strasser was no longer an obstacle in the way of diverting resources away from the North Sea theater, Hipper was having none of it. Regarding future bombing raids over Britain and the North Sea or the Mediterranean and Adriatic, Hipper advised that "the right to engage in raids and combat must not be taken away from the airship . . . but possibilities of success must not conflict with executing the mission."[47] In other words, bombing missions *could* proceed, but only if quantifiable results could be achieved without any significant airship losses—essentially never.

When Werther subsequently proposed building new, larger Zeppelins with an operational ceiling of 26,200 feet, his construction program was scrapped due to the diminished role of airships in the war and a severe shortage of raw materials. Since the *Admiralstab* now no longer believed that targets could effectively be bombed from such great heights, the only operational Zeppelin that was converted to Walther's specifications was *L 71*. Akin to *L 59*, *L 71* was cut in half and expanded by two 15-meter gas cells at the Zeppelin works in Friedrichshafen in October 1918. Although it was slated to share *L 59*'s five-engine configuration for weight savings and greater static lift, it ultimately received six engines to achieve a higher maximum speed.

Due to a hiatus on future airship projects and having only seven Zeppelins assigned for frontline service,[48] the RMA began the process of reducing the number of airships' forward operating bases and available hangars. Just like at Yambol, Wainoden, and Kovno, all airship ports within Germany, apart from Nordholz and Ahlhorn (Tondern and Jüterbog were manned by skeleton crews for emergency landings), were either decommissioned or converted to airfields for naval air service units (*Marine Feldflieger*).[49]

Thus, the loss of *L 59*—and its vision of extending the airship war to all the fronts of the Great War throughout Europe, the Middle East, Africa, and even North America—was an early signifier of the ultimate decline of the *Marine Luftschiff Abteilung* as an effective naval combat arm. The experiences of Bockholt, the crew of *L 59*, and the Zeppelin works, however, would live on in the postwar years, but not in a role that Bockholt or Strasser could have envisioned in 1917–18. *China-Sache* had proven that airships didn't have to be confined to the cooler, temperate climates of central and northern Europe and, unlike the primitive airplanes of the day, had the greatest potential to traverse the globe, establishing a novel means of aerial exploration and travel.

11

An Irenic Future for Airships

IN 1917, WHEN *L 59* COMPLETED its record-breaking flight toward German East Africa and back, the primary driving force for dirigible research and development was making airships more effective as instruments of war. The Germans needed them to fly higher, farther, and faster to hit targets deep into enemy territory and escape the rapidly evolving anti-airship defenses and intercepting aircraft. Indeed, three years prior to the *China-Sache* operation, it was considered an incredible feat that Zeppelins were even capable of crossing the English Channel and returning to bases on mainland Europe. By the end of the war, however, *L 59* had proven that countries, vast seas, and continents could be traversed with ease and swiftness and in relative safety—far exceeding the capabilities of the airplanes of the period. The proof of concept was quickly reinforced less than year after the war ended.

In July 1919, the British rigid airship *R34*—itself a carefully reverse-engineered copy of the *LZ 76 / L 33* Zeppelin that crashed in England in 1916[1]—achieved the milestone described in the *Wilnaer Zeitung* in 1917, crossing the Atlantic and reaching North America. Had Strasser still been alive to witness such an accomplishment realized by his beloved airships, he would almost certainly have been envisioning bombing raids across the Atlantic and Pacific aimed at potential enemies of the fatherland throughout the globe. He would, however, likely been alone in this sentiment. Interestingly, none of his colleagues or subordinates who survived the war appeared to share such a viewpoint.

Unlike the veterans of the U-boat service during World War I, who saw in the U-cruisers[2] a promise that submarines would become an effective, long-range tool of the German navy in imminent, future conflicts,[3] the airship veterans foresaw mostly peaceful, commercial enterprises for airships. Reinhard Scheer, representing the upper echelon of the *Kaiserliche Marine*, concluded that "we may probably look upon the military career of the airship as over and done with. But the technical side of airship navigation has been developed in such a high degree by our experience in war, that airship traffic in peace times will derive great advantages from it, and the . . . Zeppelin will be preserved as a step in the progress of civilization."[4] Those who took part in wartime endurance flights perhaps realized this sooner than others.

Obermatrose Hans Schedelmann, who was on board *L 59*'s flight to Khartoum, wrote in January 1919 that *L 59* was responsible for "paving the way for the intercontinental [travel] services to come."[5] This was echoed by Ernst Lehmann in 1937, when he, rather optimistically, claimed, "We were more than satisfied with the military performances of our airships, and we looked upon it as self-evident that the technical developments made during the war would be used for the good of peaceful world traffic when the war was over."[6] Others, while agreeing with the benign nature of future airship flights, were more realistic regarding the capabilities of airships and the increasing competition from airplanes.

One of the most eloquent assessments of the future use of airships in this respect came from Buttlar-Brandenfels in 1932, who, after first warning about—and describing in detail—the potential devastating effects of an aerial gas attack in a future war, concluded,

> As a mere weapon of war the airship has been superseded, so far as Germany is concerned. It had perhaps already been superseded as early as the end of 1917 or the beginning of 1918. The North Sea had simply become too small for us. It was not the guns of the enemy that drove us from the North Sea, or rather [flying] ever higher and higher in mid-air, but the enemy's aeroplanes. Today it has become more than ever easy to dispose quickly of a combustible airship, inflated with gas, by means of light pursuit-aeroplanes brought to the spot by a parent ship, and it would be quite impossible to build sufficiently quickly to replace losses.[7]

For him, dirigibles would be useful only to nations with vast coasts, or that otherwise were surrounded by seas, for the purposes of patrolling. Even so, he stressed that they would be successful in this endeavor only if they were filled with helium, a gas that Germany had no access to. Still, he did not completely discount commercial uses for airships.

After denigrating the *Graf Zeppelin (LZ 127)* as not representing "the ideal airship" because it was developed on compromises, he still felt that "a ship built on [helium lifting gas and light engines powered by diesel to reduce the chance of fires] . . . can, and will, prove profitable . . . provided it carries mails and goods of very high value."[8] Unfortunately, as an airship commander he didn't have any experience piloting airplanes, and his summary of the deficiencies of aircraft—namely, regarding landing and navigation—appears as both naive and a bit silly to the modern reader. Interestingly, another man, also closely associated with airships, was able to counter Buttlar's judgment of aircraft convincingly and on a scientific basis—Johannes Göbel.

Of all the people involved with Zeppelins during the Great War, Göbel provided the most realistic assessment of them, and the most criticism. He seemed to feel that *L 59* had already reached the pinnacle of airships' capabilities and that it was only a matter of time before aircraft rendered them obsolete. Writing first about *R34*'s flight from an engineer's perspective, he expanded on the concept of intercontinental travel and the foundations already laid by *L 59*, noting,

> The imitation Zeppelin ship [*R34*] was not to be used as a weapon in the future: it was rather considered as a means of transport. According to a proposal presented in Parliament, England is considering setting up transport routes to the colonies, especially in India. In this context, reference was again made to the *L 59*'s journey to Khartoum. . . . With its famous journey to America, *R34* merely proved that an airship that carries its payload in petrol reserves and uses it up en route can reach its final destination . . . with empty petrol tanks. However, England was lagging behind . . . proof had already been fully provided by *L 59* a year and a half earlier.[9]

And in reference to the future role of airships, he wrote,

> The airship will . . . in the area of economic air transport, have to take a back seat to the airplane, which has a completely different developmental potential. It will perhaps be able to retain some

"aesthetic" advantages over other aircraft, and will thus embody the elegant luxury yacht over the passenger and freight steamer . . . which is built less for comfort than economy.[10]

Göbel's prescience was shockingly accurate, particularly when considering how early in aeronautical history he arrived at his verdict, but he did appear somewhat short-sighted in the immediate potential of airships. Throughout the 1920s and early 1930s, there were still numerous frontiers for airships to cross, such as the journey to the North Pole with the Italians' *Norge* semirigid airship in 1926 and the Germans' *Graf Zeppelin*'s circumnavigation of the world in 1929.

When Douglas Robinson concluded that "it was the experiences of the men of *L 59* that first demonstrated the feasibility of the postwar global airship services,"[11] he, like Göbel, seemed to be suggesting that simply by arriving back in Yambol and setting a distance record, *L 59* had laid the groundwork for the future flights. Both men failed to elucidate on the technological, meteorological, and practical gains made on the voyage both for airship travel and aviation in general—much of which could be directly attributed to the numerous trials and errors made by Ludwig Bockholt.

It must be remembered that the flight that actually approached Khartoum was *L 59*'s third attempt at reaching German East Africa from Yambol. In that and the preceding flights, Bockholt had to make adjustments to his payload, ballast, and course on the basis of actual experiences in the air, which deviated from what weather forecasters, engineers, and other experts had predicted.

One of the most important lessons learned from the voyages was the numerous temperature inversions experienced in warmer climates under the subtropical sun and the cooling of the gas bags that followed in the evening. As Bockholt noted in his report following his first attempt, 3,200 kgs of gasoline, oil, provisions, and cargo had to be expended because the temperature conditions at 1,000 meters of altitude over Bulgaria were not in any way representative of the original estimates from *Kapitänleutnant* Sommerfeld.[12] Then, on the third flight, Bockholt realized that even more water ballast would have to be taken on board, since the temperature inversions at altitude, rising heat from the surface, and extreme radiation from the sun over the deserts of North Africa resulted in hydrogen venting during the day and condensing at night, both necessitating dumping ballast or, in *L 59*'s case, also some of her precious cargo.[13] They also led to an extremely turbulent ride, causing seasickness among the crew.

Hugo Eckener, the manager of Luftschiffbau Zeppelin and the *Graf Zeppelin*'s captain during most of her endurance flights, appeared to have studied Bockholt's reports prior to departing on his long-distance voyages. In 1929, when the *Graf Zeppelin* took off for a Mediterranean trip over Italy, the Middle East, the coast of Egypt, Greece, and central Europe, he was crossing landmarks already reached by Bockholt, and endured much of what the crew of *L 59* already went through. He thus shouldn't have been surprised at the fine weather over Naples, the blizzard near Vienna, or the navigational problems in trying to "hold the ship on her course over the Danube valley, between the great heights on both sides."[14] Indeed, when the *Graf Zeppelin* went on its tour of the world, Eckener admitted that *L 59*'s experiences over Africa prepared him for crossing the North American deserts over Texas, New Mexico, and Arizona, though apparently not well enough. He recalled:

> We were soon to experience what a continental atmosphere could produce. The opposite of the stable atmosphere which we had experienced on the flight across the broad Pacific, it was most decidedly unpleasant. . . . At dawn we were over the edge of Arizona. . . . The uncommonly clear air ahead of us above the Arizona desert was entirely stable during the cool of the early morning. . . . The sun, gradually climbing, did its work and heated the air above the ground. It rose, and the ship began to toss about. . . . The ship was lifted 600–1,000 feet at a time by the rising air-mass, and then drawn down an equal distance by down-drafts. . . . I recalled that when a naval airship was sent south during the World War, a good half of the crew . . . became seasick on the flight across the Sahara Desert. I did not actually become seasick, but I made up my mind to avoid if possible, flying over the desert in the summer by day, or at least to get across the desert as quickly as possible.[15]

With *L 59*'s lessons relearned, Eckener had much more solid grounds for establishing Zeppelin routes over North and South America and occasional flights across North Africa and the Middle East, where climates much different than central Europe could be expected.

Just as important as the temperature deviations over the desert and Mediterranean that Bockholt warned about was the understanding of how a large Zeppelin behaved transporting a wide-ranging cargo instead of merely bombs and ordnance. This was especially indispensable for

Eckener's postwar airships, which made most of their profit on intercontinental mail services. Again, Bockholt's detailed report from November 27, in which he described the "nose-heaviness" of a light ship, the "stern-heaviness" felt under dynamic lift, a wandering center of gravity, and the lack of speed and control of the rudder at inclines of 6 degrees or greater,[16] helped guide Zeppelin engineers not only with the conversion of *L 59* for combat, but also in building even-greater airships in the form of the X-class Zeppelins and the enlarged *L 71*. Indeed, the genes of the Zeppelins designed in the final year of the war, which built on the tribulations endured by *L 59* and her crew during the *China-Sache* operation, were still perceptible over a decade later with the oft-traveled *Graf Zeppelin* and *Hindenburg* airships.

Perhaps even more important than the practical advances in airship operations gleaned from the "China matter," however, is the ambition that led to *L 59*'s conception. Although Dr. Zupitza had no role whatsoever in Zeppelin design, he identified a unique purpose for the extant technology that ultimately proved to be groundbreaking. Even today, nearly a century after commercial airships have been abandoned for jet aircraft, there are still inventors and entrepreneurs who are arguing for a resurgence of dirigibles to perform roles similar to that of *L 57* and *L 59*. Besides the luxury aerial tourism market already occupied by Zeppelin NT, they feel airships are best suited to deliver supplies to areas ravaged by natural disasters, where conventional aircraft cannot land, or, at the very least, to serve as a more environmentally friendly means of transporting cargo. Utilizing solar-powered, electric engines, carbon fiber frames, and modern, synthetic, helium or hydrogen-filled gas cells, they would leave a much-smaller carbon footprint both in their construction and operation than their much-faster, economical, but gross-polluting distant jet-aircraft cousins.

While the viability of any such ventures seems doubtful at the time of writing this (in late 2024), it must be remembered that prior to *LZ 120*'s endurance trial over the Baltic, it was assumed that any relief flight to Africa was also doomed to failure. Instead, the *China-Sache* operation was the first step in establishing intercontinental aerial travel and, for a period spanning nearly two decades, the only means of speedily crossing continents and oceans. Although conceived for a very specific purpose in a time of war, *L 59* was the forerunner for the peaceful and innovative golden age of airships in the interwar years.

Epilogue

IN SEPTEMBER 1918, with the dream of airship raids over Britain bringing "perfidious Albion" to her knees all but dead, the remnants of the airship troops stationed at Yambol boarded trains bound for Germany. Since no one back home knew of the incredible feats of *L 59*, there would be no heroes' welcome or any publicized propaganda tour. In fact, the only two men still alive who bore any recognition for participating in the "China matter" were *Obermatrose* Schedelmann and *Funktelegraphie-Maat* Kettner, who, by missing the final mission to Malta, could tell their friends and family back home exactly how they earned their Iron Crosses, 2nd class, during the Great War. Their comrades who perished in *L 59*, however, would not be forgotten. Before departing Yambol, the ground crews left a somber memorial to commemorate the "passing of the crew of *L 59*" and their "last flight on the 7th of April 1918" in the form of a tall grave marker set atop a rectangular foundation, bearing a plaque for the departed crew, and adorned by an Iron Cross.

Unfortunately, that September none of the *Schutztruppen* still fighting it out in Africa were appreciative of the efforts of the *Marine Luftschiff Abteilung*, the RMA, the RKA, or the various other facets of the *China-Sache* operation. Oblivious to the fact that the fatherland was even making attempts at reaching them in late 1917, they spent nearly a year making hit-and-run attacks in Mozambique, requisitioning supplies, and watching their numbers dwindle. Then, on September 28, 1918, Lettow led 172 Germans, 1,260 Askari, and 3,000 porters and various retinue,[1] just a fraction of the colonial force's peak wartime complement, across the Rovuma and back into German East Africa. To Lettow's amazement, he found the country to be "amazing fertile," noting that "the troops were able to get thoroughly fit again."[2] However, the *Schutztruppen*, agonizingly, weren't to remain on their home soil for very long.

Correctly sensing that the enemy was on his scent, Lettow did the unthinkable. He, and what remained of his army, invaded the British Empire—crossing into northern Rhodesia in October. Here, among the scattered British outposts that never expected the Germans and Askari to mount such an offensive, the *Schutztruppe* continued to live off raids, securing foodstuffs, equipment, and even information about the state of the Western Front. The news they heard was unsettling. While some reports told of British attacks being repelled along the Siegfried Line, other, more-fantastic stories spoke of the death of Field Marshal Paul von Hindenburg and a forced peace being impressed on the Germans who still stood their ground in enemy territory. Lettow refused to accept any of it as factual and urged his troops to carry on with the struggle. He wouldn't learn the truth until *after* the armistice had already been signed.

On November 13, a day after a successful four-hour engagement against a company of the King's African Rifles in Kasama and another victorious assault on a weakly defended rubber factory near the Chambezi River, a telegram in the possession of a captured British motorcyclist sent shock waves through Lettow's ranks. It read:

> 12 Nov. 18. To be fwded [*sic*] via M.B. cable and dispatch rider. "Send following to Colonel von Lettow Vorbeck under white flag. The Prime Minister of England has announced that an armistice was signed at 5 hours on Nov. 11th, and that hostilities on all fronts cease at 11 hours on Nov. 11th. I am ordering my troops to cease hostilities forthwith unless attacked, and of course I conclude that you will do the same. Conditions of armistice will be forwarded to you immediately I receive them [*sic*]. Meanwhile I suggest you remain in your present vicinity in order to facilitate communication. —General van Deventer. As message is also being sent to Livingstone, it is important Karwunfor receives this same time as enemy; every effort must be made to get message to him to-day.[3]

Lettow couldn't believe what he was reading. Throughout his and his men's superhuman war of resistance in Africa, he was ignorant of the state of the conflict back in Europe and was thus convinced that when the war ended, "the conclusion of hostilities must have been favorable, or at least not unfavorable to Germany."[4] As it stood, he had to accept the inevitable. The *Schutztruppe* officially surrendered at Abercorn (now Mbala, Zambia) on November 25.

Unbeknown to Lettow or the late Peter Strasser was that by the war's end, the two men realized objectives that could be considered, historically, quite rare. The German airships, unlike the limited coastal bombardments of the High Seas Fleet, successfully and repeatedly brought the war to the British home front, going as far as striking the capital city as early as 1915. Likewise, while the German army occupied swathes of France, Belgium, and the Russian Empire, accessible by foot within the European continent, the *Schutztruppe* was the only ground force to physically occupy British territory during the war. Just as their aims had been similar at the war's outbreak, so were their legendary achievements at its end.

Appendixes

Appendix A

Imperial German Ranks and Their Equivalents in the US and Great Britain

Kaiserliche Marine	US Navy	Royal Navy
Großadmiral	Fleet Admiral	Admiral of the Fleet
Admiral	Admiral	Admiral
Vizeadmiral	Vice Admiral	Vice Admiral
Konteradmiral	Rear Admiral	Rear Admiral
Kommodore	Commodore	Commodore
Kapitän zur See	Captain	Captain
Fregattenkapitän	Commander	Captain
Korvettenkapitän	Lt. Commander	Commander
Kapitänleutnant	Lieutenant	Lt. Commander

Oberleutnant zur See	Lieutenant, Jr. Grade	Jr. Lieutenant
Leutnant zur See	Ensign	Sublieutenant
Oberbootsmann	Chief Petty Officer	Chief Petty Officer
Bootsmannsmaat	Petty Officer 3rd Class	Leading Rate
Steuermann	Petty Officer 1st Class	Senior Petty Officer
Obersteuermannsmaat	Petty Officer 2nd Class	Petty Officer
Funktelegraphie-Maat	Radio Petty Officer	Radio Petty Officer
Funktelegraphie-Gast	Radioman	Signalman
Obermaschinistenmaat	Engineman Petty Officer	Chief Artificer Engineer
Maschinistenmaat	Engineman	Engine Room Artificer
Obermatrose	Seaman 1st Class	Seaman 1st Class
Obersegelmachermaat	Sailmaker	Sailmaker

Heer	**US Army**	**British Army**
Generalmajor	Brigadier General	Brigadier General
Oberstmajor	Lt. Colonel	Lt. Colonel
Hauptmann	Captain	Captain
Feldwebelleutnant	First Sergeant	Sergeant Major
Oberstabarzt	Surgeon (Major)	Staff Surgeon (Major)

Appendix B

Maps

German East Africa and neighboring colonies at the outbreak of war in 1914.
Author's illustration

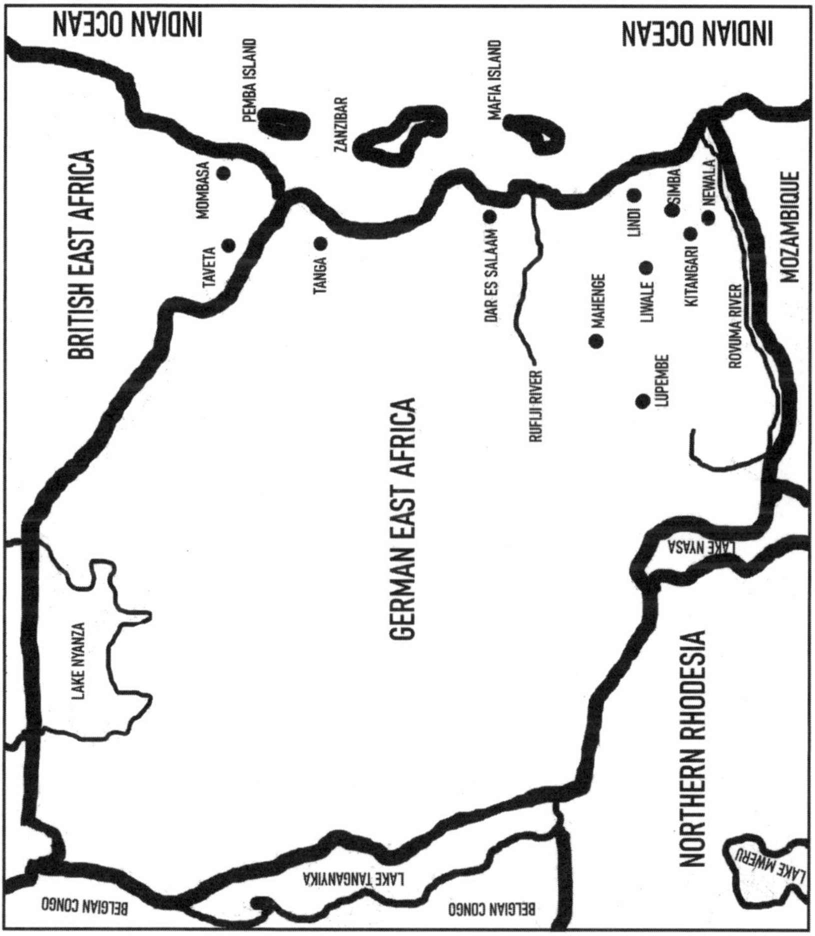

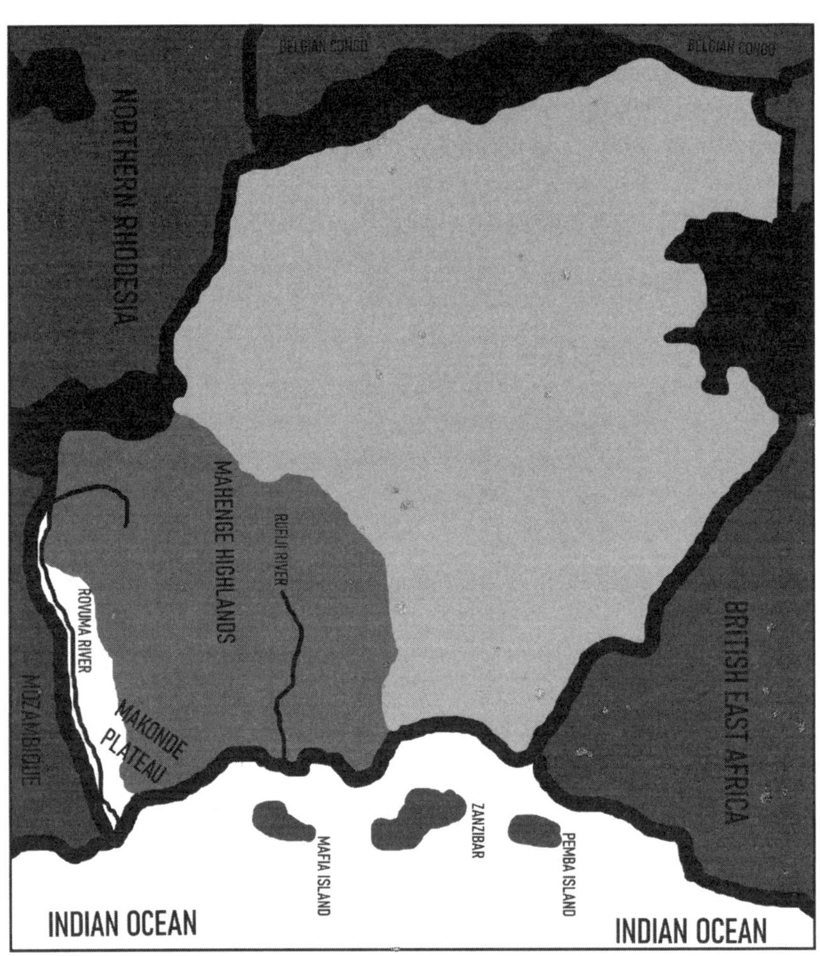

Allied incursions into and occupation of German East Africa prior to the *Schutztruppe* invading Mozambique (Portuguese East Africa). *Author's illustration*

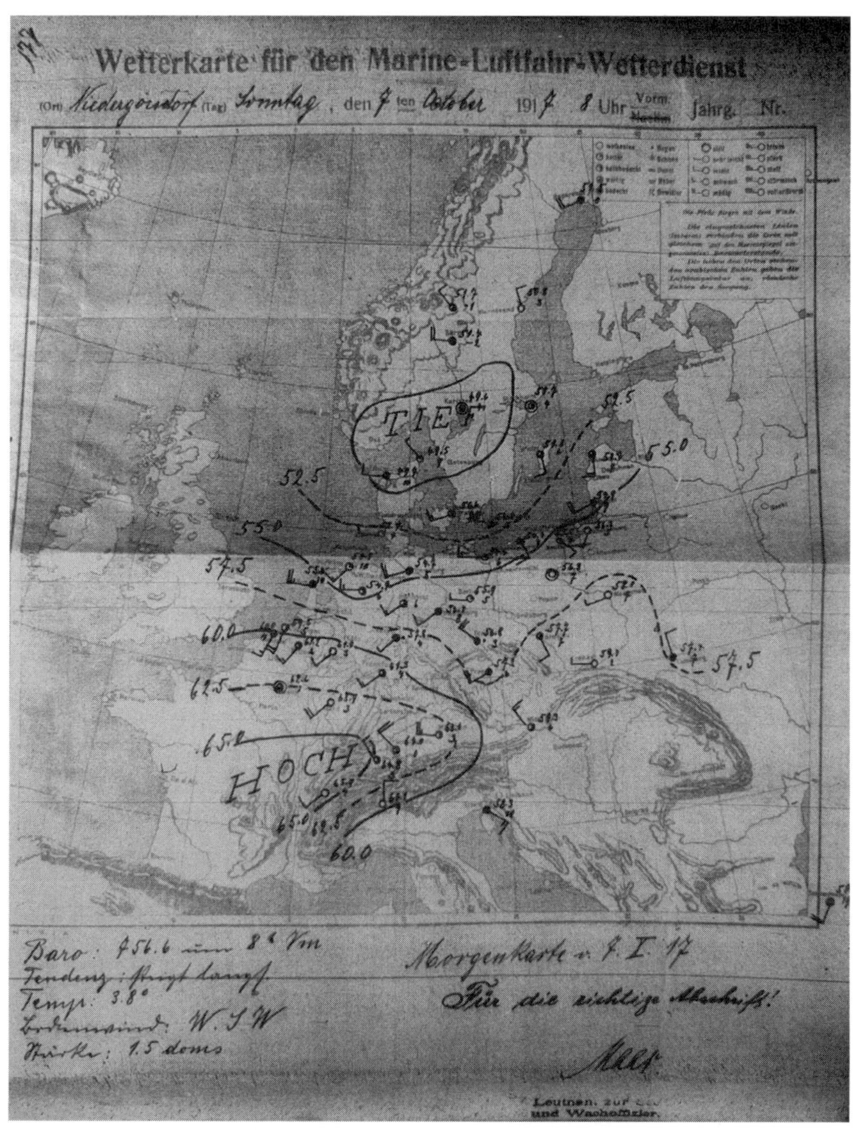

The morning weather chart indicating high (*hoch*) and low (*tief*) pressure systems over Europe prior to *L 57*s disastrous flight on October 7, 1917. Note *Leutnant* zur See Maas's signature on the lower right. *Courtesy of the National Archives and Records Administration, T1022 / 798 / PG 75204*

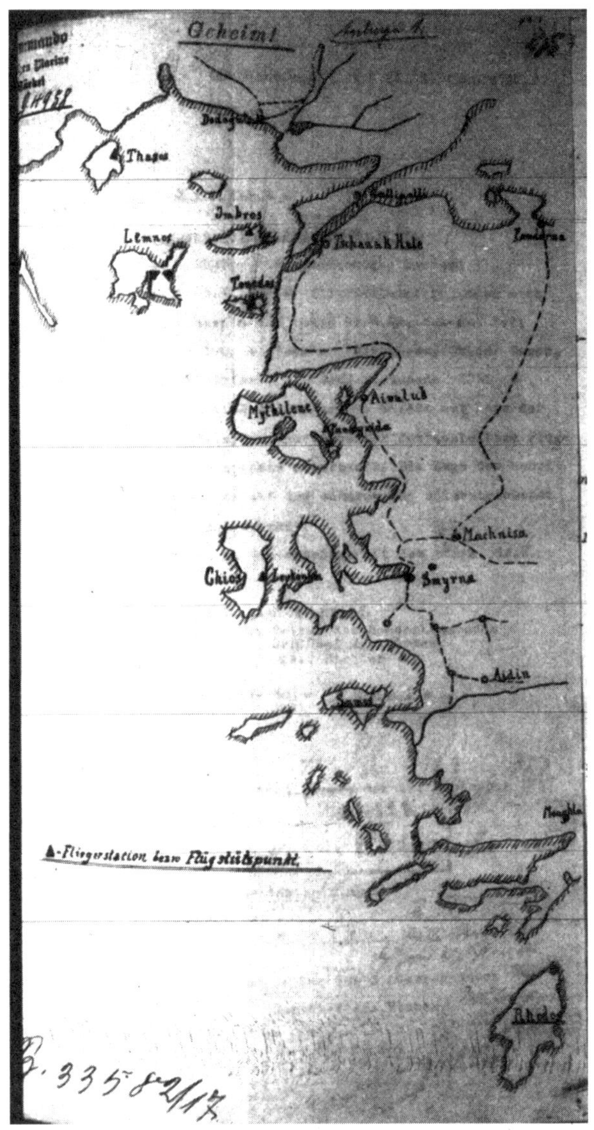

Hand-drawn sketch from the Mediterranean Division indicating Allied airfields and defensive positions in the Greek isles. This was given to Bockholt to aid in plotting *L 59*'s course over Asia Minor.
Courtesy of the National Archives and Records Administration, T1022 / 798 / PG 75204

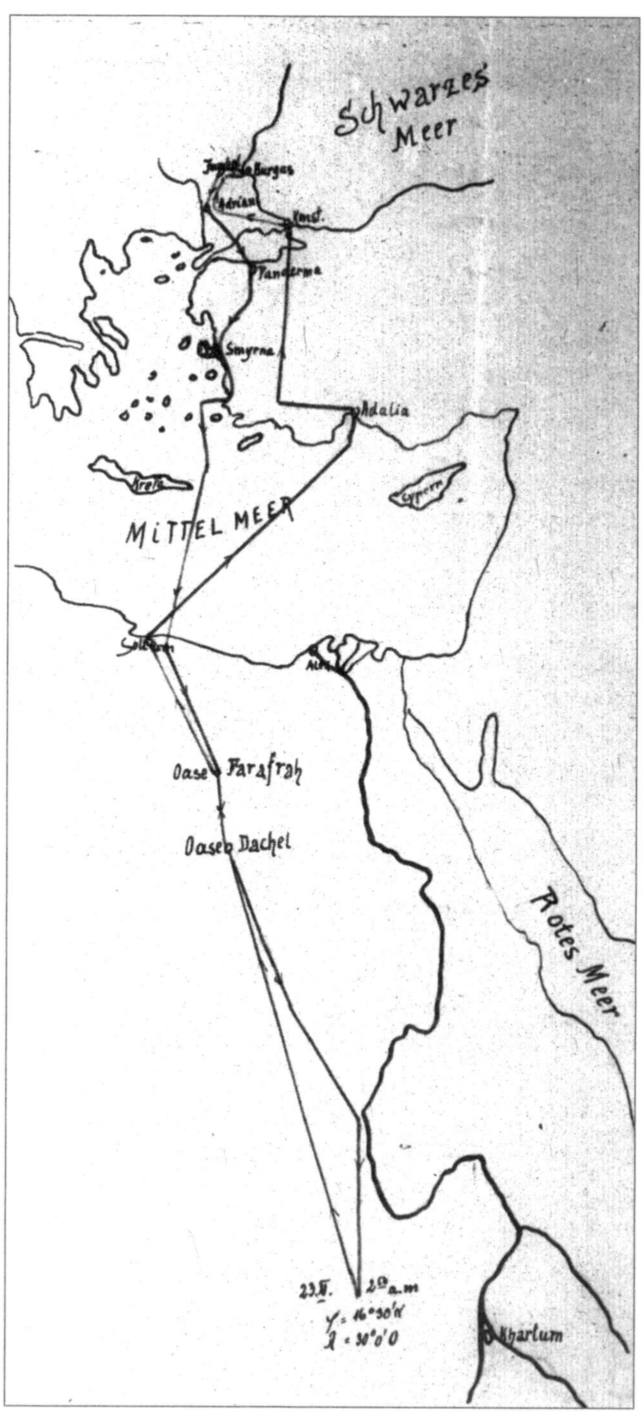

Hand-drawn map depicting *L 59*'s course during the flight to and from Africa (included within *L 59*'s war diary). Schwarzes Meer, Mittelmeer, and Rotes Meer are the Black, Mediterranean, and Red Seas, respectively. Kreta and Cypern are Crete and Cyprus. Jambol is Yambol, Konst. is Constantinople, Adrian. is Adrianople, and Oase obviously means "oasis." *Courtesy of the National Archives and Records Administration, T1022 / 798 / PG 75204*

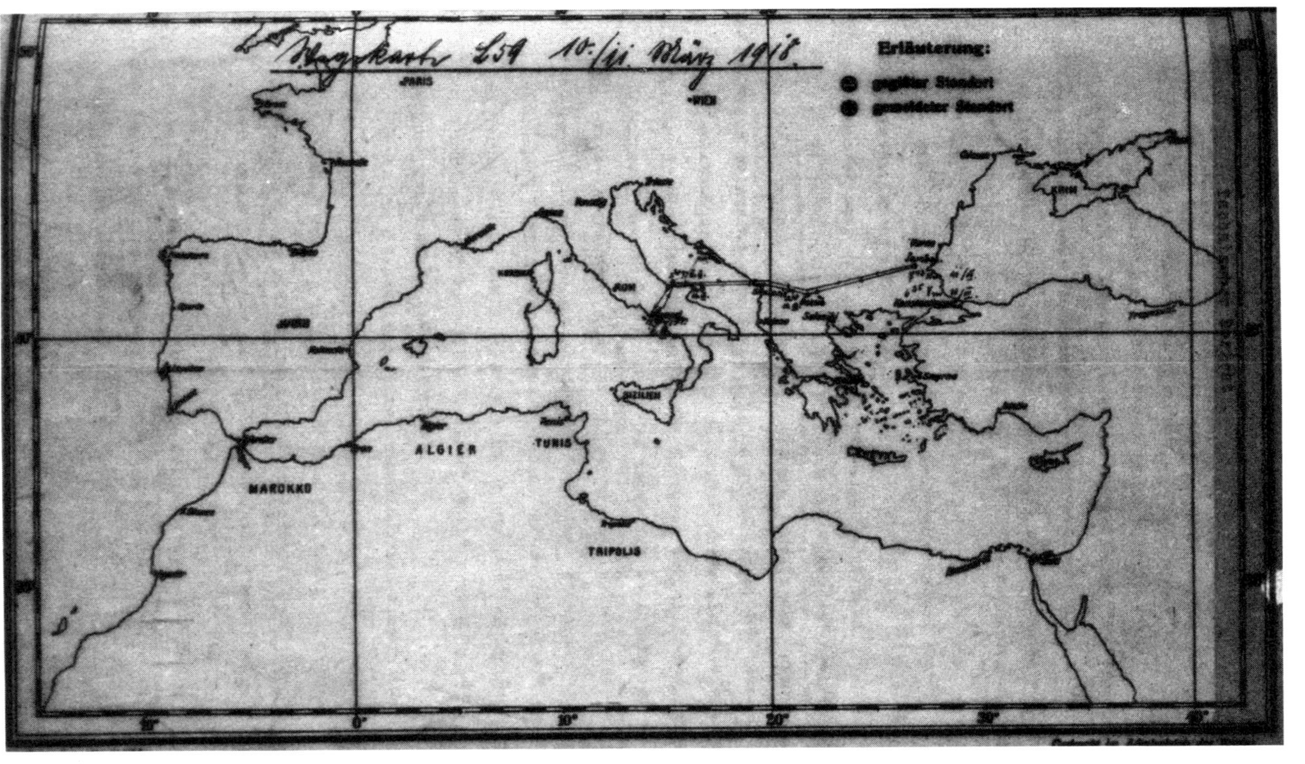

L 59's course for the raid on Naples during the night of March 10–11, 1918 (included within *L 59*'s war diary). *Courtesy of the National Archives and Records Administration, T1022 / 4316 / PG 66139b*

Appendix C

Ballast Charts

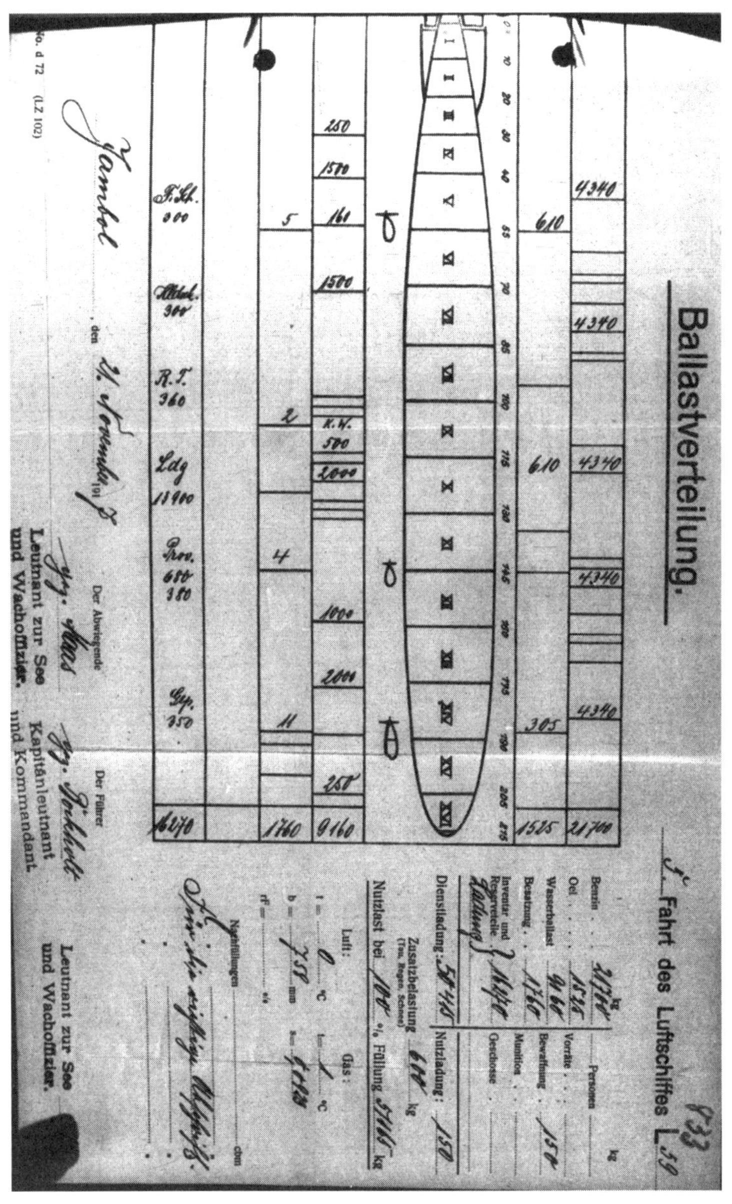

Ballastverteilung.

5. Fahrt des Luftschiffes L 59

	kg		kg
Benzin	21700	Personen	
Oel	1525	Vorräte	
Wasserballast	9160	Bewaffnung	150
Besatzung	1760	Munition	
Inventar und Reserveteile / Ladung	16470	Geschosse	
Dienstladung:	50615	Nutzladung:	150

Zusatzbelastung (Tau, Regen, Schnee) 600 kg

Nutzlast bei 100 % Füllung 51165 kg

Luft: t = 0 °C, b = 758 mm — Gas: t = 1 °C

Nachfüllungen ... cbm

F.T. 300 — R.T. 360 — Ldg 13900 — Prov. 680 380 — Gep. 350 — 16470

Jambol, den 21. November 1917

Der Abwiegende: gez. Maas, Leutnant zur See und Wachoffizier.

Der Führer: gez. Bockholt, Kapitänleutnant und Kommandant.

No. d 72 (LZ 102)

L 59's ballast chart from her "5th flight" on November 21, 1917—the third attempt at reaching German East Africa. Note Bockholt's and Maas's signatures on the bottom, the two additional gas cells, and the position of the gondolas and lateral engine nacelles. *Courtesy of the National Archives and Records Administration, T1022 / 798 / PG 75204*

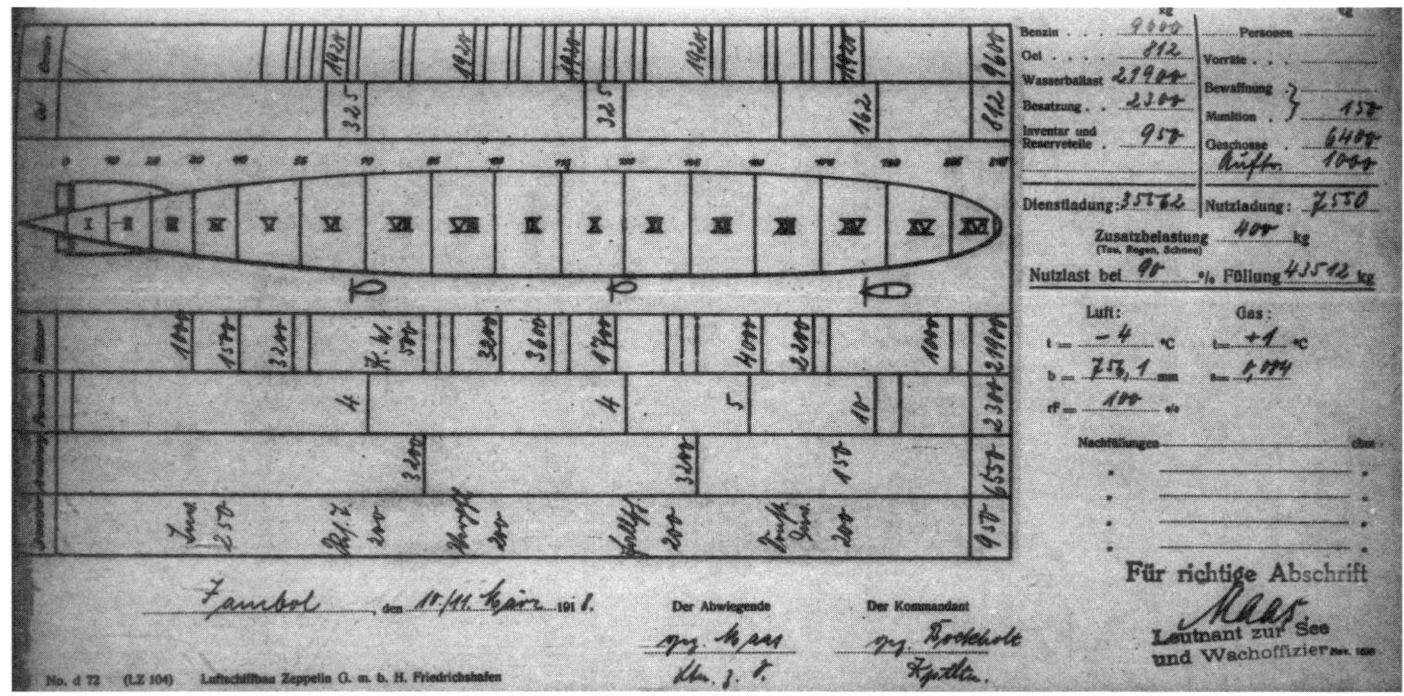

Benzin . . . 9600 kg
Oel 812
Wasserballast 21900
Besatzung . . 2300
Inventar und Reserveteile . 950

Personen
Vorräte
Bewaffnung
Munition 150
Geschosse 6400

Dienstladung: 35562
Nutzladung: 7550
Zusatzbelastung (Tau, Regen, Schnee) 400 kg
Nutzlast bei 98 % Füllung 43512 kg

Luft:
t = -4 °C
b = 756,1 mm
rF = 100 %

Gas:
t = +1 °C
s = 1,074

Nachfüllungen

Für richtige Abschrift
Leutnant zur See und Wachoffizier

Jambol, den 10./11. März 1918.

Der Abwiegende
Der Kommandant

No. d 72 (LZ 104) Luftschiffbau Zeppelin G. m. b. H. Friedrichshafen

L 59's ballast chart from the raid on Naples on March 10–11, 1918. Note that the lateral engine nacelles have been repositioned 15 meters farther aft, to the rear of cell 11, and the rear gondola has been moved 15 m forward. *Courtesy of the National Archives and Records Administration, T1022 / 4316 / PG 66139b*

Appendix D

Casualty List for L 59

1. *Kapitänleutnant* Ludwig Bockholt
2. *Funktelegraphie-Maat* Heinrich Bott
3. *Maschinistenmaat* Peter Bröcker
4. *Obermaschinistenmaat* Friedrich Engelke
5. *Feldwebelleutnant* Emil Grussendorf
6. *Obermatrose* Adolf Fuchs
7. *Obermaschinistenmaat* Bruno Heimann
8. *Maat der Luftschiff-Abteilung* Kurt Hocke
9. *Obermaschinistenmaat* Ferdinand Holland
10. *Leutnant zur See* Heinrich Maas
11. *Obermaschinistenmaat* Hans Marholz
12. *Funktelegraphie-Gast* Wilhelm Müller
13. *Obersignalmaat* Albert Nolte
14. *Obermaschinistenmaat* Heinrich Pabst
15. *Maschinistenmaat* Gustav Proll
16. *Maschinistenmaat* Albert Rieck
17. *Obersignalmaat* Karl Savoye
18. *Obermaschinistenmaat* Berthold Schilling
19. *Obermatrose der Luftschiff-Abteilung* Max Schmieder
20. *Maschinistenmaat* Karl Schmitz
21. *Obersegelmachermaat* Richard Schulz
22. *Steuermann* Emil Wald
23. *Maat der Luftschiff-Abteilung* Bernhardt Wiesemann

Appendix E

List of *L 57*'s and *L 59*'s Wartime Flights

L 57

Flight #1
Date: September 26, 1917
Description: Factory trial flight
Duration: 2 hours, 36 minutes
Maximum altitude (in feet): 6,890

Flight #2
Date: September 27, 1917
Description: Second factory trial flight
Duration: 3 hours, 18 minutes
Maximum altitude (in feet): 13,451

Flight #3
Date: September 28, 1917
Description: Transfer from Friedrichshafen to Jüterbog
Duration: Approximately 8 hours
Maximum altitude (in feet): Unknown

Flight #4
Date: October 7, 1917
Description: Test flight over Jüterbog and loss of airship
Duration: Approximately 4 hours
Maximum altitude (in feet): Unknown

L 59

Flight #1
Date: October 30, 1917
Description: Factory trial flight
Duration: 5 hours, 36 minutes
Maximum altitude (in feet): 12,139

Flight #2
Date: November 3, 1917
Description: Transfer from Staaken to Yambol
Duration: 28 hours, 30 minutes
Maximum altitude (in feet): 5,740

Flight #3
Date: November 13, 1917
Description: Aborted flight to German East Africa
Duration: 2 hours
Maximum altitude (in feet): 1,476

Flight #4
Date: November 16, 1917
Description: Second aborted flight to German East Africa
Duration: 32 hours
Maximum altitude (in feet): 7,874

Flight #5
Date: November 21, 1917
Description: Third and final attempt at reaching German East Africa
Duration: 95 hours
Maximum altitude (in feet): 12,795

Flight #6
Date: December 1, 1917
Description: Minesweeping over the Black Sea
Duration: 9 hours, 5 minutes
Maximum altitude (in feet): 4,593

Flight #7
Date: December 11, 1917
Description: Transfer from Yambol to Ahlhorn (actually landed at Niedergörsdorf [Jüterbog])
Duration: 25 hours, 12 minutes
Maximum altitude (in feet): 9,022

Flight #8
Date: December 21, 1917
Description: Transfer from Niedergörsdorf (Jüterbog) to Friedrichshafen
Duration: 8 hours, 35 minutes
Maximum altitude (in feet): 9,843

Flight #9
Date: February 6, 1918
Description: Factory trial flight after conversion to five-engined bomber
Duration: 1 hour
Maximum altitude (in feet): 2,133

Flight #10
Date: February 7, 1918
Description: Second factory trial flight after conversion
Duration: 1 hour
Maximum altitude (in feet): 2,133

Flight #11
Date: February 9, 1918
Description: Third factory trial flight and altitude test
Duration: 2 hours, 40 minutes
Maximum altitude (in feet): 22,638

Flight #12
Date: February 14, 1918
Description: Aborted transfer from Friedrichshafen to Yambol
Duration: 3 hours, 30 minutes
Maximum altitude (in feet): 4,593

Flight #13
Date: February 20, 1918
Description: Transfer from Friedrichshafen to Yambol
Duration: 24 hours, 25 minutes
Maximum altitude (in feet): 8,202

Flight #14
Date: March 3, 1918
Description: Aborted bombing raid on "southern Italy"
Duration: 35 hours, 42 minutes
Maximum altitude (in feet): 13,615

Flight #15
Date: March 10, 1918
Description: Raid on Naples from Yambol
Duration: 37 hours, 17 minutes
Maximum altitude (in feet): 17,224

Flight #16
Date: March 20, 1918
Description: Raid on Port Said from Yambol
Duration: 48 hours, 40 minutes
Maximum altitude (in feet): 17,913

Flight #17
Date: April 7, 1918
Description: Final raid on Malta that resulted in the loss of *L 59* and her crew
Duration: Unknown
Maximum altitude (in feet): Unknown

Endnotes

Prologue

1. Now Tønder, Denmark, but then part of Germany.

2. *L 23* was a naval designation. Her actual production number was *LZ 66*, with the "LZ" designating "*Luftschiff* Zeppelin" for the manufacturer (other makers were Schütte-Lanz, abbreviation "SL," and Parseval, "P"). The German army airships initially numbered their airships beginning with the maker designation "Z" for Zeppelin and a Roman numeral, such as *Z I.* Later, they utilized numbering identical to the factory, such as *LZ 17*, until June 1915, when 30 was added to the factory production number, meaning that *LZ 42* became *LZ 72.*

3. Senior helmsman's mate.

4. Rolf Marben, ed., *Ritter der Luft: Zeppelinabenteuer im Weltkrieg* (Hamburg, Germany: Verlagsbuchhandlung Broschek, 1931), 124.

5. "Kriegstagebuch des Luftschiffes '*L 23*': 16 April 1917–30 April 1917," April, 23, 1917, 0955, PG 63642, National Archives Microfilm Publication T1022, roll 395.

6. Ibid., 0936.

7. The actual quote is "*Hat man sich nicht ringsum vom Meer umgeben gesehen, so hat man keinen Begriff von Welt und von seinem Verhältnis zur Welt. Als Landschaftszeichner hat mir diese große, simple Linie ganz neue Gedanken gegeben*" ("If one has not seen oneself surrounded by the sea, one has no concept of

the world and of one's relationship to the world. As a landscape artist, this great, simple line gave me completely new ideas"). It appears in Goethe's *Italienische Reise* (*Italian Journey*) (1816).

8. "Kriegstagebuch des Luftschiffes 'L 23': 16 April 1917–30 April 1917," April 23, 1917, 1058, T1022/395/PG 63642.

9. Imperial German Navy.

10. *Hræsvelgr*, which translates to "corpse swallower," was a supernatural being in Norse mythology that took the shape of a giant eagle and was thought to be the source of the winds. Correspondingly, he was attributed to ancient shipwrecks.

11. *Kaleu* is a shortened, more familiar version of *Kapitänleutnant* used by naval crewmen.

12. *Kapitänleutnant* Horst Julius *Freiherr* Treusch von Buttlar-Brandenfels was one of the most successful airship commanders of the Great War. While under the command of *L 6*, he performed a water landing and "sailed" his airship on the Alster River in Hamburg in order to win a drunken bet.

13. A German phrase literally translating to "in an emergency, the devil eats flies." The English equivalent to the phrase is "beggars can't be choosers."

14. Marben, *Ritter der Luft: Zeppelinabenteuer im Weltkrieg*, 130.

15. "Kriegstagebuch des Luftschiffes 'L 23': 16 April 1917–30 April 1917," 23 April, 1733, T1022 / 395 / PG 63642.

16. Marben, *Ritter der Luft: Zeppelinabenteuer im Weltkrieg*, 130.

17. Ibid., 131.

18. Paul Emil von Lettow-Vorbeck, *My Reminisces of East Africa* (London: Hurst and Blackett, 1920), 180.

Chapter 1: The Wind and the Lion

1. *Oberstmajor* is the equivalent to a lieutenant colonel. This was Lettow's rank at the outset of the war; in October 1917 he was promoted to *Generalmajor*.

2. Count Zeppelin was serving in the engineering corps of the Württemberg army during this time but was given leave to act as an observer with the Army of the Potomac. While in Washington, DC, he had heard of balloons being utilized for military purposes and was interested in taking a flight with Thaddeus S. C. Lowe, inventor and chief aeronaut of the Union Army Balloon Corps, only to be denied since Lowe was not allowed to take any passengers. It was sheer chance that Zeppelin happened across the German-born balloonist John Steiner while traveling through Minnesota. Since Steiner had quit the Balloon Corps in 1862, his balloon was under no military restrictions, and Zeppelin finally got his opportunity to board a balloon, ascending to an altitude of 200–300 meters.

3. DELAG is an acronym for Deutsche Luftschiffahrts-Aktiengesellschaft, or German Airship Travel Corporation. This was a commercial venture between

Luftschiffbau Zeppelin and the Hamburg-America line and operated local pleasure flights within Germany in the prewar years. Ernst Lehmann was an early pilot for DELAG and naval reserve lieutenant, captaining the Sachsen and subsequently becoming a successful army airship commander during the war, when the Sachsen was requisitioned as *LZ 17*. He would continue serving with the army, not the navy, for the duration of the war, commanding numerous airships, including *LZ 120*, which set an endurance record of 101 hours in flight. Both Lehmann and DELAG would continue after the war, with Lehmann serving as a commanding officer on board the *Graf Zeppelin* and the *Hindenburg* (he was on board the *Hindenburg*'s final flight as an observer and died from severe burns a day after the crash).

4. *Riesenflugzeuge*, literally translating to "giant aircraft," were multiengine, strategic bombers that dwarfed the *Grossflugzeuge* (large aircraft) such as the Gotha G.V. The R.VI had four Mercedes D.IVa engines and a wingspan of just over 138 feet, whereas the Gotha G.V had two of the same Mercedes engines and a wingspan of nearly 78 feet. Likewise, the R.VI had a much-larger payload of up to 4,409 lbs. for bombs, or over five times the Gotha's payload of 840 lbs.

5. G. W. Haddow and Peter M. Grosz, *The German Giants: The German R-Planes, 1914–1918* (New York: Funk & Wagnalls, 1962), 252.

6. Aerial bombs had not yet been developed by August 1914, and Zeppelin crews had to rely on modified artillery shells for the purpose.

7. Ernst Lehmann, *Zeppelin: The Story of Lighter-Than-Air Craft* (Stroud, UK: Fonthill Media, 2015), 53.

8. Unlike the navy, at the outbreak of war the army didn't have any centralized command of their various airplane, airship, and balloon units. Each battalion and squadron fell under the command of the local army group. It wasn't until 1916 that the German Empire's army "flying troops" were consolidated into the *Luftstreitkräfte* (Air Force) under General Ernst von Hoeppner, a cavalry officer.

9. Lehmann, *Zeppelin: The Story of Lighter-Than-Air Craft*, 55.

10. *LZ 17* was the only army airship still operating on the Western Front, since the others had been transferred east.

11. Douglas Robinson, *The Zeppelin in Combat: A History of the German Naval Airship Division, 1912–1918* (Atglen, PA: Schiffer Military History, 1994), 80.

12. Reinhard Scheer, *Germany's High Seas Fleet in the World War* (New York: Peter Smith, 1934), 210.

13. Treusch von Buttlar-Brandenfels, *Zeppelins over England*, trans. Huntley Patterson (New York: Harcourt, Brace, 1932), 5–6.

14. *L 6* also took part in the raid with Strasser on board but was forced to turn around near the Dutch coast when one of her engine's crankshafts broke.

15. E. B. Ashmore, *Air Defence* (London: Longman's, Green, 1929), 158.

16. Schütte-Lanz was another rigid airship manufacturer and competitor to the Zeppelin works. While superficially similar to Zeppelins, Schütte-Lanz airships

originally employed a plywood frame instead of Duralumin, though they eventually switched to tubular aluminum frames in late 1918. Due to concerns over material degradation due to humidity, only eight wooden-framed Schütte-Lanz airships were commissioned by the navy.

17. *L 5* was shot down over Latvia by Russian antiaircraft fire, and *L 8* was shot down over Belgium. *L 12* was also lost in 1915, but not directly through combat. Although she was heavily damaged on a raid over England, she landed in the North Sea near German-occupied Ostend and was towed into port to be salvaged, where a fire later destroyed her.

18. H. A. Jones, *The War in the Air: Being the Story of the Part Played in the Great War by the Royal Air Force*, vol. 3 (Oxford: Clarendon, 1931), 158.

19. Alfred Rawlinson, *The Defence of London, 1915–1918* (London: Andrew Melrose, 1923), 14.

20. N. W. Routledge, *History of the Royal Regiment of Artillery: Anti-Aircraft Artillery, 1914–1955* (London: Brassey's, 1994), 13.

21. Jones, *The War in the Air*, 3:158.

22. The two utilized during the war were Brock and Pomeroy bullets, named after their respective inventors, Commander Frank Brock and John Pomeroy.

23. These are Zeppelin production numbers. *LZ 62* was actually *L 30*, using the naval designation, and *LZ 90* was the army airship *LZ 120* (again, adding a value of "30" to the actual production number).

24. Robinson, *The Zeppelin in Combat*, 385.

25. Pitt Klein, *Achtung! Bomben Fallen!* (Leipzig: Verlag von K. F. Koehler, 1934), 105.

26. Ibid., 106.

27. "Kriegstagebuch des Luftschiffes '*L 23*': 16 September 1916–30 September 1916, 24 September, 0220, T1022 / 395 / PG 63642.

28. "Kriegstagebuch des Luftschiffes '*L 23*': 16 September 1916–30 September 1916, 25–26 September, 1420–0315, T1022 / 395 / PG 63642.

29. Robinson, *The Zeppelin in Combat*, 211.

30. Klein, *Achtung! Bomben Fallen!*, 102.

31. Ibid., 135.

32. Robinson, *The Zeppelin in Combat*, 223.

33. Ibid., 187.

34. Ibid.

35. A total of 3,860 pounds were shed from *LZ 62 / L 30*, and as much as 4,890 lbs. was cut from *LZ 86 / L 39*, by means of shortening the control car, eliminating crew quarters, removing machine guns, reducing onboard fuel, halving the bomb-load, lightening structural girders, and replacing the rear two-engine gondola for the three-engined type. Not only was the 16,500-foot altitude achievable with this

loss of weight, it was surpassed, with *L 40* reaching 17,100 feet and *L 39* going as high as 17,700 feet on their trial flights.

36. Robinson, *The Zeppelin in Combat*, 228.

37. It was actually the V class (commissioned in August 1917 with *LZ 100 / L 53*) that set a Zeppelin altitude record of 24,900 feet (7,600 meters); however, these airships were lightened to such an extent that they were too fragile for anything other than high-altitude reconnaissance missions over the North Sea, to say nothing of the effects of such a height on the crew.

38. Although crews were issued heavy, fur-lined jackets to reduce exposure, these were still completely inadequate at such high altitudes. Even with crewmen wearing these jackets, layering their uniforms, and even going as far as stuffing newspapers in their jackets and pants, nothing could be done to alleviate the effects of the cold temperatures on the body.

39. *L 42* had Strasser on board and, contributing to his perception as a "Jonah," had to turn around off the Belgian coast when one engine failed and the other three couldn't compete with the southerly gale.

40. Robinson, *The Zeppelin in Combat*, 240.

41. "Gefechtsbericht L.43 über die Angriffsfahrt am 23–24 Mai 1917," May 26, 1917, T1022 / 4315 / PG 66198.

42. "Bericht des Kommandos 'L 42' über die Fernunternehmung am 23–24 Mai 1917," May 26, 1917, T1022 / 4315 / PG 66198.

43. "Gefechtsbericht zu der Angriffsfahrt am 23–24 Mai 1917, L.45," May 26, 1917, T1022 / 4315 / PG 66198.

44. Walter Gladisch, ed., *Der Krieg zur See 1914–1918: Der Krieg in der Nordsee*, vol. VI (Berlin: Verlag von E. S. Mittler & Sohn, 1937), 290.

45. Lehmann, Zeppelin*: The Story of Lighter-Than-Air Craft*, 174.

46. Douglas Botting, *Dr. Eckener's Dream Machine: The Great Zeppelin and the Dawn of Air Travel* (New York: Henry Holt, 2001), 81.

47. Gladisch, *Der Krieg zur See 1914–1918: Der Krieg in der Nordsee*, VI:290.

48. Ibid.

49. Buttlar-Brandenfels, *Zeppelins over England*, 308.

50. Jones, *The War in the Air: Being the Story of the Part Played in the Great War by the Royal Air Force*, 3:243–44.

51. These were actual terms used by Strasser to describe the role of the airship service. Eric Lawson and Jane Lawson, *The First Air Campaign: August 1914–November 1918* (Conshohocken, PA: Combined Books, 1996), 79.

52. Lettow-Vorbeck, *My Reminisces of East Africa*, 3.

53. The Askari were Native troops in the service of various colonial forces. The word is Swahili for "soldier." Military-strength figures are quoted from Ludwig Boell, *Die Operationen in Ostafrika* (Hamburg, Germany: Walter Dachert, 1951), 28.

54. Charles Hordern, ed., *Military Operations: East Africa Volume I, August 1914–September 1916* (London: His Majesty's Stationery Office, 1941), 575.

55. Boell, *Die Operationen in Ostafrika*, 28–29.

56. Ibid., 31–32.

57. Heinrich Schnee, *Die Deutschen Kolonien vor, in und nach dem Weltkrieg* (Leipzig: Queller & Meyer, 1939), 41–42.

58. Brian Loveman, "General Act of the Berlin Conference on West Africa, February 26, 1885," https://loveman.sdsu.edu/docs/1885GeneralActBerlinConference.pdf.

59. Schnee, *Die Deutschen Kolonien vor, in und nach dem Weltkrieg*, 36.

60. Ibid.

61. William Roger Louis, *Great Britain and Germany's Lost Colonies: 1914–1919* (Oxford: Clarendon, 1967), 37.

62. Ibid.

63. Schnee, *Die Deutschen Kolonien vor, in und nach dem Weltkrieg*, 41.

64. Lettow-Vorbeck, *My Reminisces of East Africa*, 21.

65. Edward Paice, *World War I: The African Front* (New York: Pegasus Books, 2008), 21.

66. Boell, *Die Operationen in Ostafrika*, 73.

67. Ibid., 51.

68. Karl Ernst Göring, *Meine Kriegserlebnisse in Deutsch-Ostafrika 1914–1920* (typescript of an unknown binding, 1927), 1.

69. The *Königsberg* avoided being sunk in Dar es Salaam's harbor by leaving port on July 31; however, her commerce-raiding career in the western Indian Ocean was cut short by a lack of coal and engines badly in need of repair. She retreated into the Rufiji delta in September 1914 to conduct the required overhauls but was eventually spotted and trapped by British forces. After repelling numerous attacks and retreating farther into the Rufiji, she was eventually scuttled in 1915, and her crew and salvaged guns then joined up with the *Schutztruppe*. See Max Looff, *Tufani: Sturm über Deutsch-Ostafrika* (Berlin: Bernard & Graefe, 1936), 62–117.

70. Hordern, *Military Operations: East Africa Volume I, August 1914–September 1916*, 101.

71. Boell, *Die Operationen in Ostafrika*, 134.

72. Hew Strachan, *The First World War*, vol. 1, *To Arms* (Oxford: Oxford University Press, 2003), 602.

73. Ibid., 600.

74. Boell, *Die Operationen in Ostafrika*, 91.

75. Alfred Schöffler, *Matata: A Memoir of a German Cavalryman in German East Africa Before, During, and After World War I* (Middletown, DE: Amazon Publishing Services, 2020), 343.

76. "Abschrift zu B.X.115 Gg. Reichs-Kolonialamt. Kommando der *Schutztruppe*n. Nr.M.2013/17. A.1.O.A," September 10, 1917, T1022 / 798 / PG 75204

77. Lettow-Vorbeck, *My Reminisces of East Africa,* 193.

78. Paice, *World War I: The African Front*, 304.

79. "Abschrift zu B.X.115 Gg. Reichs-Kolonialamt: Kommando der *Schutztruppe*n. Nr.M.2013/17. A.1.O.A," September 10, 1917, T1022 / 798 / PG 75204.

80. This figure excludes the number of Native porters, who died at exponentially higher rates

81. "Abschrift zu B.X.115 Gg. Reichs-Kolonialamt: Kommando der *Schutztruppe*n. Nr.M.2013/17. A.1.O.A," September 10, 1917, T1022 / 798 / PG 75204.

Chapter 2: Feasible and Promising

1. Werner von Langsdorff, *Deutsche Flagge über Sand und Palmen, 53 deutsche Kolonialkrieger Erzählen* (Gütersloh, Germany: Verlag C. Bertelsmann, 1935), 331.

2. *Wilnaer Zeitung* 136 (May 20, 1917): 1–2.

3. *Wilnaer Zeitung* 141 (May 25, 1917): 3.

4. *Wilnaer Zeitung* 166 (June 20, 1917): 3.

5. Maximilian Zupitza. "Die Hilfsexpedition für die deutsch-ostafrikanische *Schutztruppe* auf dem Luftwege." *Deutsche Kolonialzeitung* 36 (1919): 29.

6. Kurt Assmann, ed., *Der Krieg zur See 1914–1918: Die Kämpfe der Kaiserlichen Marine in den Deutschen Kolonien* (Berlin: Verlag von E. S. Mittler & Sohn, 1935), 209.

7. "Abschrift zu B.X.115 Gg. Reichs-Kolonialamt: Kommando der *Schutztruppe*n. Nr.M.2013/17. A.1.O.A," September 10, 1917, T1022 / 798 / PG 75204.

8. The *Landsturm* were essentially militia or reservist forces comprising older-aged men and relegated to duties "behind the lines."

9. Alastair Reid, ed., *Marine-Luftschiffer-Kameradschaft Newsletters, 1980–1997* (Durham, NC: Lulu, 2021), 56.

10. Langsdorff, *Deutsche Flagge über Sand und Palmen*, 331.

11. Assmann, *Der Krieg zur See 1914–1918: Die Kämpfe der Kaiserlichen Marine in den Deutschen Kolonien*, 149.

12. Ibid., 150.

13. E. Keble Chatterton, *The Königsberg Adventure* (London: Hurst and Blackett, 1932), 143.

14. Ibid., 144.

15. Lettow-Vorbeck, *My Reminisces of East Africa,* 67.

16. Schöffler, *Matata*, 340–41.

17. Sörensen actually held the rank of *Obermatrose der Reserve* (seaman 1st class)—a junior NCO. He was promoted to *Leutnant* solely for the duration of the operation.

18. Assmann, *Der Krieg zur See 1914–1918: Die Kämpfe der Kaiserlichen Marine in den Deutschen Kolonien*, 199.

19. Ibid.

20. Due to the fact that the *Marie* was not attempting to rendezvous with another vessel while at sea, Sörensen was able to maintain radio silence and thus avoid the attention of the Allied wireless stations on the route.

21. Assmann, *Der Krieg zur See 1914–1918: Die Kämpfe der Kaiserlichen Marine in den Deutschen Kolonien*, 203.

22. Wilhelm Solf, secretary of state of the Reich Colonial Office to Henning von Holtzendorff, chief of the Admiralty staff of the Navy, April 21, 1917. Assmann, *Der Krieg zur See 1914–1918: Die Kämpfe der Kaiserlichen Marine in den Deutschen Kolonien*, 206.

23. Dominic Etzold, *Reaping the Whirlwind: The U-boat War off North America During World War I* (Atglen, PA: Schiffer Military History, 2023), 33–34.

24. Wilhelm Solf, secretary of state of the Reich Colonial Office to Henning von Holtzendorff, chief of the Admiralty staff of the Navy, April 21, 1917. Assmann, *Der Krieg zur See 1914–1918: Die Kämpfe der Kaiserlichen Marine in den Deutschen Kolonien*, 206.

25. Lettow-Vorbeck, *My Reminisces of East Africa*, 68.

26. General Ludendorff, chief of the General Staff of the Army, to Wilhelm Solf, secretary of state of the Reich Colonial Office, April 28, 1917. Assmann, *Der Krieg zur See 1914–1918: Die Kämpfe der Kaiserlichen Marine in den Deutschen Kolonien*, 207.

27. Admiral von Holtzendorff, chief of the Admiralty staff, to Wilhelm Solf, secretary of state of the Reich Colonial Office, April 29, 1917. Assmann, *Der Krieg zur See 1914–1918: Die Kämpfe der Kaiserlichen Marine in den Deutschen Kolonien*, 207.

28. Reid, *Marine-Luftschiffer-Kameradschaft Newsletters, 1980–1997*, 368.

29.Lehmann, Zeppelin*: The Story of Lighter-Than-Air Craft*, 174–75.

30. Robert S. Pohl, *101 Hours in a Zeppelin: Ernst August Lehmann and the Dream of Transatlantic Flight, 1917* (Atglen, PA: Schiffer Military History, 2023), 15.

31. Ibid., 16.

32. Lehmann, *Zeppelin: The Story of Lighter-Than-Air Craft*, 175.

33. Ibid., 176.

34. The radio compass operating by receiving signals from a land-based station that set bearings within an onboard compass on the airship. This eliminated the need for airship commanders to constantly report their position or for stations to try to triangulate their location, subsequently giving away their position to the enemy. Officially, Professor Robert Wichard Pohl was taken on the endurance flight to test this experimental system, but as his grandson Robert S. Pohl noted in his work about *LZ 120*'s flight, his presence was simply "as opportunity to spend some time with an old friend." That friend was the airship's commander, Ernst Lehmann.

35. Robinson, *The Zeppelin in Combat*, 276.

36. Lehmann, Zeppelin*: The Story of Lighter-Than-Air Craft*, 177.

37. "Abschrift zu B.X.115 Gg. Reichs-Kolonialamt: Kommando der *Schutztruppe*n. Nr.M.2013/17. A.1.O.A," September 10, 1917, T1022 / 798 / PG 75204.

38. Ibid.

39. Wolfgang Meighörner-Schardt, *Wegbereiter des Weltluftverkehrs wider Willen: Die Geschichte des* Zeppelin-*Luftschifftyps "W"* (Friedrichshafen, Germany: Zeppelin Museum, 1992), 23; and Johannes Göbel and Walter Förster, *Afrika zu unsern Füßen* (Leipzig: Verlag von K. F. Koehler, 1925), 49.

40. "Abschrift zu B.X.115 Gg. Reichs-Kolonialamt: Kommando der *Schutztruppe*n. Nr.M.2013/17. A.1.O.A," September 10, 1917, T1022 / 798 / PG 75204.

41. Reid, *Marine-Luftschiffer-Kameradschaft Newsletters, 1980–1997*, 368.

42. Ibid., 369.

43. "Abschrift: Meteorologisches Gutachten zur Chinasache," T1022 / 798 / PG 75204.

44. "Abschrift: Gutachten des F.d.L. zur Unternehmung Chinasache," September 16, 1917, T1022 / 798 / PG 75204.

45. *Denkschrift zu dem Plane der Entsendung eines Luftschiffes vom Jamboli (Bulgarien) aus nach Deutsch-Ostafrika zur Hilfsleistung für die Schutztruppe*, September 19, 1917, T1022 / 798 / PG 75204.

46. "Chief of the Admiralty to Kaiser Wilhelm II, Operational Matters, China-Sache," October 1, 1917, T1022 / 798 / PG 75204.

47. Ibid.

48. Göbel and Förster, *Afrika zu unsern Füßen*, 51.

49. Meighörner-Schardt, *Wegbereiter des Weltluftverkehrs wider Willen: Die Geschichte des Zeppelin-Luftschifftyps "W,"* 27–28.

Chapter 3: The China Matter

1. Buttlar-Brandenfels, *Zeppelins over England*, 228.

2. Ibid.

3. Ibid., 229.

4. Ibid., 230.

5. Horst Julius Ludwig Otto Treusch von Buttlar-Brandenfels married Anna Agnes Wilhelmine Ilse Böhm on February 12, 1916. According to German customs of the period, you were given multiple first names and a "call name," which was usually the last given name before the surname. As such, Anna Agnes Wilhelmine Ilse was just known as "Ilse" and Horst Julius Ludwig Otto Treusch was called "Treusch." In my own, simpler, much less noble ancestral line, my great-great-grandfather was named Julius Hugo Etzold but was known only as Hugo.

6. This is a German adage that translates to "Where there is no temptation, there is no glory."

7. Buttlar-Brandenfels, *Zeppelins over England*, 230–31.

8. Stumpf recorded the first instance of these transfers occurring as early as September 7, 1914, writing, "Deep disappointment mingled with boredom is rampant. The best and most intelligent of our officers have been transferred to cruisers, torpedo boats, and submarines. They are urgently needed there." Then, on March 29, 1915, he noted that every time volunteers are sought for the submarines, or even the naval infantry in *Marinekorps Flandern*, all stepped forward. Richard Stumpf and Daniel Horn, eds., *The Private War of Seaman Stumpf* (London: Leslie Frewin, 1969), 75, 83.

9. Ibid., 292–93.

10. *L 23* was originally commanded by *Kapitänleutnant* Otto von Schubert (April 16–August 9, 1916), *Kapitänleutnant* Wilhelm Ganzel (August 9–December 15, 1916), and *Kapitänleutnant* Franz Stabbert, then was repatriated from a six-month internment in Norway after crashing *L 20* on May 3, 1916 (December 20, 1916–January 23, 1917).

11. Robert Gaudi, *African Kaiser: General Paul von Lettow-Vorbeck and the Great War in Africa, 1914–1918* (New York: Dutton Caliber, 2017), 361.

12. Ibid., 362.

13. Ibid.

14. Rather humorously, Bockholt's name is frequently misspelled as "Bockholdt" in various archival correspondence. While actual evidence that goes against Gaudi's assertions will be provided within this chapter and subsequent chapters, this simple and frequent spelling error also goes against the idea of Bockholt somehow having friends in high places.

15. Even in the 1930s, when Zeppelins had since crossed oceans and continents, Ernst Lehmann lamented not being chosen for the China-Sache mission. In his memoir, he claimed, "Even today I envy Bockholt and every one of his twenty-one men the rich experience of this flight over three continents, a flight which exceeds in audacity everything that much larger airships, with much stronger engines, have since then accomplished." Lehmann, *Zeppelin: The Story of Lighter-Than-Air Craft*, 185.

16. Buttlar-Brandenfels, *Zeppelins over England*, 235.

17. Göbel and Förster, *Afrika zu unsern Füßen*, 51.

18. Robinson, *The Zeppelin in Combat*, 285.

19. Like Buttlar-Brandenfels's crew, Bockholt's crew too unanimously volunteered for the mission. There was, however, one critical crew member missing—*Obersteuermannsmaat* Ernst Fegert, the leader of *L 23*'s boarding party. Although he took part in *L 57*'s first flight to Jüterbog, his wife of six weeks died before *L 57* made its flight to Yambol, and he was instead replaced by Steuermann Emil Wald.

20. "Brieftelegramm an den Chef des Admiralstabes der Marine," September 19, 1917, T1022 / 798 / PG 75204.

21. Göbel and Förster, *Afrika zu unsern Füßen*, 12.

22, Ibid., 4.

23. Ibid., 18.

24. Ibid., 22.

25. "Strasser to the state secretary of the Reichsmarineamt Marine Luftschiffs Abteilung, Berlin," September 21, 1917, T1022 / 798 / PG 75204.

26. Jones, *The War in the Air*, 3:61.

27. Lettow-Vorbeck, *My Reminisces of East Africa*, 143.

28. "Memo," September 26, 1917, T1022 / 798 / PG 75204.

29. Göbel and Förster, *Afrika zu unsern Füßen*, 51.

30. "Telegram copy," September 25,1917, T1022 / 798 / PG 75204.

31. Yambol had only a single airship hangar. This originally housed the Schütte-Lanz *SL X,* and when that was lost on a mission to Sevastopol, the Zeppelin *LZ 101*. The base was used primarily for reconnaissance missions over the Black Sea and for bombing missions over Greece, Romania, and the Russian Empire.

32. "Abschrift zu D 9180 VI," September 29, 1917, T1022 / 798 / PG 75204.

33. "RMA to Kaiser Wilhelm II," October 1, 1917, T1022 / 798 / PG 75204.

34. Ibid.

35. "*Kapitänleutnant* Mangelsdorff, leader of the Marine Special Command in Yambol, to FdL Strasser," October 24, 1917, T1022 / 798 / PG 75204.

36. "*Reichskolonialamt*, Command of the *Schutztruppe* to Reichsmarineamt," October 2, 1917, T1022 / 798 / PG 75204.

37. "*Reichskolonialamt*, Command of the *Schutztruppe* to Reichsmarineamt," October 6, 1917, T1022 / 798 / PG 75204.

38. "Abschrift: Anlage zum Bericht einer Luftschiffahrt Jambol-Mahenge," October 21, 1917, T1022 / 798 / PG 75204. The specifics regarding the ammunition supplies, rifles, machine guns, and medical equipment were taken from Meighörner-Schardt, *Wegbereiter des Weltluftverkehrs wider Willen: Die Geschichte des* Zeppelin-*Luftschifftyps "W,"* 23.

39. "Abschrift: Telegramm für Gouverneur Ostafrika," October 6, 1917, T1022 / 798 / PG 75204.

40. Paice, *World War I: The African Front*, 350.

41. Room 40 was the World War I precursor to World War II's Bletchley Park. It was, quite literally, room number 40 in the Admiralty's Old Building in Whitehall (London) and was a secret division within British naval intelligence responsible for decoding German wireless signals. While most of their work involved deciphering signals from the High Seas Fleet and the U-boat flotillas, they also intercepted Zeppelin transmissions.

Chapter 4: Disaster over Jüterbog

1. With *L 57* being lengthened by 30 meters, there was a greater surface area and thus more resistance from the air. Even with the addition of another Maybach engine, it was expected that maneuverability and dynamic lift would be reduced.

2. Meighörner-Schardt, *Wegbereiter des Weltluftverkehrs wider Willen: Die Geschichte des Zeppelin-Luftschifftyps "W,"* 21.

3. Ibid., 21.

4. Ibid.

5. Eckener took over the Zeppelin factory in the postwar years and remained the strongest advocate for airship travel. He pushed for the construction of LZ 126 to be used as war reparations under the Treaty of Versailles and personally captained the airship on its voyage to Lakehurst, New Jersey, where it was awarded to the US Navy as USS *Los Angeles* (ZR-3). He also piloted the *Graf Zeppelin* for most of its flight when it circumnavigated the globe.

6. Testimony of Ludwig Bockholt, "Bericht über den Totalverlust des Luftschiffes L.57," October 8, 1917, T1022 / 798 / PG 75204.

7. Testimony of Hugo Eckener, "Bericht über den Totalverlust des Luftschiffes L.57," October 9, 1917, T1022 / 798 / PG 75204.

8. Airship hangars were traditionally known as sheds in English speaking countries in the early twentieth century. The Germans used the word *Halle*, which literally translates to "hall" and is, perhaps, a more fitting word. I've used the word "hangar" predominantly in this work since that is a term more familiar to modern American readers.

9. Testimony of Ludwig Bockholt, "Bericht über den Totalverlust des Luftschiffes L.57," October 9, 1917, T1022 / 798 / PG 75204.

10. Ibid.

11. For brevity's sake, I've utilized the shortened, familiar forms of the technical ranks more commonly used by the *Kriegsmarine* during World War II. The official rank of *Funkmaat* in the *Kaiserliche Marine* was *Funktelegraphie-Maat*. Likewise, *Funker* was formally *Funktelegraphie-Gast*.

12. Testimony of Ludwig Bockholt, "Bericht über den Totalverlust des Luftschiffes L.57," October 8, 1917, T1022 / 798 / PG 75204.

13. Ibid.

14. Testimony of Emil Grussendorf, "Bericht über den Totalverlust des Luftschiffes L.57," October 9, 1917, T1022 / 798 / PG 75204.

15. Testimony of Ludwig Bockholt, "Bericht über den Totalverlust des Luftschiffes L.57," October 8, 1917, T1022 / 798 / PG 75204.

16. Ibid.

17. Testimony of Heinrich Maas, "Bericht über den Totalverlust des Luftschiffes L.57," October 9, 1917, T1022 / 798 / PG 75204.

18. Meighörner-Schardt, *Wegbereiter des Weltluftverkehrs wider Willen: Die Geschichte des* Zeppelin-*Luftschifftyps "W,"* 24.

19. Testimony of Ludwig Bockholt, "Bericht über den Totalverlust des Luftschiffes L.57," October 8, 1917, T1022 / 798 / PG 75204.

20. Ibid.

21. Testimony of Heinrich Maas, "Bericht über den Totalverlust des Luftschiffes L.57," October 9, 1917, T1022 / 798 / PG 75204.

22. Testimony of Ludwig Bockholt, "Bericht über den Totalverlust des Luftschiffes L.57," October 8, 1917, T1022 / 798 / PG 75204.

23. Ibid.

24. Sommerfeld was then the commander of the experimental airship *L 35*, based in Jüterbog. This airship was withdrawn from combat service in September 1917 and was currently at the base to trial new Maybach high-altitude engines. As an aside, in 1918, *L 35* tested the release of an Albatros D.III fighter plane from altitude as a means of defending airships from British seaplane patrols over the North Sea. The concept was abandoned until a suitable seaplane could be developed in lieu of a land-based fighter that would only be able to land on the ground. Interestingly, *Kapitänleutnant* Herbert Ehrlich ceded command of *L 35* to Sommerfeld since he was slated to take command of *L 59*, only to have to give it up to Bockholt for the African mission.

25. Testimony of Heinrich Maas, "Bericht über den Totalverlust des Luftschiffes L.57," October 9, 1917, T1022 / 798 / PG 75204.

26. Testimony of Emil Grussendorf, "Bericht über den Totalverlust des Luftschiffes L.57," October 9, 1917, T1022 / 798 / PG 75204.

27. "Memo," October 11, 1917, T1022 / 798 / PG 75204.

28. Ibid.

29. Ibid.

30. Meighörner-Schardt, *Wegbereiter des Weltluftverkehrs wider Willen: Die Geschichte des* Zeppelin-*Luftschifftyps "W,"* 27.

31. "Memo," October 11, 1917, T1022 / 798 / PG 75204.

32. *Kapitänleutnant* Herbert Ehrlich began his service with the *Kaiserliche Marine* in 1901 and joined the *Marine Luftschiff Abteilung* in May 1915. Here he commanded the Zeppelins *L 5* (August–October 1915), *L 17* (October 1915–October 1916), *L 35* (October 1916–September 1917), and *L 61* (October 1917, after losing command of *L 59* to May 1918). In June 1918 he ceased combat operations and joined the Admiralty staff in Berlin. He survived the war but died during surgery in 1921.

33. "Gutachten der Bericht über den Totalverlust des Luftschiffes L.57," October 11, 1917, T1022 / 798 / PG 75204.

34. "RMA to his Excellence the chief of the Admiralty," October 15, 1917, T1022 / 798 / PG 75204.

35. "*Reichskolonialamt*, Kommando der *Schutztruppe*n an den Kaiserlichen Admiralstab," October 11, 1917, T1022 / 798 / PG 75204.

36. Ibid.

37. "Memo," October 11, 1917, T1022 / 798 / PG 75204.

38. Meighörner-Schardt, *Wegbereiter des Weltluftverkehrs wider Willen: Die Geschichte des* Zeppelin-*Luftschifftyps "W,"* 22.

39. "Transcript, Lt. Elias, Inspection of Airship Troops, to the State Secretary of the RMA," October 11, 1917.

40. Ibid.

41. Meighörner-Schardt, *Wegbereiter des Weltluftverkehrs wider Willen: Die Geschichte des Zeppelin-Luftschifftyps "W,"* 22.

42. Edwin T. Woodhall, *Spies of the Great War: Revelations of the Secret Service* (London: Mellifont, 1925), 172.

43. Ibid., 175.

44. Robinson, *The Zeppelin in Combat*, 301.

45. Ibid.

46. Ibid., 302.

47. Ibid.

48. Paice, *World War I: The African Front*, 350.

49. W. D. Downes, *With the Nigerians in German East Africa* (London: Methuen, 1919), 232.

50. Paice, *World War I: The African Front*, 350.

Chapter 5: The Battle of Mahiwa and a Change of Plans

1. 2012 Census, the United Republic of Tanzania, National Bureau of Statistics, https://www.nbs.go.tz/nbs/takwimu/census2012/Village_Statistics(ondoa).pdf.

2. The Nigerian Brigade in Mahiwa consisted of the 1st, 2nd, and 4th Battalions of the Nigerian Regiment, the Nigerian Battery, and the Stokes Mortar section of the brigade.

3. Lettow-Vorbeck, *My Reminisces of East Africa*, 209.

4. Göring, *Meine Kriegserlebnisse in Deutsch-Ostafrika 1914–1920*, 131.

5. Lettow-Vorbeck, *My Reminisces of East Africa*, 210.

6. Göring, *Meine Kriegserlebnisse in Deutsch-Ostafrika 1914–1920*, 131.

7. Ibid., 132.

8. Downes, *With the Nigerians in German East Africa*, 221.

9. Lettow-Vorbeck, *My Reminisces of East Africa*, 211.

10. Ibid.

11. Göring, *Meine Kriegserlebnisse in Deutsch-Ostafrika 1914–1920*, 132–134.

12. Downes, *With the Nigerians in German East Africa*, 221.

13. Ibid.

14. Lettow-Vorbeck, *My Reminisces of East Africa*, 212.

15. The total sum of the forces employed by the *Schutztruppe* before the battle of Mahiwa was 3,146 men (501 Europeans and 2,645 Askaris). Those who took in part in the battle numbered 1,243 (155 Europeans and 1,088 Askaris), which, as mentioned in the text, amounted to 39.5 percent of the *Schutztruppe*. The casualties at Mahiwa, which totaled 499 men, while much fewer than the 2,700 lost by the British, were still just over 40 percent of the companies' fighting strength, to say nothing of the materiel and supplies lost. Figures from Boell, *Die Operationen in Ostafrika*, 342.

16. Göring, *Meine Kriegserlebnisse in Deutsch-Ostafrika 1914–1920*, 134.

17. Lettow-Vorbeck, *My Reminisces of East Africa*, 212.

18. Downes, *With the Nigerians in German East Africa*, 229.

19. Lettow-Vorbeck, *My Reminisces of East Africa*, 213.

20. Ibid., 216.

21. Schöffler, *Matata*, 441.

22. Paice, *World War I: The African Front*, 332.

23. Lettow-Vorbeck, *My Reminisces of East Africa*, 222.

24. The Boma was a multistory setup of buildings constructed by the Germans to serve as an outpost and an enclosure for livestock. It subsequently became a customhouse under the British, then a police station and office building in the independent Tanzania. It is currently still standing but is abandoned and in a state of decay.

25. Meighörner-Schardt, *Wegbereiter des Weltluftverkehrs wider Willen: Die Geschichte des Zeppelin-Luftschifftyps "W,"* 41.

26. "*Reichskolonialamt*, Kommando der *Schutztruppen* an den Chef des Admiralstabes," October 16, 1917, T1022 / 798 / PG 75204.

27. Meighörner-Schardt, *Wegbereiter des Weltluftverkehrs wider Willen: Die Geschichte des Zeppelin-Luftschifftyps "W,"* 30.

28. Anton Friedrich Heinen was another Zeppelin factory pilot who flew for DELAG in the prewar years and assisted in the training of naval airship commanders during the war. Following World War I, he moved to the United States, where he served as an advisor for the US Navy's "lighter-than-air" program.

29. Göbel and Förster, *Afrika zu unsern Füßen*, 51.

30. Meighörner-Schardt, *Wegbereiter des Weltluftverkehrs wider Willen: Die Geschichte des Zeppelin-Luftschifftyps "W,"* 31.

31. "Reichsmarineamt zum J.V.," November 3, 1917, T1022 / 798 / PG 75204.

32. Göbel and Förster, *Afrika zu unsern Füßen*, 52.

33. Ibid., 53.

34. Ibid., 55. It should be noted that the peak of the Shipka Pass was noted in this book as being 1,273 meters (4,177 feet). I have substituted the modern, more accurate measurement of 1,150 meters (3,820 feet).

35. "Telegramm vom Marine-Sonderkommando an den Admiralstab," November 4, 1917, T1022 / 798 / PG 75204.

36. "Reichsmarineamt zum J.V.," November 3, 1917, T1022 / 798 / PG 75204.

37. "*Reichskolonialamt*, Kommando der *Schutztruppen* an den Kaiserlichen Admiralstab," November 6, 1917, T1022 / 798 / PG 75204.

38. Apparently, Bockholt didn't respond to the RKA's initial telegram. Instead, a telegram sent on the eleventh, the day after the RKA's second request for confirmation, indicates that he was notified of the new landing zone.

39. "Telegrammabschrift, Admiralstab der Marine," November 6, 1917, T1022 / 798 / PG 75204.

40. Göbel and Förster, *Afrika zu unsern Füßen*, 66.

41. "Kommando '*L 59*' an den Admiralstab," November 14, 1917, T1022 / 798 / PG 75204.

42. Meighörner-Schardt, *Wegbereiter des Weltluftverkehrs wider Willen: Die Geschichte des* Zeppelin-*Luftschifftyps "W,"* 43.

43. Discerned through correspondence with the late Elisabeth Bliesener, the granddaughter of Ernst Fegert.

44. The SMS *Goeben*, commanded by Konteradmiral Wilhelm Souchon, was a Moltke-class battle cruiser that, along with the light cruiser SMS *Breslau*, was assigned to the *Kaiserliche Marine's Mittelmeer-Division* (Mediterranean Division) in Pola at the outbreak of World War I. After bombarding the port of Philippeville, then in French Algeria, she was transferred to Constantinople—outrunning the pursuing Royal Navy battle cruisers HMS *Indefatigable* and *Indomitable* in the process. Upon reaching Turkish waters, Souchon was offered command of the Ottoman fleet, and the *Goeben* and *Breslau*, and their German crews, entered Ottoman service as the *Yavuz Sultan Selim* and *Midilli*, respectively, swapping both flags and crew uniforms, but otherwise remaining German vessels. See Jeffrey Judge, *The Imperial German Navy of World War I*, vol. 1, *Warships* (Atglen, PA: Schiffer Military History, 2016), 108; and Franz von Rintelen, *The Dark Invader: Wartime Reminiscences of a German Naval Intelligence Officer* (New York: Macmillan, 1933), 24–33.

45. Göbel and Förster, *Afrika zu unsern Füßen*, 51.

46. "Kommando '*L 59*' an den Admiralstab," November 14, 1917, T1022 / 798 / PG 75204.

47. Ibid.

48. Ibid.

49. Ibid.

50. Göbel and Förster, *Afrika zu unsern Füßen*, 59.

51. Ibid., 58.

52. Ibid.

53. Ibid.

54. "*Kapitänleutnant* Bockholt an den Admiralstab," November 15, 1917 (received at 0046, November 16), T1022 / 798 / PG 75204.

Chapter 6: The Next Attempt

1. "Bericht über die Fahrt L.59 am 16 und 17.11.17," November 28, 1917, T1022 / 798 / PG 75204.

2. As early as December 25, 1914, the British had flown into Germany territory to attack airship bases. The first attack utilized seaplanes that were carried by naval tenders and successfully reached Cuxhaven and Wilhelmshaven, although they caused only minimal damage to the sheds. The most successful attack occurred in 1918, when the battle cruiser HMS *Furious* was converted to an aircraft carrier and launched seven Sopwith Camel fighters to attack the base at Tondern. During this raid, a captive balloon was destroyed along with the Zeppelins *L 54* and *L 60.*

3. Although *L 59* had an unusual, tan-colored canvas shell, it still retained the typical German markings of iron crosses on each side and the alphanumeric identity of the airship on its nose. In addition to these marks, *L 59* also had the imperial German war ensign painted on its sides (with the colonial flag replacing the *Reichsflagge* in its top-left corner), aft of the rear gondola. Later, additional markings were painted on in the form of massive Ottoman and German flags located on the Zeppelin's underside, just in front of the control car.

4. Göbel and Förster, *Afrika zu unsern Füßen*, 59.

5. "Bericht über die Fahrt L.59 am 16 und 17.11.17," November 28, 1917, T1022 / 798 / PG 75204.

6. Ibid.

7. Some signals did actually reach Yambol, but in mutilated form. A transmission sent by *L 59* upon reaching Asia Minor was transcribed as "13:45? / Panderma / . . . [?] . . . [?] 3 . . . [?]" (Admiralstab der Marine Chiffrierbureau [Cypher Bureau], Telegrammabschrift K.Z.67664). Later in the flight, the radiotelegraph appeared to be functioning well, since Bockholt's message on aborting the mission was transcribed accurately, reading "Central / Asia Minor / shot at / by / rifle / thrown up / by / strong thunderstorms / reduced weight / water ballast / 4(?) tons / petrol / 2 tons of ammunition / dropped / turned around. Tuesday clear." ("Telegrammabschrift, Admiralstab der Marine," received in Berlin, November 18, 1917), T1022 / 798 / PG 75204.

8. "Bericht über die Fahrt L.59 am 16 und 17.11.17," November 28, 1917, T1022 / 798 / PG 75204.

9. Göbel and Förster, *Afrika zu unsern Füßen*, 60.

10. Ibid., 61.

11. "Bericht über die Fahrt L.59 am 16 und 17.11.17," November 28, 1917, T1022 / 798 / PG 75204.

12. Göbel and Förster, *Afrika zu unsern Füßen*, 64.

13. Ibid.

14. The report noted weak resistance from the Germans (the *Westtruppen*) and that following a skirmish "on the heights east of the train station," 46 Germans and 425 Askaris were captured. Additionally, it noted that since November 1, 473 Germans and 1,072 Askaris were killed or captured, and numerous ship guns (from the SMS *Königsberg*), machine guns, and miscellaneous war materiel had been seized. "*Reichskolonialamt*, Kommando der *Schutztruppe*n, 'Bericht aus Ostafrika,'" November 19, 1917, T1022 / 798 / PG 75204.

15. The territorial gains claimed by the British were accurate, as were the numbers of Germans and Askaris captured. What the British report didn't disclose, however, was that most of the captured forces represented troops that were willingly given up, since they were either too sick or too wounded to fight. As the *Westtruppen* continued their retreat to the southeast, in order to link up with Lettow's main forces, they were successfully able to break through British and Belgian forces, escaping with nearly 2,000 officers and troops, a dozen machine guns, and more than 500,000 rounds of ammunition. See Paice, *World War I: The African Front*, 332–36; and Boell, *Die Operationen in Ostafrika*, 392–96.

16. "*Reichskolonialamt*, Kommando der *Schutztruppe*n, 'Bericht aus Ostafrika,'" November 19, 1917, T1022 / 798 / PG 75204.

17. "Telegrammabschrift, Admiralstab der Marine," November 18, 1917, 0855, T1022 / 798 / PG 75204.

18. "Telegrammabschrift, Admiralstab der Marine," November 18, 1917, 1150, T1022 / 798 / PG 75204.

19. "Telegrammabschrift, Admiralstab der Marine," November 20, 1917, 0130, T1022 / 798 / PG 75204.

20. "Bericht über die Fahrt L.59 am 16 und 17.11.17," November 28, 1917, T1022 / 798 / PG 75204.

Chapter 7: Into the Winds of Destiny

1. The figures of 9,000 kg for the water ballast and 13.9 metric tons of cargo were estimates given by Bockholt in his report following the completion of the flight. See "Bericht über die Fernfahrt des L.59 vom 21.–25.11.17 nach Afrika," November 27, 1917, T1022 / 798 / PG 75204. The actual figures, taken from *L 59*'s ballast distribution chart from the morning of the twenty-first, indicate that 9,160 kg of water ballast was on board, and cargo (including spare parts) equated to 16,240 kg. Including the complement of the crew, oil, gasoline, and supplies, plus an additional 600 kg taken into account for rain or snow soaking the envelope, *L 59* had a payload totaling 51,465 kg (113,461 lbs.). See "Ballastverteilung, 5. Fahrt des Luftschiffs *L 59*," November 21, 1917, T1022 / 798 / PG 75204.

2. “Bericht über die Fernfahrt des L.59 vom 21.–25.11.17 nach Afrika,” November 27, 1917, T1022 / 798 / PG 75204.

3. Göbel and Förster, *Afrika zu unsern Füßen*, 66.

4. A telegram from November 25 indicates that it took nearly three days for the correspondence to actually reach Germany. According to the message, Panderma received the drop on the twenty-second but didn’t wire the encrypted telegraphs to the Mediterranean Division and Yambol until 0440 on the twenty-fifth. The former subsequently telegraphed the material at 1100. See “Kriegstagebuch für die Fahrt vom 21.11–25.11.17 nach Afrika,” November 21, 1917, 1145, and “Telegrammabschrift, Admiralstab der Marine,” November 25, 1917, 1100, T1022 / 798 / PG 75204.

5. Göbel and Förster, *Afrika zu unsern Füßen*, 73.

6. *Korvettenkapitän* Wolfram von Knorr had a storied naval career prior to his service with the Admiralstab, which included serving on the SMS *Königsberg* and becoming a naval attaché in Japan prior to the outbreak of war. After making his way back to Germany in 1915, he commanded an auxiliary cruiser (the *Meteor*) and eventually took over the SMS *Breslau*, then in Ottoman service. In July 1917 he was assigned back to Germany to serve in the Admiralstab in Berlin. As an interesting aside, he was the son of *Korvettenkapitän* Eduard von Knorr, who as an officer of the Kaiserliche Marine in the nineteenth century played an essential role in forcing the sultan of Zanzibar’s hand in ceding the mainland of East Africa to the Germans. See Hans Hildebrand, Albert Röhr, and Hans-Otto Steinmetz, *Die deutschen Kriegsschiffe: Biographien—ein Spiegel der Marinegeschichte von 1815 bis zur Gegenwart* (Herford, Germany: Koehler, 1993), 6:102.

7. “Reichs-Kolonialamt, Kommando der *Schutztruppe*n. Abschrift. Englischer Bericht aus Ostafrika,” November 22, 1917, T1022 / 798 / PG 75204.

8. “Brieftelegramm für Seine Majestät den Kaiser,” November 22, 1917, T1022 / 798 / PG 75204.

9. “Fernschreiben an Marinesonderkommando Jambol für *L 59*,” November 21, 1917, 1528, T1022 / 798 / PG 75204.

10. “Telegrammabschrift, Admiralstab der Marine,” November 21, 1917, 1820, T1022 / 798 / PG 75204.

11. Bernard John Leggett, *Wireless Telegraphy, with Special Reference to the Quenched-Spark System* (London: Chapman and Hall, 1921), 294.

12. “Kriegstagebuch für die Fahrt vom 21.11–25.11.17 nach Afrika,” November 21, 1917, 1745 T1022 / 798 / PG 75204.

13. Göbel and Förster, *Afrika zu unsern Füßen*, 70.

14. Ibid., 74.

15. Ibid.

16. Ibid.

17. "Bericht über die Fernfahrt des L.59 vom 21.–25.11.17 nach Afrika," November 27, 1917, T1022 / 798 / PG 75204.

18. Göbel and Förster, *Afrika zu unsern Füßen*, 75.

19. This range is mentioned in Göbel and Förster, *Afrika zu unsern Füßen*, 75, but is confirmed in the altitude charts attached to *L 59*'s war diary, T1022 / 798 / PG 75204.

20. Ibid.

21. St. Elmo, or Saint Erasmus of Formia, is the patron saint of sailors. When seamen observed St. Elmo's fire forming around masts and sails, it was regarded as a good omen.

22. "Kriegstagebuch für die Fahrt vom 21.11–25.11.17 nach Afrika," November 21, 1917, 2225; and "Bericht über die Fernfahrt des L.59 vom 21.–25.11.17 nach Afrika," November 27, 1917, T1022 / 798 / PG 75204.

23. A great explanation of how *Peilbomben* were utilized can be found in a 1930 issue of *Flugsport*. Concerning their use with a transoceanic flight on a seaplane, the article reads: "It is important to determine the drift over the sea. To do this, you use tracking bombs with floats; the wind direction can be determined from the plume of smoke; the speed over the ground can be measured from a certain height using a stop watch. The difference between the measured and the known flight speed is the wind strength." Oskar Ursinus, ed., "Von Gronaus Transozeanflug auf Dornier Wal," *Flugsport* 2, no. 18 (September 1930).

24. "Bericht über die Fernfahrt des L.59 vom 21.–25.11.17 nach Afrika," November 27, 1917, T1022 / 798 / PG 75204.

25. Göbel and Förster, *Afrika zu unsern Füßen*, 76.

26. "Bericht über die Fernfahrt des L.59 vom 21.–25.11.17 nach Afrika," November 27, 1917, T1022 / 798 / PG 75204.

27. Ibid.

28. Ibid.

29. Meighörner-Schardt, *Wegbereiter des Weltluftverkehrs wider Willen: Die Geschichte des* Zeppelin-*Luftschifftyps "W,"* 59.

30. Göbel and Förster, *Afrika zu unsern Füßen*, 81.

31. "Kriegstagebuch für die Fahrt vom 21.11–25.11.17 nach Afrika," November 21, 1917, 1230, T1022 / 798 / PG 75204.

32. "Bericht über die Fernfahrt des L.59 vom 21.–25.11.17 nach Afrika," November 27, 1917, T1022 / 798 / PG 75204.

33. Göbel and Förster, *Afrika zu unsern Füßen*, 81.

34. "Bericht über die Fernfahrt des L.59 vom 21.–25.11.17 nach Afrika," November 27, 1917, T1022 / 798 / PG 75204.

35. "Kriegstagebuch für die Fahrt vom 21.11–25.11.17 nach Afrika," November 21, 1917, 1230, T1022 / 798 / PG 75204.

36. "Bericht über die Fernfahrt des L.59 vom 21.–25.11.17 nach Afrika," November 27, 1917, T1022 / 798 / PG 75204.

37. Reid, *Marine-Luftschiffer-Kameradschaft Newsletters, 1980–1997*, 387.

38. "Brieftelegramm für Seine Majestät den Kaiser," November 22, 1917, T1022 / 798 / PG 75204.

39. Göbel and Förster, *Afrika zu unsern Füßen*, 88–89.

40. "Bericht über die Fernfahrt des L.59 vom 21.–25.11.17 nach Afrika," November 27, 1917, T1022 / 798 / PG 75204.

41. Meighörner-Schardt, *Wegbereiter des Weltluftverkehrs wider Willen: Die Geschichte des* Zeppelin-*Luftschifftyps "W,"* 58.

42. According to Bockholt, "The navigation through the desert was carried out astronomically during the day and at night with the help of the shadow table. In the moonlight, especially at night, the shadow provided a good means of orientation." "Bericht über die Fernfahrt des L.59 vom 21.–25.11.17 nach Afrika," November 27, 1917, T1022 / 798 / PG 75204.

43. Ibid.

44. Göbel and Förster, *Afrika zu unsern Füßen*, 91.

45. This sequence of events is described in Ernst Lehmann's memoir, which, according to him, was "repeated verbatim" from members of the operation who told him about the flight (Lehmann himself did not participate in China-Sache). On the basis of some of the wording regarding personnel and the description of areas flown over on the flight, it is obvious that much of his account was heard from Förster. See Lehmann, *Zeppelin: The Story of Lighter-Than-Air Craft*, 185–88.

46. "Kriegstagebuch für die Fahrt vom 21.11–25.11.17 nach Afrika," November 23, 1917, 0045, T1022 / 798 / PG 75204.

47. Ibid.

48. The *U-Deutschland* being referenced by Göbel and Förster was the first of a fleet of merchant U-boats developed by a private consortium, consisting of Norddeutscher Lloyd, Deutsche Bank, and Friedrich Krupp Germaniawerft, to subvert the British blockade on Germany and reestablish trade with the United States. It departed Bremen on June 14, 1916, and arrived in Baltimore, Maryland, to much fanfare on July 9. Although her sister ship, the *U-Bremen*, was sunk on her maiden voyage, the *U-Deutschland* returned to the United States on November 1, this time in New London, Connecticut. It was a huge, although short-lived, propaganda victory for Germany; however, once the US showed signs of joining the Allies against Germany, all the merchant U-boats were converted for combat use as U-cruisers, with the *U-Deutschland* becoming SM *U-155*, and the others becoming *U-151*, *U-152*, *U-153*, *U-154*, *U-156*, and *U-157*. See Etzold, *Reaping the Whirlwind: The U-Boat War off North America During World War I*, 16–66.

49. See Göbel and Förster, *Afrika zu unsern Füßen*, 96–97; and Carl Henze, *Kolonial-Bücherei Heft 32: Mit "L 59" nach Afrika* (Berlin: Steiniger Verlage, 1941), 27.

50. The Prince of Homburg referred to Bockholt is the one portrayed in Heinrich von Kleist's play instead of the actual historical figure. In the play *Der Prinz von Homburg*, the prince gets distracted and fails to hear his orders. As a result, he disobeys a direct order, wins a battle, and is summarily court-martialed and condemned to death. See Henze, *Kolonial-Bücherei Heft 32: Mit "L 59" nach Afrika*, 27.

51. Göbel and Förster, *Afrika zu unsern Füßen*, 97.

52. A discrepancy exists between Bockholt's postmission report and both his own log book and Göbel and Förster's account of the mission. In the former, he describes nearly touching down on the plateau and then receiving the order to turn back; the latter sources describe the inverse. By comparing the coordinates given in the log book, it is clear that the sudden drop in altitude occurred on the return leg of the journey, and not prior to receiving the callback notification as Bockholt's report suggests.

53. Bockholt described this process in his postmission report and how such a maneuver was nearly disastrous when a sudden increase of temperature was experienced. He estimated the weight of a single ballast cable as being 1 kg and felt that for future endeavors, it wouldn't be "any problem" to make the addition. "Bericht über die Fernfahrt des L.59 vom 21.–25.11.17 nach Afrika," November 27, 1917, T1022 / 798 / PG 75204.

54. This figure is another discrepancy that exists between the log book and Bockholt's report. The former gives a number of 3,800 kg and the latter notes 2,800 kg as being released. Due to the log book recording the weight at the time of the occurrence instead of nearly a week later, when the report was submitted, the larger figure has been assumed as being correct.

55. "Kriegstagebuch für die Fahrt vom 21.11–25.11.17 nach Afrika," November 24, 1917, 0000, T1022 / 798 / PG 75204.

56. Ibid., November 24, 1917, 1200.

57. Meighörner-Schardt, *Wegbereiter des Weltluftverkehrs wider Willen: Die Geschichte des Zeppelin-Luftschifftyps "W,"* 67.

58. Ibid.

59. Göbel and Förster, *Afrika zu unsern Füßen*, 106.

60. "Telegrammabschrift, Admiralstab der Marine," November 26, 1917, T1022 / 798 / PG 75204.

61. Göbel and Förster, *Afrika zu unsern Füßen*, 105.

62. Meighörner-Schardt, *Wegbereiter des Weltluftverkehrs wider Willen: Die Geschichte des Zeppelin-Luftschifftyps "W,"* 68.

63. "Telegrammabschrift, Admiralstab der Marine," Received in Berlin, November 25, 1917, 2335, T1022 / 798 / PG 75204.

64. "Telegrammabschrift, Admiralstab der Marine," November 22, 1917, 2300, T1022 / 798 / PG 75204.

65. Bockholt places the arrival of *L 59* in Constantinople as being at 2130 in his report, but his log notes the airship's position as being over the city at 2220. He may have meant that Constantinople was spotted at 2130 but not actually reached until later. "Bericht über die Fernfahrt des L.59 vom 21.–25.11.17 nach Afrika," November 27, 1917, T1022 / 798 / PG 75204.

66. Göbel and Förster, *Afrika zu unsern Füßen*, 106.

67. "Kriegstagebuch für die Fahrt vom 21.11–25.11.17 nach Afrika," November 25, 1917, 0305, T1022 / 798 / PG 75204.

68. Ibid.

69. Meighörner-Schardt, *Wegbereiter des Weltluftverkehrs wider Willen: Die Geschichte des Zeppelin-Luftschifftyps "W,"* 69.

70. "Bericht über die Fernfahrt des L.59 vom 21.–25.11.17 nach Afrika," November 27, 1917, T1022 / 798 / PG 75204.

71. The exact distance covered by Lehmann on *LZ 120*'s endurance trial is speculative, and most sources note only the time spent aloft as opposed to mileage traveled. Since a direct flight from Seerappen (Lyublino) to the submarine base in the Åland Islands, which constituted a normal patrol for the army airship, is only 375 miles, an estimate of 500 miles each way can safely be assumed, especially since Lehmann was known to have made pit stops along the way at various sites. See Pohl, *101 Hours in a Zeppelin*.

72. "Interview between von Knorr and Bockholt—Telegrammabschrift, Admiralstab der Marine Kriegszentrale," November 27, 1917, T1022 / 798 / PG 75204.

73. "Telegraphie des Deutschen Reichs, Berlin, Haupt-Telegraphenamt," Received in Berlin from *L 59* on November 27, 1917, T1022 / 798 / PG 75204.

74. "Interview between von Knorr and Bockholt—Telegrammabschrift, Admiralstab der Marine Kriegszentrale," November 27, 1917, T1022 / 798 / PG 75204.

75. Ibid.

Chapter 8: Confusion, Disinformation, and Decision-Making

1. "Bericht über die Fernfahrt des L.59 vom 21.–25.11.17 nach Afrika," November 27, 1917, T1022 / 798 / PG 75204.

2. Ibid.

3. Ibid.

4. Ibid.

5. "Interview between von Knorr and Bockholt—Telegrammabschrift, Admiralstab der Marine Kriegszentrale," November 27, 1917, T1022 / 798 / PG 75204.

6. "Telegrammabschrift, Admiralstab der Marine," November 26, 1917, 1830, T1022 / 798 / PG 75204.

7. Bockholt actually had less than half his initial fuel supply, since of the 21,700 liters on board at the departure, 9,025 remained. A total of 11,775 liters had been consumed during the trip, and 900 liters had to be dumped for buoyancy on the return leg. See "Technischer Bericht," November 30, 1917; and "Interview between von Knorr and Bockholt—Telegrammabschrift, Admiralstab der Marine Kriegszentrale," November 27, 1917, T1022 / 798 / PG 75204.

8. Bockholt informed Knorr that one of his machinists was already ill, and, given that malaria was so prevalent in Bulgaria, he needed at least two reserve machinists and another experienced helmsman. While nothing is mentioned about Grussendorf falling ill, or leaving the operation to return to the army, Bockholt placed particular emphasis on having a replacement on standby.

9. "Interview between von Knorr and Bockholt—Telegrammabschrift, Admiralstab der Marine Kriegszentrale," November 27, 1917, T1022 / 798 / PG 75204.

10. *Ettappendienst* literally translates to "staging service," and the *Ettappendienst der Marine* was essentially the German naval intelligence / spy network abroad.

11. "Report to Kaiser Wilhelm II concerning abandoning China-Sache operation," November 28, 1917, T1022 / 798 / PG 75204.

12. *Kapitänleutnant* Humann, unlike other officers serving in the Mediterranean, was born and raised in Türkiye and thus had a command of both the Turkish language and culture. He had previously met Enver Pasha during the latter's stay in Berlin and was a natural fit to serve the German Empire's interests in Asia Minor. See Klaus Wolf, *Victory at Gallipoli, 1915: The German-Ottoman Alliance in the First World War* (Barnsley, UK: Pen & Sword, 2020), 12.

13. "Telegrammabschrift, Admiralstab der Marine Chiffrierbureau," November 28, 1917, 2030, T1022 / 798 / PG 75204.

14. "Fernschreiben, Admiralstab an den FdL—Ahlhorn," November 28, 1917, 1646–1715, T1022 / 798 / PG 75204.

15. "Telegrammabschrift, Admiralstab der Marine Kriegszentrale," November 29, 1917, 1130, T1022 / 798 / PG 75204.

16. "Telegrammabschrift, Admiralstab der Marine Chiffrierbureau," December 2, 1917, 2020, T1022 / 798 / PG 75204.

17. Wolf, *Victory at Gallipoli, 1915: The German-Ottoman Alliance in the First World War*, 8.

18. Meighörner-Schardt, *Wegbereiter des Weltluftverkehrs wider Willen: Die Geschichte des Zeppelin-Luftschifftyps "W,"* 81.

19. "Telegrammabschrift, Admiralstab der Marine Kriegszentrale," November 27, 1917, 1720, T1022 / 798 / PG 75204.

20. Ibid.

21. Ibid.

22. Woodhall, *Spies of the Great War*, 177.

23. Ibid., 176.

24. Brian Garfield, *The Meinertzhagen Mystery: The Life and Legend of a Colossal Fraud* (Washington, DC: Potomac Books, 2007), 126.

25. Leonard Mosley, *Duel for Kilimanjaro: Africa, 1914–1918—the Dramatic Story of an Unconventional War* (New York: Ballantine Books, 1964), 165.

26. Göbel and Förster, *Afrika zu unsern Füßen*, 102.

27. Marben, *Ritter der Luft: Zeppelinabenteuer im Weltkrieg*, 161.

28. Buttlar-Brandenfels, *Zeppelins over England*, 237.

29. Lehmann, Zeppelin*: The Story of Lighter-Than-Air Craft*, 187.

30. Marben, *Ritter der Luft: Zeppelinabenteuer im Weltkrieg*, 161.

31. Lettow-Vorbeck, *My Reminisces of East Africa*, 220.

32. Ibid.

33. "Reichs-Kolonialamt, Kommando der *Schutztruppe*n. Abschrift. Englischer Bericht aus Ostafrika," November 22, 1917, T1022 / 798 / PG 75204.

34. Lettow-Vorbeck, *My Reminisces of East Africa*, 224.

35. Boell, *Die Operationen in Ostafrika*, 399.

36. Ibid.

37. Tafel's troops, although not locating the main forces of the army under Lettow, had actually crossed the Rovuma farther to the west. Finding neither friendly forces nor supplies, all the *Westtruppen*, besides Hauptmann Ernst Otto's detachment of fourteen Germans and twenty-three Askari, reentered German East Africa and surrendered to the British on November 28. Otto remained within Mozambique and later met up with Göring's forces—both rejoining Lettow nearly a month later.

38. Identified as Major Cohen in Paice, *World War I: The African Front*, 339.

39. See Boell, *Die Operationen in Ostafrika*, 399; Lettow-Vorbeck, *My Reminisces of East Africa*, 232; and Paice, *World War I: The African Front*, 340.

40. Lettow-Vorbeck, *My Reminisces of East Africa*, 232.

41. "Abschrift, W.T.B vom 29 November 1917: Englischer Bericht aus Ostafrika," November 29, 1917, T1022 / 798 / PG 75204. Confirming the report, Bockholt forwarded a similar transmission intercepted from Malta to the RMA on the thirtieth.

42. "Report to Kaiser Wilhelm II concerning abandoning China-Sache operation," November 28, 1917, T1022 / 798 / PG 75204.

43. Repeating the trip to East Africa, flying to Yemen, mine searching in the Bosphorus and Black Sea, or transferring *L 59* back to Germany to be converted to a seven-engine reconnaissance airship.

44. "Kriegstagebuch des Luftschiffes '*L 59*': 3 November 1917–19 Februar 1918," November 26–29, 1917, T1022 / 4316 / PG 66139b.

45. "Kriegstagebuch des Luftschiffes '*L 59*': 3 November 1917–19 Februar 1918," December 1, 1917, 1037–1535, T1022 / 4316 / PG 66139b.

46. Bockholt's report began with the line "As the Mediterranean Division has wired here, it has applied to the Admiralty staff for the '*L 59*' to be left here for attack purposes on the Suez Canal." Again, it appeared that while Strasser and the RMA in Berlin were busy discussing *L 59*'s fate, the Mediterranean Division had been devising their own plans and had been in Bockholt's ear.

47. "Bericht des Kommandanten '*L 59*' des Luftschiffhafens Jambol mit einem Marineluftschiff von großen Aktionradius zu Angriffsfahrten über das Mittelländische Meer," December 4, 1917, T1022 / 1060 / PG 76863.

48. Ibid.

49. Ibid.

50. Ibid.

51. "Stellungnahme zum Bericht des Kommandanten '*L 59*' des Luftschiffhafens Jambol mit einem Marineluftschiff von großen Aktionradius zu Angriffsfahrten über das Mittelländische Meer," December 20, 1917, T1022 / 1060 / PG 76863.

52. Ibid.

53. Ibid.

54. Ibid.

55. Ibid.

56. Ibid.

57. See Robinson, *The Zeppelin in Combat*, 287–303.

58. Ibid., 287.

59. The bombing mission over England on October 19–20, 1917, is known by British historians as the "silent raid" because the airships taking part flew at such a high altitude that their engines were never heard from the ground.

60. Robinson, *The Zeppelin in Combat*, 302.

61. "Report to Kaiser Wilhelm II concerning abandoning China-Sache operation," November 28, 1917, T1022 / 798 / PG 75204.

62. Meighörner-Schardt, *Wegbereiter des Weltluftverkehrs wider Willen: Die Geschichte des Zeppelin-Luftschifftyps "W,"* 83.

63. The Ritterkreuz mit Schwertern des Hohenzollernschen Hausordens, or Knight's Cross with Swords of the House of Hohenzollern, was a Prussian medal awarded both before and during World War I. In the hierarchy of German military awards, it would have fallen between the Eisernes Kreuz I. Klasse (Iron Cross, 1st class) on the lower end and the Pour le Mérite (the highest Prussian award for bravery).

64. "Chef des Admiralstabes der Marine an den Chef des Marine-Kabinetts," December 19, 1917, T1022 / 798 / PG 75204.

65. "Chef des Marine-Kabinetts an den Chef des Admiralstabes der Marine," December 29, 1917, T1022 / 4316 / PG 66139b.

66. Following the return to Yambol on November 25, on the twenty-seventh Bockholt submitted a list of crewmen whom he recommended for the Eisernes Kreus II. Klasse or Iron Cross 2nd class. These were *Feldwebelleutnant* Grussendorf, *Obermaschinistenmaat* Holland, *Obermaschinistenmaat* Heimann, *Obermaschinistenmaat* Bröcker, *Maschinenmaat* Proll, *Maschinenmaat* Schmitz, *Obermatrose* Hocke, *Obermatrose* Fuchs, *Obermatrose* Schedelmann, and *Funktelegraphie-Maat* Kettner. "Vorschläge zur Verleihung des Eisernen Kreuzes II.Klasse," November 27, 1917, T1022 / 798 / PG 75204.

67. "Chef des Marinekabinetts, Großhauptquartier an den Chef des Admiralstabes der Marine (mit 10–Eis.Krz.2.Kl.)," December 15, 1917, T1022 / 798 / PG 75204.

Chapter 9: Relighting Vulcan's Forge

1. Meighörner-Schardt, *Wegbereiter des Weltluftverkehrs wider Willen: Die Geschichte des* Zeppelin-*Luftschifftyps "W,"* 85.

2. "Der Staatsekretär der Reichs-Kolonialamts, Kommando der *Schutztruppe* an den Chef des Admiralstabes der Marine, Betrifft: Auflösung–Chinasache," December 12, 1917, T1022 / 798 / PG 75204.

3. "Kriegstagebuch des Luftschiffes '*L 59*': 3 November 1917–19 Februar 1918," December 11, 1917, 1130, T1022 / 4316 / PG 66139b.

4. Ibid., December 11, 1917–December 12, 1917, 0115, 1130, T1022 / 4316 / PG 66139b.

5. Ibid., December 12, 1917, 0115, 1130, T1022 / 4316 / PG 66139b.

6. Ibid., December 12, 1917, 0810.

7. Ibid., December 20, 1917, T1022 / 4316 / PG 66139b.

8. "Belegung des Luftschiffhafens Jambol mit einem Marineluftschiff von großen Aktionradius zu Angriffsfahrten über das Mittelländische Meer," December 16, 1917, T1022 / 4316 / PG 66139b.

9. Ibid.

10. Although nominally similar to the Mb.IV engines already equipped to *L 59* and the earlier "height climber" classes of Zeppelins, the Mb.IVa was an entirely different design intended to perform at altitudes approaching 20,000 feet. Strasser desired that all new airships be equipped with the Mb.IVa, but "the new power plants were [only] being hand-made in small quantities." See Robinson, *The Zeppelin in Combat*, 317.

11. Meighörner-Schardt, *Wegbereiter des Weltluftverkehrs wider Willen: Die Geschichte des Zeppelin-Luftschifftyps "W,"* 83.

12. Ibid.

13. Although the armistice signed on December 15. 1917, essentially took Russia temporarily out of the war, no significant German army units departed the front, since the armistice guaranteed a ceasefire for only thirty days, which would be extended another thirty days in perpetuity unless one party informed the other that they wished to resume hostilities. This being said, other, less critical assets, such as airship troops in Bulgaria, were being transferred to the Western Front, where they were more urgently required. Ultimately, negotiations for a final peace did break down in February 1918, but devastating German offensives soon brought a permanent peace with the signing of the Treaty of Brest-Litovsk on March 3, 1918.

14. "Abschrift, Kriegsministerium, Allgemeines Kriegsdepartment an das Reichs-Marine-Amt," December 24, 1917, T1022 / 4316 / PG 66139b.

15. Ludendorff actually gave a figure of 102 army personnel being present at the Yambol base and associated gasworks. "Chef des Generalstabes des Feldheeres an den Herrn Chef des Admiralstabes der Marine," December 29, 1917, T1022 / 4316 / PG 66139b.

16. The German U-boat flotilla in Pola, later designated *Unterseebootsflottille Mittelmeer* (U-boat Flotilla Mediterranean Sea), housed, for most of their careers, the greatest U-boat aces of World War I, including *Kapitänleutnant* Lothar von Arnauld de la Perière, *Kapitänleutnant* Otto Hersing, *Korvettenkapitän* Waldemar Kophamel (at one point the commander of the base), *Kapitänleutnant* Walter Forstmann, and *Kapitänleutnant* Max Valentiner—with Arnauld, Kophamel, and Valentiner going on to command the massive *U-Kreuzer* submarines.

17. Following the RMA's decision to keep *L 59* in its current five-engine layout and merely install bomb bays and related equipment, nothing further is heard from Strasser regarding the conversion. Instead, throughout the period that *L 59* was being modified, there was a flurry of activity among the RMA, the army, and the naval attaché in Sofia. Although Bockholt was summoned for a consultation on January 9, 1918 ("*T*elegraphie des Deutschen Reichs, Berlin Haupt-Telegraphenamt," January 9, 1918, 1230, T1022 / 4316 / PG 66139b), he too was no longer mentioned in any correspondence. As the state secretary for the RMA intimated on January 29, 1918, the Mediterranean Division was essentially taking over the tactical decisions regarding *L 59*.

18. The RMA calculated that 2 officers and 164 men would be required to man the Yambol base. The officers would consist of an *Oberleutnant* or *Leutnant zur See*, taking overall command of the troops, and a doctor. The enlisted personnel would consist of 146 NCOs and sailors for airship operations, and the remaining 18 men would be slated for operating the hydrogen production plant. An additional five men, not included in the overall tally, would be allocated to be directly subordinate to the officers. These included a tailor, a shoemaker, a cook, and two drivers. Five hundred Bulgarians would compose the ground "holding crews," just as they had during the China-Sache operation. See "Kriegsstärkenachweisung für den Marine-Luftschifftrupp Jambol in Bulgarien," January 29, 1918; and "Telegraphie des Deutschen Reichs, Berlin Haupt-Telegraphenamt," January 18, 1918, 1230, T1022 / 4316 / PG 66139b.

19. "Der Staatsekretär des Reichs-Marine-Amts an den Admiralstab," January 29, 1918, T1022 / 4316 / PG 66139b.

20. "Der Gerichtsherr und Chef der Mittelmeerdivision an den Chef des Admiralstabes der Marine," April 8, 1918, T1022 / 1060 / PG 76863.

21. See Meighörner-Schardt, *Wegbereiter des Weltluftverkehrs wider Willen: Die Geschichte des Zeppelin-Luftschifftyps "W,"* 85; Reid, *Marine-Luftschiffer-Kameradschaft Newsletters, 1980–1997*, 394; and "Ballastverteilung, *L 59*," March 10–11, 1918, T1022 / 4316 / PG 66139b.

22. Maybach engines were handbuilt, and thus every component within the engine (crankshafts, camshafts, pistons, etc.) was given an identical number associated its specific engine case.

23. Meighörner-Schardt, *Wegbereiter des Weltluftverkehrs wider Willen: Die Geschichte des Zeppelin-Luftschifftyps "W,"* 87.

24. See "Telegrammabschrift, Führer der Luftschiffe an den Admiralstab," January 16, 1918, 1130; "Telegraphie des Deutschen Reichs, Berlin Haupt-Telegraphenamt," January 18, 1918, 1230; "Telegrammabschrift, Kommandant *L 59* an den Admiralstab," January 18, 1918, 1752; "Telegrammabschrift, Führer der Luftschiffe an den Admiralstab," January 19, 1918, 2120; "Telegrammabschrift, Admiralstab der Marine Kriegszentrale," January 25, 1918, 0645; "Telegrammabschrift, Kommando *L 59*, FdL an den Admiralstab," January 27, 1918, 1040; and "Telegrammabschrift, Kommando *L 59*, FdL an den Admiralstab," January 30, 1918, 2220, T1022 / 4316 / PG 66139b.

25. Meighörner-Schardt, *Wegbereiter des Weltluftverkehrs wider Willen: Die Geschichte des Zeppelin-Luftschifftyps "W,"* 88.

26. Ibid.

27. *L 59*'s war diary, in the period from February 10 through the thirteenth, reads only "Ready to fly, didn't take off due to weather conditions and Yambol port still not being ready for occupancy." On the basis of telegrams being sent back and forth between Berlin and Sofia, Yambol was sorely lacking in food supplies, provisions, and even cutlery, which had been sold off following *L 59*'s return to Friedrichshafen. All had to be procured before *L 59* could return. "Kriegstagebuch des Luftschiffes '*L 59*': 3 November 1917–19 Februar 1918," February 10–13, 1918, T1022 / 4316 / PG 66139b.

28. *L 59* actually departed Friedrichshafen for Yambol on February 14, but the flight lasted just over three hours. As the war diary reads, "While searching for the ground in the Kempten area [the cloud ceiling was at the low altitude of 800 meters at the time], the antenna was knocked off. Turned around to get a new one, landed in worsening weather conditions. Trip canceled." Poor weather in the period from February 15 through 19 further delayed the transfer until the twentieth. "Kriegstagebuch des Luftschiffes '*L 59*': 3 November 1917–19 Februar 1918," February 14, 1918, 0815–1120, T1022 / 4316 / PG 66139b.

29. Lake Constance is referred to as Bodensee in German and actually refers to three bodies of water situated between Germany, Switzerland, and Austria. The lake being referred to by Bockholt was specifically Upper Lake Constance (Obersee Bodensee), on whose shore Friedrichshafen lies.

30. "Kriegstagebuch des Luftschiffes '*L 59*': 3 November 1917–19 Februar 1918," February 20, 1918, 1415, T1022 / 4316 / PG 66139b.

31. Ibid., February 20–21, 1918, 2000–0200.

32. Ibid., February 21, 1918, 0600.

33. The war diary specifies only "southern Italy" as being the destination for the raid. Although Brindisi could also have been the intended target, given the route taken by Bockholt, it is likely that the true goal of the mission was to bomb Naples, especially given the fact that a second raid, just a week later, had this as its objective.

34. "Kriegstagebuch des Luftschiffes '*L 59*': 3 November 1917–19 Februar 1918," March 3, 1918, 0625, T1022 / 4316 / PG 66139b.

35. Bockholt had been following the same methodology he had used during the African voyage, in which one engine was always kept offline while the others ran. Without the heat from the engine, its coolant froze and necessitated *L 59* descending to a lower altitude to thaw it.

36. "Kriegstagebuch des Luftschiffes '*L 59*': 3 November 1917–19 Februar 1918," March 3, 1918, 1630, T1022 / 4316 / PG 66139b.

37. Ibid., March 3, 1918, 1730.

38. Ibid., March 4, 1918, 1215.

39. Ibid., March 5–7, 1918.

40. Ibid., March 10, 1918, 0630; and "Ballastverteilung, *L 59*," March 10–11, 1918, T1022 / 4316 / PG 66139b.

41. "Kriegstagebuch des Luftschiffes '*L 59*': 3 November 1917–19 Februar 1918," March 10, 1918, 1420–1930, T1022 / 4316 / PG 66139b.

42. Ibid., 2215.

43. Ibid., March 11, 1918, 0055–0115.

44. Ibid., 0115.

45. "Technischer Bericht," March 16, 1918, T1022 / 4316 / PG 66139b.

46. Ibid.

47. The Austro-Hungarian armed forces were referred to as being "*Kaiserlich und Königlich*," or "imperial and royal," in reference to the dual monarchy that existed within the empire. This has historically been shortened to K.u.K.

48. "Abschrift, Fernschreiben an den 1) Admiralstab Berlin 2) Mittelmeerdivision—Germania Ettape Konstantinopel 3) Luftschiffführer Nordholz," March 11, 1918, T1022 / 4316 / PG 66139b.

49. This was likely because Bockholt took the same direct route home that he had on his outbound journey instead of flying south of Greece, going over Asia

Minor, and circling back to Yambol, as he suggested would be necessary in his earlier report.

50. "Interview between Bockholt, Hagen, and Eichel—Telegrammabschrift, Admiralstab der Marine Kriegszentrale," March 12, 1918, T1022 / 1060 / PG 76863.

51. Ibid.

52. Ibid.

53. Ibid.

54. Ibid.

55. Ibid.

56. *La Stampa* listed the victims from the press release as being "seven poor old women hospitalized in the hospice of the Little Sisters at Arco Mirelli, whose names are still unknown," and "Pasquale Coppola, Maria Coppola, Maria Tibaldi, Giulia Borlenza, Maria Borlenza, Maria Rimonti, Emma Garozzi, Salvatore Arimondi, Arturo Maglione, Maria Gandolfo, [and] the director of the San Carlo theater, Grataretta, as well as a man in his sixties who was previously unknown. Among the wounded is the wife of one of our colleagues from *Il Giorno*, Mrs. Leonilde Berino, who fortunately was only slightly injured. Among the other wounded we were able to collect the following names: Alfonso Bocci, Edoardo Gianturfi. Maria Mugnone, Arturo Cariogena, Minervino Giovanni, Aurelio Nino, Rimondi Maria, Luigia Corneli, Canonica Francesco, Maestro De .Simone." "Napoli bombardata dal Cielo," *La Stampa*, March 11, 1918, 1.

57. Ibid. A similar report was also published by the *New York Times*; see *New York Times*, March 13, 1918, 2.

58. "Napoli bombardata dal Cielo," *La Stampa*, March 11, 1918, 1. Interestingly, the *New York Times*, going against the consensus of Italian newspapers, reported a lower figure of sixteen deaths; see *New York Times*, March 14, 1918, 3.

59. Ibid.

60. "L'encomio ai segnalatori del dirigibile nemico," *La Stampa*, March 14, 1918, 2.

61. Ibid.

62. Göbel and Förster, *Afrika zu unsern Füßen*, 110.

63. Reid, *Marine-Luftschiffer-Kameradschaft Newsletters, 1980–1997*, 397; and Göbel and Förster, *Afrika zu unsern Füßen*, 111.

64. Göbel and Förster, *Afrika zu unsern Füßen*, 112.

65. Ibid.

Chapter 10: The Fall of Icarus

1. Erich Gröner, *German Warships, 1815–1945*, vol. 2, *U-Boats and Mine Warfare Vessels* (Annapolis, MD: Naval Institute Press, 1991), 26.

2. "WWI U-boat Commanders: Robert Sprenger," https://uboat.net/wwi/men/commanders/336.html. Accessed November 24, 2024.

3. "Aufgabe," *Kriegstagebuch SM UB-53: 7 April 1918–6 Mai 1918* (Cuxhaven-Altenbruch, Germany: Freundeskreis Traditionsarchiv Unterseeboote e.V).

4. *Kriegstagebuch SM UB-53: 7 April 1918–6 Mai 1918*, April 7, 1918, 2000.

5. Ibid.

6. Ibid.

7. Reid, *Marine-Luftschiffer-Kameradschaft Newsletters, 1980–1997*, 397.

8. *Kriegstagebuch SM UB-53: 7 April 1918–6 Mai 1918*, April 7, 1918, 2000.

9. Ibid.

10. Ibid., 2030.

11. Ibid., 2050.

12. Ibid.

13. Reid, *Marine-Luftschiffer-Kameradschaft Newsletters, 1980–1997*, 398.

14. *Obermatrose* Hans Schedelmann and *Obersteuermannsmaat* Ernst Fegert were the only crewmen not on board *L 59* on its final flight. Schedelmann was on scheduled leave, and Fegert had been on medical leave since March 9, 1918 (per correspondence with his granddaughter Elisabeth Bliesener).

15. *Kriegstagebuch SM UB-53: 7 April 1918–6 Mai 1918*, April 7, 1918, 2050.

16. "Telegrammabschrift, FdU Pola an den Admiralstab Berlin," April 9, 1918, 1620, T1022 / 1060 / PG 76863.

17. "Telegrammabschrift, von Arnim an den Admiralstab," April 11, 1918, T1022 / 1060 / PG 76863.

18. The Austrian report notes that *K.177* suffered engine failure and crash-landed in the Adriatic, denting the bottom of the seaplane in the process. *K.183* then landed next to *K.177* at 0710, radioed a tender to come and pick up the downed seaplane, and then took off to return to base. *K.183* flew back to the area at 1100 to assist the torpedo boats and tender in looking for the crashed seaplane and located it. By 1400 the tender, with the rescued pilots and aircraft, returned to base.

19. "Marinestationkommando Durazzo an das K.u.K Kreuzerflottillekommando," April 8, 1918, T1022 / 1060 / PG 76863.

20. "Obersten Heeresleitung an den Admiralstab," April 11, 1918, T1022 / 1060 / PG 76863.

21. "Telegrammabschrift, Admiralstab der Marine, M.L.T g20 an den Admiralstab," April 10, 1918, 1230, T1022 / 1060 / PG 76863.

22. "Telegrammabschrift, Admiralstab der Marine, FdL an den Admiralstab," April 12, 1918, 1008, T1022 / 1060 / PG 76863.

23. "Bericht des Kommandos 'L.42' über die Fernunternehmung am 23–24 Mai 1917, " 26 May 1917, T1022 / 4315 / PG 66198.

24. According to Douglas Robinson, *L 42* was actually struck three times. In his account, deviating from the actual postmission report, Robinson states, "On the homeward flight *L 42* found a wall of black thunderclouds reaching up to 23,000 feet barring her way. Dietrich had no choice but to fly through them . . . at 4:45 a.m. a blinding flash of lightning struck the ship. The metal structure was so heavily charged that a machinist's mate . . . got a severe shock when he touched the duralumin gondola wall. There was a strong smell of ozone . . . and its personnel believed that the electrical charge left the airship along the port propeller bracket. Ten minutes later the Zeppelin was staggered by a second lightning bolt. This time the top lookout saw it strike near him and along the course of the ship's back, while people in the rear gondola saw the flash shooting out of the tail. . . . Fifteen minutes later there was a weaker stroke which was seen from the control car to hit forward." See Robinson, *The* Zeppelin *in Combat*, 244–45.

25. "Telegrammabschrift, FdU Pola an den Admiralstab," May 11, 1918, 1230, T1022 / 1060 / PG 76863.

26. Meighörner-Schardt, *Wegbereiter des Weltluftverkehrs wider Willen: Die Geschichte des Zeppelin-Luftschifftyps "W,"* 107.

27. Göbel and Förster, *Afrika zu unsern Füßen*, 117.

28. Italy lost nine airships in total by the end of the war. The Città di Ferrara and Città di Jesi were shot down on June 8, 1915, and August 14, 1915, respectively, the former by an Austro-Hungarian seaplane and the latter through antiaircraft fire while the airship was bombing the naval base at Pola. On May 4, 1916, the M.4 was shot down by Austro-Hungarian aircraft. In 1917, the M.12 was downed by antiaircraft fire during a bombing run, and M.13 and M.8 were lost during raids on their hangars in July in Jesi and Ferrara, respectively. In 1918, the U.5 went missing on May 2, after returning from an escort mission, and A.1 crashed on August 16, following a bombing raid on Cattaro, assumed to have crashed into the sea near Cape Rodon.

29. Erich Gröner's authoritative, and oft-cited, study on U-boats states that *UB-53* was armed with an 8.8 cm SK L/30 deck gun; however, *UB-53*'s *Kriegstagebuch* from April 7 through May 6, notes only 10.5 cm ammunition taken on board. This indicates that at some point prior to the patrol, *UB-53*'s deck gun had been upgraded to a 10.5 cm SK L/45 gun, already being installed on other UB III submarines. See Gröner, *German Warships, 1815–1945*, 2:26.

30. Norman Friedman, *Naval Weapons of World War One* (Barnsley, UK: Seaforth, 2011), 145.

31. "Munitionsverbräuche," *Kriegstagebuch SM UB-53: 7 April 1918–6 Mai 1918.*

32. "Kommando L.59 an RMA.B.X, Admiralstab, FdL, Betrifft Benzinunfall in hinterer Gondel und Trägerbrüche bei L.59," April 3, 1917, T1022 / 1060 / PG 76863.

33. Alastair Reid, *DELAG: A History* (Durham, NC: Lulu, 2025), 446.

34. Meighörner-Schardt, *Wegbereiter des Weltluftverkehrs wider Willen: Die Geschichte des Zeppelin-Luftschifftyps "W,"* 108.

35. "Abschrift, Staatsekretär des Reichs-Marine-Amts an den Führer der Marine-Luftschiffe," April 20, 1918, T1022 / 1060 / PG 76863.

36. Robinson, *The Zeppelin in Combat*, 315.

37. "Seekriegsleitung Großhauptquartier an den Admiralstab," September 15, 1918, 1325, T1022 / 1060 / PG 76863.

38. "Telegrammabschrift, Admiralstab der Marine Kriegszentrale," September 30, 1918, 2050, T1022 / 1060 / PG 76863.

39. Ibid.

40. Robinson, *The Zeppelin in Combat*, 353.

41. Prior to the raid on England, Loßnitzer had flown only a single mission—commanding *LZ 120* for reconnaissance during Operation Albion. Before that, he headed the airship school in Nordholz and flew the antiquated *L 16*.

42. Robinson, *The Zeppelin in Combat*, 353.

43. Kenneth Munson, *Aircraft of World War I* (New York: Doubleday, 1968), 16.

44. Cadbury was responsible for shooting down *L 21* on November 28, 1916, and Leckie was credited with the destruction of *L 22* on May 14, 1917.

45. Lehmann, *Zeppelin: The Story of Lighter-Than-Air Craft*, 193.

46. Robinson, *The Zeppelin in Combat*, 355.

47. Ibid., 364.

48. *L 73* and *L 74,* which were already under construction when the reduction of the *Marine Luftschiff Abteilung* took place, were allowed to proceed to completion; however, the war ended before they could be put into service. Thus, the seven frontline Zeppelins in service in October 1918 were *L 56*, *L 61*, *L 63*, *L 64*, *L 71*, and *L 72*.

49. Robinson, *The Zeppelin in Combat*, 365.

Chapter 11: An Irenic Future for Airships

1. See Pohl, *101 Hours in a* Zeppelin, 177; Göbel and Förster, *Afrika zu unsern Füßen*, 122; and Guillaume de Syon, Zeppelin*! Germany and the Airship, 1900–1939* (Baltimore: Johns Hopkins University Press, 2002), 116.

2. Following the United States' entry into World War I, the Germans converted their merchant U-boats into U-cruisers, which were then sent to the coast of Africa in 1917 and to North America in 1918. Besides the merchant submarines, the Germans also developed a U-cruiser concept from the ground up (the U-139 class) and large, oceangoing minelayers (the U-117 class), which also patrolled off the east coast of Canada and the United States in the summer of 1918.

3. Etzold, *Reaping the Whirlwind*, 333–338.

4. Scheer, *Germany's High Seas Fleet in the World War*, 212.

5. Paice, *World War I: The African Front*, 349.

6. Lehmann, *Zeppelin: The Story of Lighter-Than-Air Craft*, 198.

7. Buttlar-Brandenfels, *Zeppelins over England*, 314–15.

8. Ibid., 316–17.

9. Göbel and Förster, *Afrika zu unsern Füßen*, 122.

10. Ibid., 123.

11. Robinson, *The Zeppelin in Combat*, 315.

12. "Kommando '*L 59*' an den Admiralstab," November 14, 1917, T1022 / 798 / PG 75204.

13. "Bericht über die Fernfahrt des L.59 vom 21.–25.11.17 nach Afrika," November 27, 1917, T1022 / 798 / PG 75204.

14. Hugo Eckener, *My Zeppelins*, trans. Douglas Robinson (London: Putnam, 1958), 65.

15. Ibid., 90–91.

16. "Bericht über die Fernfahrt des L.59 vom 21.–25.11.17 nach Afrika," November 27, 1917, T1022 / 798 / PG 75204.

Epilogue

1. In January 1916, the *Schutztruppe* was composed of 17,121 men (3,026 Europeans, 11,465 Askaris, and 2,630 porters and auxiliary troops). For 1918 figures, see Paice, *World War I: The African Front*, 383.

2. Lettow-Vorbeck, *My Reminisces of East Africa*, 304.

3. Ibid., 315.

4. Ibid., 316.

Bibliography

Books

Aeronautical Chamber of Commerce of America. *Aircraft Year Book: 1922*. New York: Aeronautical Chamber of Commerce of America 1922.

Ashmore, E. B. *Air Defence*. London: Longman's, Green, 1929.

Assmann, Kurt, ed. *Der Krieg zur See 1914–1918: Die Kämpfe der Kaiserlichen Marine in den Deutschen Kolonien.* Berlin: Verlag von E. S. Mittler & Sohn, 1935.

Beesly, Patrick. *Room 40: British Naval Intelligence, 1914–1918*. Oxford: Oxford University Press, 1984.

Boell, Ludwig. *Die Operationen in Ostafrika*. Hamburg, Germany: Walter Dachert, 1951.

Botting, Douglas. *Dr. Eckener's Dream Machine: The Great* Zeppelin *and the Dawn of Air Travel*. New York: Henry Holt, 2001.

Brose, Eric Dorn. *Clash of the Capital Ships: From the Yorkshire Raid to Jutland.* Annapolis, MD: Naval Institute Press, 2021.

Buttlar-Brandenfels, Treusch von. Zeppelin*s over England.* Translated by Huntley Patterson. New York: Harcourt, Brace, 1932.

Chatterton, E. Keble. *The Königsberg Adventure*. London: Hurst and Blackett, 1932.

Christensen, Christen P. *Blockade and Jungle*. London: Robert Hale, 1941.

Christiansen, Carl. *Durch! Mit Kriegsmaterial zu Lettow-Vorbeck*. Stuttgart: Verlag für Volkskunst, 1918.

Downes, W. D. *With the Nigerians in German East Africa*. London: Methuen, 1919.

Dürr, Ludwig. *Fünfundzwanzig Jahre* Zeppelin-*Luftschiffbau*. Berlin: V.D.I.-Verlag GmbH, 1924.

Eckart, Wolfgang Uwe. *Medizin und Kolonialimperialismus: Deutschland 1884–1945*. Paderborn, Germany: Ferdinand Schönigh, 1997.

Eckener, Hugo. *My Zeppelins*. Translated by Douglas Robinson. London: Putnam, 1958.

Eckermann, Erik, Wilhelm Treue, and Stefan Zima. *Technikpionier Karl Maybach: Antriebssysteme, Autos, Unternehmen, 4. Auflage*. Wiesbaden, Germany: Springer, 2023.

Etzold, Dominic. *Reaping the Whirlwind: The U-boat War off North America During World War I*. Atglen, PA: Schiffer Military History, 2023.

Fendall, C. P. *The East African Force, 1915–1919*. London: H. F. & G. Witherby, 1921.

Friedman, Norman. *Naval Weapons of World War One*. Barnsley, UK: Seaforth, 2011.

Garfield, Brian. *The Meinertzhagen Mystery: The Life and Legend of a Colossal Fraud*. Washington, DC: Potomac Books, 2007.

Gaudi, Robert. *African Kaiser: General Paul von Lettow-Vorbeck and the Great War in Africa, 1914–1918*. New York: Dutton Caliber, 2017.

Gladisch, Walter, ed. *Der Krieg zur See 1914–1918: Der Krieg in der Nordsee*. Vol. VI. Berlin: Verlag von E. S. Mittler & Sohn, 1937.

Göbel, Johannes, and Walter Förster. *Afrika zu unsern Füßen*. Leipzig: Verlag von K. F. Koehler, 1925.

Goote, Thor. *Peter Strasser: Der Führer der Luftschiffe*. Frankfurt am Main: Breidenstein Verlagsgesellschaft, 1938.

Göring, Karl Ernst. *Meine Kriegserlebnisse in Deutsch-Ostafrika 1914–1920*. Typescript of an unknown binding, 1927.

Gröner, Erich. *German Warships, 1815–1945*. 2 vols. Annapolis, MD: Naval Institute Press, 1991.

Groos, Otto, ed. *Der Krieg zur See 1914–1918: Der Krieg in der Nordsee*. Vols. I–V. Berlin: Verlag von E. S. Mittler & Sohn, 1920–27.

Hacker, Georg. *Die Männer von Manzell Erinnerungen des ersten* Zeppelin-*Kapitäns*. Frankfurt am Main: Frankfurter Societäts-Druckerei, 1936.

Haddow, G. W., and Peter M. Grosz. *The German Giants: The German R-Planes, 1914–1918*. New York: Funk & Wagnalls, 1962.

Henze, Carl. *Kolonial-Bücherei Heft 32: Mit "L 59" nach Afrika*. Berlin: Steiniger Verlage, 1941.

Hildebrand, Hans, Albert Röhr, and Hans-Otto Steinmetz. *Die deutschen Kriegsschiffe: Biographien—ein Spiegel der Marinegeschichte von 1815 bis zur Gegenwart.* 6 vols. Herford, Germany: Koehler, 1993.

Hordern, Charles, ed. *Military Operations: East Africa Volume I, August 1914–September 1916*. London: His Majesty's Stationery Office, 1941.

Horne, Charles, and Walter Austin, eds. *Source Records of the Great War*. 7 vols. New York: National Alumni, 1923.

Jones, H. A. *The War in the Air: Being the Story of the Part Played in the Great War by the Royal Air Force*. Vol. 3. Oxford: Clarendon, 1931.

Judge, Jeffrey. *The Imperial German Navy of World War I*. Vol. 1, *Warships*. Atglen, PA: Schiffer Military History, 2016.

Klein, Pitt. *Achtung! Bomben Fallen!* Leipzig: Verlag von K. F. Koehler, 1934.

Knudsen, Knud. *Fahrt nach Ostafrika*. Leipzig: Otto Lenz, 1918.

Krüsmann, Jochen, and Simon Schnetzke. *Expedition "Mirr": Eine Darstellung der Tätigkeit deutscher U-Boote im Rahmen der osmanischen Kriegsführung in Tripolitanien und der Cyrenaika im Ersten Weltkrieg (1915–1918)*. Oldenburg, Germany: Arbeitkreis Krieg zur See, 1914–18, e.V., 2020.

Langsdorff, Werner von. *Deutsche Flagge über Sand und Palmen, 53 deutsche Kolonialkrieger Erzählen*. Gütersloh, Germany: Verlag C. Bertelsmann, 1935.

Latimer, Elizabeth. *Europe in Africa in the 19th Century*. 3rd ed. Chicago: A. C. McClurg, 1898.

Lawson, Eric, and Jane Lawson. *The First Air Campaign: August 1914–November 1918*. Conshohocken, PA: Combined Books, 1996.

Leggett, Bernard John. *Wireless Telegraphy, with Special Reference to the Quenched-Spark System*. London: Chapman and Hall, 1921.

Lehmann, Ernst. *Zeppelin: The Story of Lighter-Than-Air Craft*. Stroud, UK: Fonthill Media, 2015.

Lettow-Vorbeck, Paul von. *My Reminisces of East Africa*. London: Hurst and Blackett, 1920.

Lettow-Vorbeck, Paul von, and Walter von Ruckteschell. *Heia Safari! Deutschlands Kampf in Ostafrika*. Leipzig: K. F. Koehler, 1920.

Looff, Max. *Tufani: Sturm über Deutsch-Ostafrika*. Berlin: Bernard & Graefe, 1936.

Louis, William Roger. *Great Britain and Germany's Lost Colonies: 1914–1919*. Oxford: Clarendon, 1967.

Marben, Rolf, ed. *Ritter der Luft:* Zeppelin*abenteuer im Weltkrieg*. Hamburg, Germany: Verlagsbuchhandlung Broschek, 1931.

Martel, Gordon. *The Origins of the First World War*. 3rd ed. Harlow, UK: Pearson Education, 2003.

Meighörner-Schardt, Wolfgang. *Wegbereiter des Weltluftverkehrs wider Willen: Die Geschichte des Zeppelin-Luftschifftyps "W."* Friedrichshafen, Germany: Zeppelin Museum, 1992.

Meinertzhagen, Richard. *Army Diary: 1899–1926.* London: Oliver and Boyd, 1960.

Methner, Wilhelm. *Unter drei Gouverneuren: 16 Jahre Dienst in deutschen Tropen.* Breslau, Germany: W. G. Korn Verlag, 1938.

Meyer, Peter. *Das grosse Luftschiffbuch.* Mönchengladbach, Germany: Elsbeth Rütten Verlag, 1976.

Miller, Charles. *Battle for the Bundu: The First World War in German East Africa.* New York: Macmillan, 1974.

Mosley, Leonard. *Duel for Kilimanjaro: Africa, 1914–1918—the Dramatic Story of an Unconventional War.* New York: Ballantine Books, 1964.

Munson, Kenneth. *Aircraft of World War I.* New York: Doubleday, 1968.

Neumann, Georg, ed. *The German Air Force I Knew, 1914–1918: Memoirs of the Imperial German Air Force in the Great War.* Barnsley, UK: Pen & Sword, 2014.

Occleshaw, Michael. *Armour Against Fate: British Military Intelligence in the First World War, and the Secret Rescue from Russia of the Grand Duchess Tatiana.* London: Columbus Books, 1989.

Paice, Edward. *World War I: The African Front.* New York: Pegasus Books, 2008.

Pasha, Djemal. *Memories of a Turkish Statesman, 1913–1919.* London: Hutchinson, 1922.

Pohl, Robert S. *101 Hours in a Zeppelin: Ernst August Lehmann and the Dream of Transatlantic Flight, 1917.* Atglen, PA: Schiffer Military History, 2023.

Rawlinson, Alfred. *The Defence of London, 1915–1918.* London: Andrew Melrose, 1923.

Reid, Alastair. *DELAG: A History.* Durham, NC: Lulu, 2025.

Reid, Alastair, ed. *Marine-Luftschiffer-Kameradschaft Newsletters, 1980–1997.* Durham, NC: Lulu, 2021.

Rintelen, Franz von. *The Dark Invader: Wartime Reminiscences of a German Naval Intelligence Officer.* New York: Macmillan, 1933.

Robinson, Douglas. *The Zeppelin in Combat: A History of the German Naval Airship Division, 1912–1918.* Atglen, PA: Schiffer Military History, 1994.

Routledge, N. W. *History of the Royal Regiment of Artillery: Anti-Aircraft Artillery, 1914–1955.* London: Brassey's, 1994.

Samson, Anne. *Britain, South Africa and East African Campaign, 1914–1918: The Union Comes of Age.* International Library of Colonial History 4. London: Taurus Academic Studies, 2006.

Scheer, Reinhard. *Germany's High Seas Fleet in the World War.* New York: Peter Smith, 1934.

Schmalenbach, Paul. *Die Deutschen Marine-Luftschiffe*. Herford, Germany: Koehlers Verlagsgesellschaft mbH, 1977.

Schnee, Heinrich, ed. *Deutsches Kolonial-Lexikon*. 3 vols. Leipzig: Quelle & Meyer, 1920.

Schnee, Heinrich. *Die deutschen Kolonie vor, in und nach dem Weltkrieg*. Leipzig: Quelle & Meyer, 1939.

Schöffler, Alfred. *Matata: A Memoir of a German Cavalryman in German East Africa Before, During, and After World War I*. Middletown, DE: Amazon Publishing Services, 2020.

Spinazzola, Giuseppe Pignatelli. "Un dirigibile nel golfo: Il bombardamento aereo del 1918 e i danni al patrimonio architetttonico napoletano." In *Epilogo della Grande Guerra: Scenari italiani ed internazionali*. Edited by Simonetta Conti, Luigi Loreto, and Federico Scarano. Santa Maria Capua Vetere, Italy: DiLBeC Books, 2021.

Strachan, Hew. *The First World War*. Vol. 1, *To Arms*. Oxford: Oxford University Press, 2003.

Stumpf, Richard, and Daniel Horn, eds. *The Private War of Seaman Stumpf*. London: Leslie Frewin, 1969.

Syon, Guillaume de. *Zeppelin! Germany and the Airship, 1900–1939*. Baltimore: Johns Hopkins University Press, 2002.

Tarrant, V. E. *Jutland: The German Perspective; A New View of the Great Battle, 31 May 1916*. Annapolis, MD: Naval Institute Press, 1995.

Thornhill, Christopher. *Taking Tanganyika: Experiences of an Intelligence Officer, 1914–1918*. London: Stanley Paul, 1937.

Wolf, Klaus. *Victory at Gallipoli, 1915: The German-Ottoman Alliance in the First World War*. Translated by Thomas P. Iredale. Barnsley, UK: Pen & Sword, 2020.

Woodhall, Edwin. *Spies of the Great War: Revelations of the Secret Service*. London: Mellifont, 1925.

Logs, War Diaries, and Other Archival Primary Sources

"Akten der Kaiserlichen Marine, Reichs-Marine-Amt: Akten betreffend die Unternehmung *L 57*/59 vom September 1917 bis Dezember 1917." PG 75204, National Archives Microfilm Publication T1022, roll 798.

"Akten der Kaiserlichen Marine, Reichs-Marine-Amt: Akten betreffend *L 59* vom 20 Dezember 1917 bis 30 September 1918." PG 76863, National Archives Microfilm Publication T1022, roll 1060.

"Akten der Kaiserlichen Marine, Reichs-Marine-Amt: Akten Luftschiffahrt und Flugwesen betreffend Mobilmachung 1916/1917. Luftkriegunternehmungen Gegen England und Russland, Beiheft zu Heft 4." PG 66167, National Archives Microfilm Publication T1022, roll 4315.

"Akten der Kaiserlichen Marine, Reichs-Marine-Amt: Akten Luftschiffahrt und Flugwesen betreffend Mobilmachung 1916/1917. Luftkriegunternehmungen Gegen England und Russland, Beiheft zu Heft 5." PG 66137, National Archives Microfilm Publication T1022, roll 4315.

"Akten der Kaiserlichen Marine, Reichs-Marine-Amt: Akten Luftschiffahrt und Flugwesen betreffend Mobilmachung 1916/1917. Luftkriegunternehmungen Gegen England und Russland, Beiheft zu Heft 6." PG 66198, National Archives Microfilm Publication T1022, roll 4315.

"Akten der Kaiserlichen Marine, Reichs-Marine-Amt: Akten Luftschiffahrt und Flugwesen betreffend Mobilmachung 1917/1918. Luftkriegunternehmungen Gegen England und Russland, Heft 7." PG 66139, National Archives Microfilm Publication T1022, roll 4316.

"Akten der Kaiserlichen Marine, Reichs-Marine-Amt: Akten Luftschiffahrt und Flugwesen betreffend Mobilmachung 1917/1918. Luftkriegunternehmungen Gegen England und Russland, Heft 8." PG 66139b, National Archives Microfilm Publication T1022, roll 4316.

"Kriegstagebuch des Luftschiffes 'L 23': 16 April 1917–30 April 1917." PG 63642, National Archives Microfilm Publication T1022, roll 395.

"Kriegstagebuch des Luftschiffes 'L 23': 16 September 1916–30 September 1916." PG 63642, National Archives Microfilm Publication T1022, roll 395.

"Kriegstagebuch des Luftschiffes '*L 59*': 3 November 1917–19 Februar 1918." PG 66139b, National Archives Microfilm Publication T1022, roll 4316.

"Kriegstagebuch des Luftschiffes '*L 59*': 20 Februar 1918–30 Marz 1918." PG 66139b, National Archives Microfilm Publication T1022, roll 4316.

"Kriegstagebuch SM UB-53: 7 April 1918–6 Mai 1918." Cuxhaven-Altenbruch, Germany: Freundeskreis Traditionsarchiv Unterseeboote e.V.

Newspapers

La Stampa (Turin, Italy).

Morgenbladet (Oslo).

New York Times (New York City, United States).

Wilnaer Zeitung (occupied Vilnius, Lithuania).

Periodicals

Larson, Lorne. "Disease, Science and Religiosity: A Case Study of Leprosy in German East Africa." *Tanzania Zamani* 13, no. 1 (2021).

Mahncke, J. O. E. O. "Aircraft Operations in the German Colonies, 1911–1916: The Fliegertruppe of the Imperial German Army." *Military History Journal* 12, no. 2 (December 2001).

Noppen, Ryan K. "The 'China Matter.'" *Dirigible: The Journal of the Airship Heritage Trust* 62 (Spring 2011).

Ursinus, Oskar, ed. "Von Gronaus Transozeanflug auf Dornier Wal." *Flugsport* 2, no. 18 (September 1930).

Zupitza, Maximilian. "Die Hilfsexpedition für die deutsch-ostafrikanische *Schutztruppe* auf dem Luftwege." *Deutsche Kolonialzeitung* 36 (1919).

Online Sources

Bliesener, Elisabeth. "Im Namen des Kaisers . . . mein Opa der Pirat." Geschichte der Kölner Luftfahrt. www.luftfahrtarchiv-koeln.de/fegert_pirat.htm. Accessed January 22, 2024.

Buddecke—Flieger und Luftschiffer. https://www.buddecke.de.

De Broglio, Bernard. "Zeppelin over Moudros: The Night a German Airship Bombed Moudros." *Neokosmos*, August 23, 2021. https://neoskosmos.com/en/2021/08/23/life/Zeppelin-over-moudros-the-night-a-giant-german-airship-bombed-moudros/. Accessed September 5, 2022.

The Kaiser's Cross. "Blockade Breakers: The Two German Ships That Eluded the Royal Navy and Brought Welcome Weapons and Supplies to the German Army in East Africa During 1915 and 1916." http://www.kaiserscross.com/188001/476201.html. Accessed January 28, 2023.

Kujawsko-Pomorska Digital Library. https://kpbc.umk.pl/dlibra.

La Stampa, Archivo Storico dal 1867. www.archiviolastampa.it.

Loveman, Brian. "General Act of the Berlin Conference on West Africa, 26 February 1885." https://loveman.sdsu.edu/docs/1885GeneralActBerlinConference.pdf.

Mason, Hannah. "Next-Generation Airship Design Enabled by Modern Composites." https://www.compositesworld.com/articles/next-generation-airship-design-enabled-by-modern-composites. Accessed February 28, 2024.

Schäfer, Karl-Wilhelm. "Einige Aspekte zur Afrika-Fahrt des Marine-Luftschiffs *L 59*." Traditionsverband ehemaliger Schutz und Überseetruppen—Freunde der Früheren deutschen Schutzgebiete e.V. https://www.traditionsverband.de/download/pdf/aspekte_afrika.pdf. Accessed August 11, 2022.

Sjøhistorie. "Bark Royal." https://www.sjohistorie.no/en/skip/24469/dokumenter. Accessed January 17, 2023.

Thamm, Gerhardt B. "Mie Askari mdachi: I Am a German Askari." HistoryNet. https://www.historynet.com/mie-askari-mdachi-german-askari/. Accessed December 1, 2022.

U-Boat.net. https://uboat.net/.

Wreck Site. https://wrecksite.eu.

Index

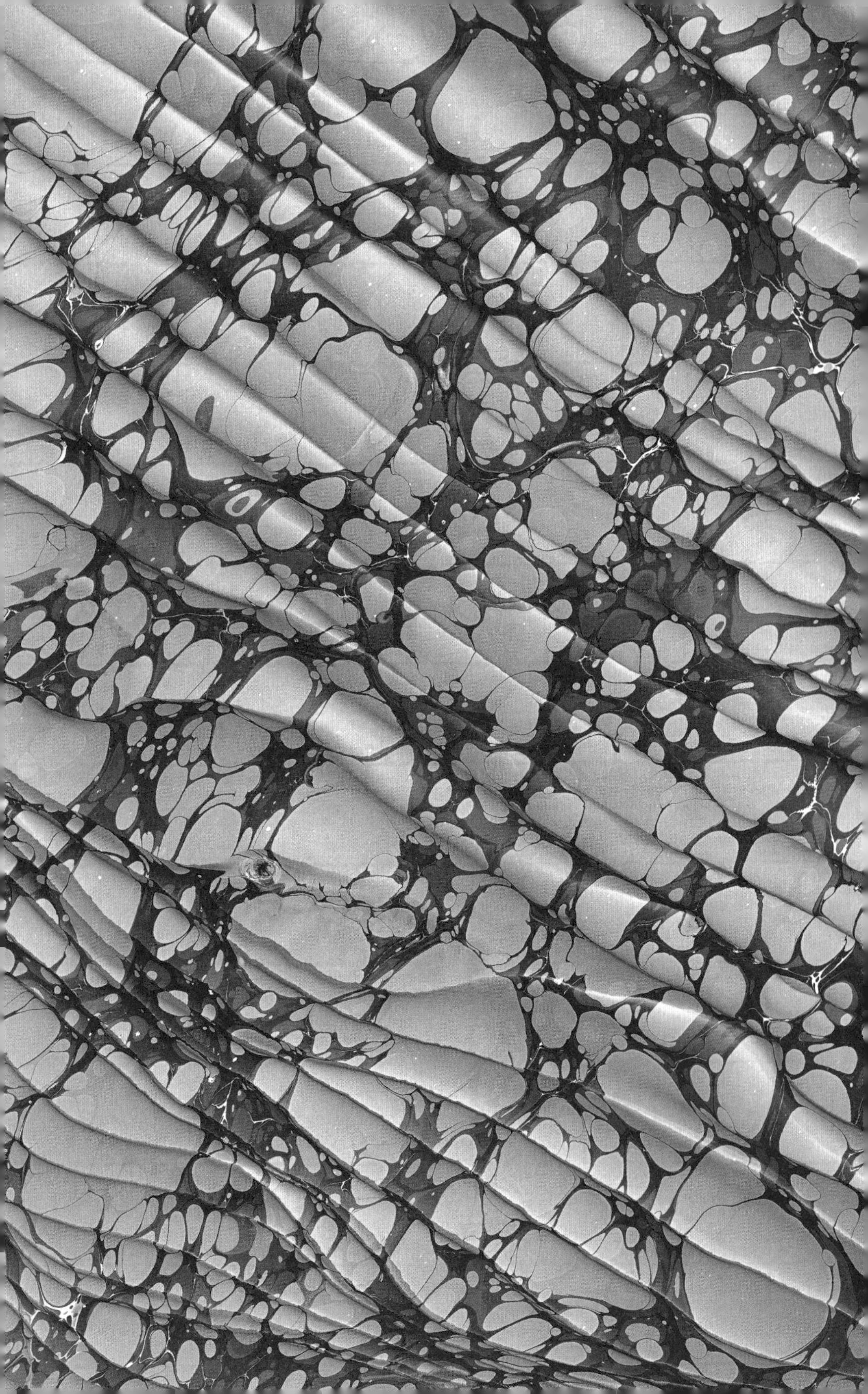